DYEING FOR FIBRES AND FABRICS

Edited by Janet De Boer

Kangaroo Press

Dedication

This book is dedicated to Inga Hunter, whose contribution to contemporary textile arts in Australia as teacher, dyer, author and maker has been as inspired as it has been generous.

Introduction

This book is a survey of both ancient and contemporary dye techniques for fibres and fabrics. It began life with the first edition of *Fibre Forum* magazine (which has since become *Textile—Fibre Forum)*, a national textiles magazine for Australia and regions which commenced publication in 1981. A number of articles are reprinted from that edition, which is long since out of print, but a great deal of new material from Australia and overseas has also been added. The reader will learn techniques and background information, and be able to choose from among the many dye types according to interest, need, and available resources.

The Australian Forum for Textile Arts (P.O. Box 77, University of Queensland, St Lucia, 4067) is the publisher of *Textile—Fibre Forum.* To obtain a sample copy of the magazine just write for details.

AFTA is grateful to the authors of articles in this book for their steadfast assistance.

Janet De Boer, Editor

Dyeing for fibres and fabrics.

Rev. ed.
Bibliography.
Includes index.
ISBN 0 86417 123 4.

1. Dyes and dyeing. I. De Boer, Janet.

667'.2

Cover: Detail of 'Balloonist's Bag' by Inga Hunter. Indigosol dyes, hand quilting and beading on silk.

This revised edition first published by Kangaroo Press Pty Ltd
3 Whitehall Road (P.O. Box 75) Kenthurst 2156
Typeset by T. & H. Bayfield
Printed in Hong Kong by Colorcraft Ltd

ISBN 0-86417-123-4

Contents

Basics
Some Definitions for Dyeing   Janet De Boer   4
Equipment Tips   Janet De Boer   6
Dye Hazards   Janet De Boer   8
Dye Waste Disposal   Jenni Dudley   9
Scouring Fibres   Janet De Boer   10
Mordanting Yarn for the Natural Dyes   Janet De Boer   13
Alternative Heat Sources   Janet De Boer   15

Synthetic Dyes   17
Synthetic Dye Korner   17
Synthetic Dyestuffs and Their Use   Eduards Voitkuns   18
Pre-Metallised Dyes   Wilmma Hollist and
                                                         Roy Russell   25
Fibre Reactive Dyes   Inga Hunter   29
Fibre Reactive Dyes for Wool   Margaret Sandiford 30
Disperse Dyes for Transfer Printing   Inga Hunter   35
Soga Discharge Dyeing   Inga Hunter   38
Indigosol Dyes   Eve Vonwiller et al. 41
Use of Naphthol Dyes   Inga Hunter   43

Methods of Dye Application   47
Synthetic Dyes for Spinners   Elizabeth Simm   48
Direct Dyeing with Cold Water Dyes   Inga Hunter   49
Adapting Wool for the Indonesian
   Batik Industry   H.D. Pleasance   55
Hand Dyeing Wool and Silk with   Barry Bassett and
   Earth Palette Cold Dyes   Elizabeth Lindsay   58
Cold Pad Batch Dye Process   Rhonda O'Meara   59
   Applied to Wool Warps
Marbling Cloth   Janet De Boer   65
Prussian Blues: Blueprinting   Alvena Hall   68
   for Textile Artists
The Silk Dyes   Marie-France Frater 71

Dyes in Nature   72
Drying for Dyeing   Edith Neilsen   72
Organising a Dye Day   Edith Neilsen   74
The Eucalypt Dyes   Jean Carman   75
Extension of the Eucalypt Dyes   Jean Carman   78
A Eucalypt Dyer's Handbook   Mikki and Ian Glasson 81
Vegetable Dyeing   Alick Smith   83

The Mineral Dyes   James N. Liles   85
Dyes Used in the 19th Century Before 1857   Neta Lewis   89
Bancroft's Mordant   Jame N. and Dale Liles   94
Traditional Indian Dyes — The World's   Joyce Burnard   97
    First Fast Dyes!

Indigo   100
Indigo Science and Art   F.H. Gerber   100
Shibori: An Introduction   Inga Hunter   102
Yoshiko Wada and the Art of Synthetic   Janet De Boer   106
    Indigo Dyeing

Suppliers   108
Magazines   108
Bibliography   109
Index   111

Basics

Some Definitions for Dyeing

Janet De Boer

Top Dyeing

The re-dyeing of already dyed yarn to deepen or alter the colour. This is the method used with natural dyes to secure secondary colours. The re-dyeing method has its place if the original colour is unsatisfactory as well, and the dyer wishes to change it.

Cross Dyeing

Cross dyeing is the dyeing of a yarn containing two different types of fibres which take the dye differently, or one of which resists the dye completely, producing a two-colour yarn.

Union Dyeing

The dyeing of a blend fibre containing two different fibres which take the dye identically. (Rayon and cotton blend is an example.)

Spot Dyeing

A mechanical means for colouring the body of a yarn while leaving spots undyed through a resist. The skein is tied tightly at the spaces determined for the undyed spots, to prevent the dyebath from penetrating it at these points. To make long undyed spots on the yarn, wrap the desired length tightly

with yarn or rags. This method is highly developed among handweavers in many parts of the world for producing elaborate or simple patterns in the finished cloth through tie-dyeing the warp and/or weft yarns, by the method variously known as *ikat*, or *kasuri*. Sections of skeins can also be made to resist the dye by covering them with bicycle inner-tubing which is then secured at either end.

Mottled Dyeing

Used to heighten the effect of surface texture through the use of mottled or unlevel yarn, so it may be intentional if designed accordingly. (Can also be unintentional as a result of poor dyeing techniques!) Achieved through crowding the pot by using a low ratio of dye liquor to fibre, and then doing a minimum of stirring during the dyeing. It may also be achieved through raising the dyebath temperature very quickly or not using a levelling agent, or through using an excess of acid in benzyl chemical dyeing, to force the dye to grab more quickly. In general, mottled dyeing results from sloppy dyeing methods!

Varicoloured Dyeing

Dye several pots of different colours simultaneously and as soon as the maximum dyeing temperature is reached, transfer the skein to a larger pot at the same temperature, with the same acid or salt concentration, and finish the dyeing with a minimum of yarn moving. There will be a certain amount of moving of the dye from one skein to another, giving varicoloured, mottled effects, though each skein will be different. A more reliable method is to top-dye skeins which have been previously spot dyed, retying the spots as desired. Experimenting will reveal many interesting effects from this method. It is also possible to suspend only part of the skein in the dyebath, and repeat this as many times as desired with different colours.

Stock Dyeing

Dyeing the fibre before it has been carded and spun. This method is much used industrially and is useful to the spinner. Mottled and colour-blended yarns can be spun, blending several colours of the fibre together in carding. Varicoloured yarns are spun through the judicious use of more than one colour of carded fibres.

Liquor Ratio

The designation 'liquor ratio' invites so many terrible jokes. We hesitate to bring it up, but most dyes require you to know what the term means. It is the amount of water you need to use — that simple. If you have weighed fibre or material (and you certainly should have) you multiply that quantity by 30, 40 or whatever the L/R (liquor ratio) tells you to do. And that's how much water you add.

Example: The L/R is given as 40:1.

Let's say your fibre or fabric weighs 50 gm. 40 × 50 is 2000 gm which is the same as 2000 ml of water (see below). And of course 2000 ml is the same as 2 litres (because there are 1000 ml in 1 litre).

So to dye 50 gm fibre or fabric at a liquor ratio of 40:1 you will need 2 litres of water.

For most dyeing methods it is helpful if you can make your peace with the metric system! Commonly used abbreviations are—

gm (gram) ml (millilitre)

gm/L (grams per litre)

One litre contains 1000 ml

1 ml can be treated as the equivalent of 1 gm.

That's why, if your recipe calls for a 30:1 liquor ratio, and you know your yarn weighs 100 gm, then you need 3000 gm water (or 3000 ml or 3 litres)! Simple, isn't it? Believe me, it is.

Equipment Tips

Janet De Boer

Equipment varies somewhat, depending on the type of dyeing you wish to do. Over the years I have found that nothing beats using adequate equipment for the job. These are some tips I've accumulated in my 'dyeing life'.

Scales

Balance scales are a lot more accurate than spring scales. If you don't want to invest much, look into 'Ohaus' school scales. Or write to Batik Oetero about their Japanese balance scales. Accurate scales are most important for weighing out dye powders, so if you can't invest in them, find a dye supplier who sends the dyes in relatively small, accurately weighed amounts. Put these into stock solution and you're all set.

Accurate scales aren't so important for weighing up salt or washing soda, for example — just so they're not too far out.

Stirring Rods and Spoons

Glass stirring rods and stainless steel spoons really are great to use. However, the glass can break during dyeing, so wooden sticks are all right. Well sanded dowelling is useful for example, and any old spoons you don't want to eat off can be used in place of stainless steel ones (which are easiest to obtain through chemical supply houses).

Glass Measures

A heat resistant glass measure (such as a Pyrex 1 litre measuring cup) is essential, unless you are doing all cold water dyeing. I like to use the Pyrex 250 ml beakers as well for a lot of my dyeing, but they are a luxury. If you do much dyeing, you will probably come to having a number of different sized glass measures, I really like using a pipette

for measuring out small quantities of dye solution (mine is graduated in 1 ml for a total of 10 ml). And yes, I have sucked dye solution into my mouth. So, find a source of used syringes and you're in business. Just watch for air bubbles, and use the same syringe for the same colour each time, as they're hard to rinse thoroughly. Brown glass jars are recommended for storing dye solutions, but you can use old bottles with good lids — store well away from light though. Baby bottles can be recycled to store dyes too (accurately labelled).

Skein Winders

A skein winder is so useful I don't know what people do without them. I don't mean 'swifts' which are best used to hold skeins which are being unwound. I mean something which quickly and accurately winds skeins, preferably something with very adjustable arms, that can be set up in a sensible working position, and is easy to wind. Something that permits you to literally wind hundreds of skeins with ease.

Dyepots

Dyebaths can present a problem, especially if enamel or stainless steel must be used, and you want to dye in any quantity. This is where one becomes tempted to use a good stainless steel cooking pot for dyeing, scrub it well, and cook with it again. Please don't do this. If you can't afford stainless steel dyepots (and many of us can't!) then look

for enamel pots. For sampling, the cheap Chinese imports often sold at Coles will do, as they can be discarded when the enamel chips. Keep an eye out for sales at places like Myers, where enamel cookware is often going for bargain prices. If you can get a group organised to buy dyepots you can probably get some good ones (such as 'Mirror Maid') at wholesale prices, and this is the best long-term solution. I prefer nappy pails for cold water dyeing, but they are not essential. However, if you dye a lot, have a separate plastic container for each dye colour.

Common sense and experience will be your best guides as to what you may need for the kind of dyeing you like to do.

If You Live in an Isolated Area

It may seem to you that equipment and ingredients for dyeing processes are extremely hard to get. In actual fact most of them are just as easy for country folk to get, as for us city folk. In other words, it can involve a lot of scrounging, ordering, and ingenuity. Your first task is to determine your mail order sources. It's useful to have catalogues from major dye suppliers (listed at the end of the book) and to locate a chemical supply house which mails orders. About the only limitation here is that particularly dangerous substances can't be sent through the mails.

Consult your nearest chemist for many chemical supplies too. They have acetic acid, sodium sulphate, and lots of other goodies. Also look into fertiliser supplies (urea, ammonium sulphate) and feed suppliers (Glauber's salts).

You can use your old washing copper for pre-metallised dyes. Nappy pails and baby baths are suitable for naphthol and fibre reactive dyeing. You can stir the bath with wooden sticks or old spoons (just don't use the spoons again for eating or cooking!).

As for scales, you can make up a simple balance system if you have some items you know the exact weight of. It is also common to find scales used for weighing gun powder in country areas. These often weigh in 'grains' but it's not too hard to make the conversion.

Dye solutions can be stored in 1 litre Coke bottles for example, provided the bottle is clearly labelled. And it's entirely possible to use most dyes by the 'teaspoon method of dyeing'. It's just that once you're used to some exactness you find it's every bit as easy as the teaspoon method, it's just a different way of thinking. There are a lot of rules in dyeing which can be bent, and some which absolutely cannot. Once you sort this out you can choose the method that suits your needs, and your locale.

Dye Hazards

Janet De Boer

Dyeing with both synthetic and natural dyestuffs can involve risks to health and safety. Dyeing need not be any more a hazard than cooking. We include some guidelines here, derived in part from personal experience, and in part from work done by Dr. Catherine L. Jenkins, Information Centre Director for Occupational Hazards, Inc., 56 Pine Street, N.Y., 10005, U.S.A.

The long-term toxicology, or carcinogenic potential has not been well studied for most dyes. Allergies have been reported after prolonged use of some dyes. Observing good precautions at all times will help diminish future health problems.

Be careful with dye powders. Don't tear open packets — snip them, and disperse slowly. Paste up dye powder in the bottom of a cup with a little water, and add the concentrate to the dyebath.

Always wear rubber gloves during this, and many other dye procedures. Surgeon's gloves are good because they let you feel through them better than other gloves. Whatever gloves you use, keep a supply on hand, and discard an old pair as soon as dyes appear to be getting through.

Cover hair with a scarf while dyeing, and wear a full smock. Leave the gear in your dye area when you are finished — don't drag dye clothing through the house. Use a toxic dust mask if you work with quantities of powder over a period of time. Pottery suppliers often carry cheap masks which are satisfactory for many uses. Avoid eating or smoking in the dye studio. Practise good housekeeping — wet mop instead of sweeping for example. Store dye containers adequately, after labelling and covering tightly. An old metal trunk with padlock is very useful for this as it also admits no light.

If using acids, keep bicarbonate of soda handy to neutralise spills. Caustic soda (sodium hydroxide) can cause ulcerative burns. Again, keep vinegar handy if using caustic. Always add acids and caustic soda *to* water and not vice versa. If you have trouble remembering this rule, think of your container of acid or caustic as a potential explosion. A little water added to it will make it want to explode very much. But adding the acid to a lot of water will diminish the explosive potential.

Natural dyers must first of all observe caution when dealing with plants themselves. In the actual dye process, mordant salts are usually the toxic problem, with potassium dichromate being the most dangerous as it can cause burns on the skin and possible perforation of the nasal septum if the dust is inhaled. In fact, potassium dichromate is so environmentally undesirable that Jean Carman states she will no longer use it for natural dye experiments.

Close doors and windows when weighing out dye powders. But be sure to open them again as most dyeing requires good ventilation, once dyes are in solution.

People who wear contact lenses should exercise extreme care with dye powders.

We hope everyone who has ever considered dyeing knows enough to keep dye materials away from children. Again, exercise the same common sense you use with the medicine cabinet or household cleaners. *Also, do not use dye equipment for cooking or preparing food.*

Contact your State Library for a Merch Index. It lists the majority of known chemicals and trade names. It describes their properties, dangers and uses.

Dye Waste Disposal

Jenni Dudley

Some years ago I had to think about the problem of dye waste disposal without modern sewerage as I moved to the country. Telephone enquiries to various dye companies and the Engineering and Water Supply yielded various solutions — one of which was the evaporating tank idea. Another was to have a deep storage tank for the dye liquors only and to pump from this into a tank mounted on a trailer, and cart the whole thing about 15 miles — where my tiny offering could join their vast traps and settlement ponds before being pumped into the main sewer to Adelaide. Rinsing water was to be evaporated.

More recent research has indicated that none of this is necessary — provided I stick to *Azoic, fibre-reactive, soluble vat* and *acid dyes.*

A friend who is an industrial chemist obligingly did a bit of homework for me. His former area of study for his Masters and PhD science degrees was dye chemistry, so I feel I can trust his judgment. The dye chemist at Actil also confirmed this method. So here it is.

All modern industrial dyes are at their most dangerous when in the powdered, non-reacted form. Once baths have been reacted and the dyestuffs have precipitated out, the solution left is water of varying degrees of hardness. Note: this only applies if correct standards are adhered to between baths.

Modern industrial dyes which are water-soluble do not present great problems.
(1) Exhaust all baths (in the case of azoics and vats, tip the 1st and 2nd baths together; let reactives stand for an hour after dyeing is complete).
(2) Strain through scraps of fabric to remove most of precipitated dye from water.
(3) Keep with 1st and 2nd rinsing waters in a suitably large holding tank (mine is 24 gallons buried in the ground). Only the dye liquors and rinses go into this. All other soapy waters just go out onto the hillside. You must naturally use only biodegradable soaps for this. I've tried dairy detergent (Bio-Gleem) and Amway coconut-oil based all-purpose cleanser. The problem here is that they bio-degrade very rapidly, during the dyeing process. However detergents recommended for dyeing, such as 'Lissapol' and 'Teepol' are all right only when they go through the treatment works.
(4) Test PH of holding tank effluent with indicator strips (Merck — I get them from Selbys). Any chemical supply store should have them.
    If PH too acid — add caustic soda.
    If PH too alkaline — add hydrochloric acid.
(5) Discharge onto land — your garden will love it! It's wise to strain effluent through fabric before discharging.

Natural dyestuffs using heavy metal mordants (chrome, copper, iron) and pigment printing pastes (Permaset and the like) containing chrome and cadmium require careful waste disposal. *Waste from these processes must not be put through septic systems or thrown out on the ground. Heavy metals contaminate* (This also applies to photographic wastes.) Any plumbing which copes with modern industrial dye wastes must *not* be used for disposal of heavy metal mordants, printing pastes, or photographic chemicals. You must keep these wastes entirely separate.
(1) All baths must be settled.
(2) An evaporating pit (sealed concrete base and sides with mesh cover) is the best receptable.
(3) Final sludge must be disposed of in the most appropriate manner. (No-one could tell me what was the best manner. Do not trust waste disposal companies. See what CSIRO says on this one and let me know). If there is anything else you use — solvents, optical brighteners, etc., check these separately with CSIRO for analysis.

Scouring Fibres

Janet De Boer

The scouring of fibres and fabrics is frequently suggested as a step to be taken prior to dyeing. This may be because a fabric contains sizing used when it was woven at the mill, or because natural waxes are left in a fibre, or because something has gotten dirty — there can be many reasons why scouring is desirable, in addition to the standard wetting out of material before dyeing.

I have assembled several recipes from literature of recent years, and will reprint them. You can then choose what seems to suit your own needs. Where appropriate the reason behind what you are doing will be given.

Most scouring recipes call for some kind of soap/detergent to be used, so we'll take a look at that first. In the area of detergent, you will often see 'nonionic' detergents referred to. These are preferred as a scouring assist. Most household detergents are anionic and will react with water softeners and/or dyestuffs if not thoroughly rinsed out. Terric BL8 is one brand name of a nonionic detergent, Lissapol is another; and there is also Teepol. These are useful as wetting agents — they help the fibre get wet clear through. They are usually supplied as concentrates, by people who sell synthetic dyes, and a little goes a long way. Most people are far too heavy-handed with nonionic detergents in the home dyeing situation. Please refer to Jenni Dudley's section on the disposal of dye water and dye wastes. She specifically recommends Bio-Gleem or Amway as detergents for people living in non-sewered areas.

Beware of washing powders containing optical brighteners (domestic washing-up detergents often have brighteners too). Wool containing optical brighteners will look white, but may turn brownish in the sun.

If scouring with soap, always use soft water to avoid scum buildup. Soap is not as efficient as the nonionic detergents. Use washing soda with it, in small quantities, when scouring wool.

Scouring Wool

Two dye recipes from Wilmma Hollist and Roy Russell, for scouring fleece

To Scour New Merino

Open out the fleece as much as possible before starting the scouring. Merino usually contains a lot of sand (or dust). Scour the fleece in small bundles (about 2 oz each) which can be put in individual mesh bags for easier handling.

First Bath This is a 3% detergent solution, or 30ml of detergent to 1 litre of water, with the water temperature at 65°C (as hot as the hand can bear). Leave fleece in this bath for a few minutes, take it out, turn it over, put it back in for a few more minutes. Before putting it in the second bath, drain out excess water, and squeeze gently — don't rub or wring it. Putting the bags of fleece in the centrifuge of a washing machine is the most efficient way to get out excess moisture.

Second bath This is a 1% detergent solution, or 10 ml detergent in every 1 litre of water. Let fleece soak a few minutes in the bath which is at 60°C. Turn, let soak again. Then drain excess water, and rinse fleece in 3 or 4 rinse buckets, with the temperature gradually dropping to 40°C. Again, if you can spin out the water in a centrifuge between each rinse, this is most effective. Spread fleece to dry after final rinse.

When the first bath becomes too dirty, empty it and use the second bath as the first, by adding more detergent to it, and more hot water. Create a new second bath, and continue.

This should remove most of the grease, and with merino, 55% of the fleece weight can be lost through scouring. The fleece should retain its staple formation in this treatment, and when dry it can be combed.

Note: Household detergent is about 10% strength so if you are using one, raise your detergent solution to 10-15%.

To Scour Very Dirty New Crossbred

First bath:
1% detergent solution (nonionic detergent, used at 10 ml for every 1 litre of water)
¼% washing soda (2.5 gm for every 1 kilo of fleece)
1% salt (household salt can be used. 10 gm for every 1 kilo of fleece)

Water at 54°C. Let fleece soak a few minutes, turn and let soak again. For a very dirty fleece, repeat the first bath before going on to the second.

Second bath
¼% detergent (nonionic, used at 2.5 ml for every 1 litre of water)
1/8% washing soda (1.25 gm for every 1 kilo of fleece)

The bath temperature again is 54°C. Let fleece soak, turn, let soak, drain excess moisture, and proceed with rinsing. Use at least 3 rinse buckets, with the temperature gradually decreasing.

The washing soda has the effect of 'saponifying' the grease. It turns it into a water soluble form which can be rinsed away. Be sure to rinse all the soda off, as alkali is not good for wool, and it may also affect the dyebath.

Fleeces prepared by these instructions should be clean enough to be dyed. If grease is still present when fleece is dyed, it will affect the evenness of the dyeing.

There is a tendency to want to play with the fleece when it is in the scouring baths, squeezing it and so on. Resist this tendency! Handle as little as possible.

A lot of extraneous dirt and 'sweat salts' can be removed from a fleece by soaking it in plain hot water before starting the scouring. This preliminary treatment will keep your scouring baths cleaner longer. Do not crowd the baths, as dirt will drop to the bottom, given room.

Francis Mayer, Manager of the Dyeing and Finishing Services of the Wool Bureau, New York City, gives this recipe for scouring wool in *The Weaver's Journal*, Vol. II, No. 3, Jan 1978.

'A typical scouring procedure would be as follows: Set the scouring bath at 120°F with:
½% detergent (suitable nonionic or anionic agent)
1% ammonia
0.1% Calgon
Note: percent is calculated on weight of wool
Enter the goods
Run 20 minutes while gently agitating
Drop bath
Rinse warm, rinse cold
Proceed with dyeing.'

She recommends doubling quantities if the wool is especially greasy or dirty. The words 'run' and 'drop' as used above are industrial terms. Basically they mean you start the scouring process, and then you stop it.

Anton Viditz-Ward, laboratory and research chemist and colourist gives this recipe in *Interweave*, Spring 1978.

'A practical scouring formulation for wool, based on the weight of fibre, is listed here with some additional variations:
Liquor ratio 40:1
Initial bath temperature 105°F-125°F (32°C-41°C)
Alkali: 1-2% ammonia (ammonium hydroxide)
Water conditioner: 2% trisodiumphosphate (TSP), also some Calgon if the water is very hard
Soap: ½-1½% neutral soap (such as Ivory)'

This scouring bath is meant to be used once, for a given quantity of wool. He also gives a recipe for a 'standing bath', or one that can be used several times over. In this case, ingredients are based on a fixed ratio, and he recommends:

'...a 5 gallon bath together with 4½-5½ ounces of soda ash (sodium carbonate, NA_2CO_3) along with 1½ ounces of any one of hundreds of nonionic agents ... The interesting result from a standing bath is that the older the bath, the better the wool will feel, but also the poorer the cleansing of the wool. Probably not more than 5 to 6 washings should be attempted from any standing bath.'

Scouring Cotton and Linen

Max Simmons gives a recipe for scouring cotton in his very handy book *Dyes and Dyeing* (Van Nostrand Reinhold, Melbourne, 1978). This recipe applies to linen as well, as both fibres contain wax and pectin which require strong scouring to remove. Alkalis do not damage cellulose fibres as they do wool, and Simmons suggests using caustic soda, which is a very potent alkali.

Liquor ratio: 10:1   Fibre: 500 gm cotton or flax
Caustic soda: 1.5% (7.5 gm for 500 gm fibre)
Detergent type A (nonionic): 1/5% (7.5 ml for 500 gm fibre)

Temperature: bring to the boil and boil for 2 hours. Top up water as evaporation lowers the level. Rinse under hot running water 15 minutes, then 15 minutes in cold water. Adjust the pH of the bath to 6 (may need to use acetic acid to do this). The fibres are now ready to be dyed.

Harry and Olive Linder give these recipes in their book *Handspinning Cotton* available from Cotton Squares, 1347 East San Miguel Ave, Phoenix, Arizona, 85014, U.S.A.:

'Scouring with washing soda' — 'Use a generous amount of warm water for bulk of fibre to be scoured. If water is hard, add water softener until the water feels slick. Add enough soap to make a good suds when stirred. Then add washing soda — one tablespoon per ounce of fibre or 24% of dry weight of fibre. Add wetted skeins and boil for one or two hours depending on the density of the yarn. Cool in solution and rinse. Fibres are now ready to mordant or dry' (or dye).

They also give a cold water method of scouring with caustic soda:

Step 1: Weigh dry yarn and record weight. You will need this when you mordant (or dye).
Step 2: Weigh out caustic soda — 15% of the dry weight of yarn.
Step 3: Dissolve caustic soda in a sufficient amount of cool water to cover yarn in an enamelled container.
Step 4: Enter wetted yarn and allow to steep in solution for 30 to 45 minutes depending on coarseness of yarn.
Step 5: Remove yarn with glass, wood, or plastic rod and rinse thoroughly. *Wear rubber gloves.*

Then wash in hot, soapy water. Rinse and mordant immediately (or dye).

Scouring Silk

There are a number of approaches to scouring silk, but this one was chosen because bicarb soda is readily available. The information is taken from an article by Kay Bromberg in *The Weaver's Journal*. Use 5% sodium bicarbonate (bicarb soda) to the dry weight of fibre. For example, if your silk weighs 100 gm when dry, you'll need 5 gm bicarb soda. And you dissolve the soda in 40 parts water (4 litres for 100 gm silk) to make the scouring bath.

Prepare your skeins carefully for scouring. As an example, tie two to three skeins of silk together loosely using a cotton string. Then twist all of the skeins together, loosely turning them inside out several times. Place the bound skeins in a bag, which could be of cheesecloth or loosely woven cotton — don't crowd the skeins! Let the ends of the cotton string hang outside the bag, and tie another piece of string around the mouth of the bag.

Scouring is easier if you pre-soak the skeins, to help soften the 'sericin' (which is what you want to remove). This may not be necessary, but if you wish to try, use 2% soda ash (sodium carbonate) to the dry weight of fibre, and a water temperature of 40°C (110°F). Soak the skeins for thirty minutes without handling them.

Start to heat the scouring bath. At this point, remove the silk from the 'soaking' bath if you used one, and enter it into the scouring bath. In any case, the skeins should be prepared as above, and be held in a bag. Watch the heat carefully and *do not boil* — instead you will *simmer* the bath for 1-2 hours. The time needed depends on the type of silk; judge by its 'feel'. If it feels stiff, more time is needed. When it feels limp it has been over-scoured. If it feels 'squeaky' then it's just right.

Note: if you are going to dye silk after scouring it's best to stop while it is still a bit stiff, as the subsequent dyeing will also remove some of the sericin.

Take the bag out, let it cool, and wring it lightly; remove the skeins carefully. Rinse the skeins in 40°C water once or twice, followed by tap water, 4-5 times. Wring the yarn out well and hang it to dry. If you 'slap' the skeins against a firm surface it will further straighten the fibres and remove tangles prior to drying.

Mordanting Yarn for the Natural Dyes

Janet De Boer

Many handbooks on the natural dyes indicate the procedure for mordanting yarn; in this description I have drawn chiefly from the book *A Handbook of Dyes From Natural Materials* by Anne Bliss (USA). The mordants are metallic salts that form a bond between the dyestuff and the fibre. Some natural materials can be used without mordants and will still result in fastness to light and washing that is quite acceptable (see the article on eucalypts for example). In other cases, the dyes can be very fugitive without the bonding accomplished through mordanting.

Caution: metallic salts are poisonous. Label carefully; store carefully; use carefully. Moreover, many plants can be toxic or induce allergies, so do some studying before you launch your career in natural materials for dyes. Also, some plants take a long time to grow (e.g. lichens) or are protected (e.g. in National Parks) — be aware of this. Also, follow recipes and observe the quantities; over-mordanting can have a bad effect on fibres. Do not use mordants in your kitchen and do not store them there. And do not use the same utensils for cooking and eating that you use for mordanting and/or natural dyeing. Establish a dye workplace *away* from your kitchen, and especially away from young children.

Pre-Mordanting Wool, Silk, and Other Protein Fibres

(1) Weigh the dry fibre (or fabric). When using yarn in skeins, tie loosely in several places to keep the skeins from tangling. Plastic meat trays can be cut into squares and attached to one of the skein ties; write on this 'tag' with waterproof ink to identify skeins.
(2) Soak the fibre in warm water before dyeing. You must check to be sure it gets wet clear through; a 'wetting agent' such as detergent may be needed to assist this process.
(3) For each 500 gm fibre, allow 15 litres of water,

and the specified amount of mordant. It is best to dissolve the mordant separately (heating helps it to dissolve in some cases). Use a 'non-reactive' pot (such as stainless steel or enamel). Sometimes fibre is dyed intentionally in a 'reactive' pot such as a cast iron pot, copper, or aluminium pot. To begin with, stick to enamel if you can, and experiment later on.
(4) Put the dissolved mordant into the pot, which has the correct amount of water in it (for the dry weight of fibre). Take the fibre from its soaking bath, gently squeeze out the excess, and put it in too. Place a lid on the pot.

(5) Raise the temperature gradually to simmering (about 180°F, or 82°C). You can stir very gently if you wish. Keep at a simmer for one hour (unless another time period is recommended in your dye manual). Again, stir gently from time to time. *Never* stick your face right over the bath or inhale the fumes. Keep the lid on except for the brief times when you stir, and work in a well ventilated area.
(6) The fibre can cool in the bath; or you can lift it out to cool. It's easiest to let it cool overnight; then rinse it the next day in tap water. Whatever you do, don't plunge a hot skein under cold tap water. Let the skein cool; rinse it in water the same temperature as the skein. It may take three rinses until no mordant can be seen 'bleeding' into the rinse water.
(7) After rinsing you can immediately dye the skein, or you can dry it, label it, and store it away from the light until you are ready to dye.

Note: quantities of mordant to fibre are not given here. There are many useful booklets on dyeing with natural materials (including the one by Anne Bliss) and it is best to obtain at least one such book or booklet and do some studying. You can dye other than protein materials of course (such as cotton, linen or rayon) but these have special requirements.

One-Pot Mordanting of Wool, Silk and Other Protein Fibres

(1) Rather than pre-mordanting, you can do everything at once.
(2) Prepare the dyebath by boiling up the dyestuff until the colour is extracted. Strain.
(3) Wet out the clean fibre separately.
(4) Measure the needed amount of mordant and dissolve it.
(5) Add the mordant to the dyebath and stir.
(6) Enter the fibre into the dyebath and follow normal processes.

Post-Mordanting Wool, Silk and Other Protein Fibres

(1) Dye your fibre using only the dye liquor (no mordant).

(2) Prepare a solution of the dissolved mordant separately.
(3) Take the dyed, wet fibre out of the dyebath and enter it into the mordant bath. Gently raise heat to a simmer and leave for one hour. Allow the skein to cool in the mordant bath. Rinse thoroughly.

Note: post-mordanting is generally used to alter the colour of the dye (e.g. iron will 'brown' or 'grey' the dye shade; tin often brightens colours; copper can turn a bright yellow to an olive). Fifteen or thirty minutes in the post-mordant bath may be enough (rather than a whole hour). Base this on the colour you are getting.

Additives
Some of the substances dyers add will heighten or alter colours. These include cream of tartar, salt, vinegar, urea, ammonia and so on. You can add another ingredient while mordanting, while dyeing, or as a rinse bath. The usual effect is to change the pH (acidity or alkalinity) and the results can be quite marked. Some dye recipes give a fair indication of what will happen. In other cases, you can only rely on experimentation and your own records.

Alternative Heat Sources

Janet De Boer

Dyeing in the Microwave Oven

Dyeing in the microwave oven can save you time and energy; only relatively small quantities can be done of course. And you must make allowances for the requirements of the dyestuff. Joan Fletcher, a dyer from New Zealand likes to use small quantities of silk yarn for miniature weavings, but her colour needs are very specific. For her purpose, microwave dyeing is the answer — there is the added advantage that the skeins don't move about during dyeing so there is no tangling of the fine silk.

Katherine Sylvan is also experienced in microwave dyeing and some of these ideas came from her (in an article which first appeared in *The Textile Artists' Newsletter*, formerly published in the USA by 'Straw Into Gold').

Before doing any experiments, be sure you understand the safe use of microwave ovens. For example, only glass or plastic can be used; *metal containers must never be used* (including metal 'twistems', metal clamps or clips, zippers on bags). Only thermometers made for use in the microwave can be used while the oven is on. When taking covers off containers that have been at boil in the microwave, you must be very careful of the steam. Also be very careful that liquids used do not dry out entirely as this could ruin the magnetron (the dye process often involves steaming, when this becomes a real danger).

Dyeing in the kitchen is *always to be discouraged*. Since microwave ovens live in kitchens (but are often very portable) have a think about this and see if you can take the microwave to your dye studio for use. Of course any utensils used for dyeing will never again be used for cooking. With care you can keep any spills off the oven itself.

Acid milling and acid levelling dyes are common hot water dyes. You can stop and start the dye process to add the 'acid' (usually vinegar) which assists the dye process. Katherine Sylvan mixes her stock solution of acid levelling dye, adds the amount she wants to water (she has a 4-quart plastic container), and puts in the washed, wetted out yarn. She 'cooks' on full power for five minutes — then stops to add acetic acid and gently turn the skein over. Another five minutes on full power; stop and turn the skein; and a final five minutes 'cooking' completes the dyeing. N.B. *Cooking continues for several minutes after you take the dyepot out of the oven*. This is a characteristic of microwave cooking.

This same method works well for oven-dyeing commercial yarns or yarns you have dyed and wish to change. If you have done your homework and know your dyes (from the usual top of stove method) you can translate this information successfully to the microwave.

Space Dyeing and Sprinkle Dyeing

Because you can localise the colour easily in microwave dyeing it lends itself to spotty and striped colour effects. For this process you must use a steamer (one made for microwaves is simplest. As an alternative, punch holes in a plastic lid, as this will let steam through to the yarn, which sits on top of the lid.) Be sure the rack is big enough to allow the skein to be spread out. Put the skein on the rack. You are going to squirt liquid dye solution on the skein (with an eye dropper, syringe or squirt bottle) so the colour should not be too concentrated. Try a 0.5% to begin with for solution strength. Squirt on as many colours as you want, in the places you want them to appear on the skein. Cover the steamer and be sure there is one-quarter to one-half inch of water on the bottom of the steamer container. Do the three, five-minute cycles, stopping after each five minute interval to check on water level; you also turn the skein so the dye can penetrate right through.

When is the acid added by this method? You must *pre-soak* the skein in a vinegar and water solution before dyeing (do not rinse out the vinegar; just lightly squeeze and place the skein on the steaming rack).

Note: you don't have to turn the skein; there will be less spottiness if you just leave it alone. Another possibility is sprinkling dye powder right onto the yarn, which can give a little 'colour explosion'. *Be very careful with the dye powder*; don't let it get on anything but the yarn, and don't let it get up your nose! Katherine Sylvan suggests using an old, dry toothbrush to gather up dry dye particles; put a piece of screening over the yarn and draw the toothbrush across this. Obviously you need a separate toothbrush and screen for each colour. Another idea is to mix the dye powder with table salt first. Sprinkle this mixture on, using an old, discarded salt shaker or a plastic cup (use a lot more salt than dye in the mixture).

Once again, the skein of yarn should be clean, and pre-soaked in a vinegar and water solution; put it on the steaming rack and follow the instructions above: have about one-quarter inch of water below the rack and dye in three, five-minute intervals, turning the skein at intervals if you wish.

Solar Dyeing

It's only logical for Australian dyers to think about using the sun as a heat source, just as many Americans presently do. Merilyn Lorance is the source of much of the information printed here (she first wrote for the USA publication *Shuttle, Spindle and Dyepot* about her experiments). On the appeal of solar dyeing for her she says, 'It is a quality of light that sun dyeing gives that conventional cooking methods somehow do not share with your eye'.

You can extract dye from plants by solar methods, prior to the actual dyeing. Or you can toss everything in a glass jar — yarn, plants, mordants and let it go. It is of course important to experiment and keep records. You will probably find it easiest to work with wool (or mohair). This method can be very good for commercially prepared rovings or scoured wool fleece which you don't want to mat through the agitation caused in conventional dyeing. Lorance has found that root crops do not yield up their colour as well as aboveground plants (for example, that old reliable, the onion is a disappointment in solar dyeing). Use a clear glass jar for your 'dyepot'; plastic is not as effective.

Mixed Pot Method   Put water, mordant (measure this very carefully to the dry weight of fibre — *don't overdo it!*), dye materials and fibre all in the same jar. Cover; put in the sun; observe; test; rinse when satisfied with the colour.

Semi-mixed Pot Method   Pre-mordant your wool; then add it to the jar along with the dye materials and water. Cover; put in the sun.

Pre-cooked Method   Use either pre-mordanted wool; or put wool and mordant in the jar with water; add dye liquid. In this method you extract the dye from the plants first. Cover; put in the sun. Here are some hints from Lorance's experiments:

1. *Wait.* Her first try was with aspen leaves and it took nine days before any colour appeared in the jar.
2. Some dyes need 'starting' — for example with nuts and hulls, barks and woods (and cochineal) you can gently simmer the materials first and then place them in the sun for further 'developing'.
3. When using delicate materials such as flowers, gather the wilted ones each morning before the dew is gone and put them in a glass jar to steep. When 'exhausted', strain out the old flowers and add more. Keep adding flowers each day until you get an intense colour; then proceed.
4. The colour in the jar will not always be the colour on the yarn. Some bright colours turn to brown as they 'dye'; this is very common with plants.
5. Metal jar tops are all right but plastic lids stand up better. Mould will not get in if you use a tight cover. In other cases you may wish to leave a jar uncovered to bring about fermentation (some colours only happen due to fermenting). You may very well get bad smells and mould; if the smell and mess wash out you haven't 'spoiled' anything.
6. It is very hard to duplicate colours this way.
7. If you use a large mayonnaise jar (restaurant-sized), about four ounces of wool can be dyed; more would crowd the jar too much.
8. The dyebath is 'finished' when you find a colour you like. You *can* lose a good colour by letting the dyebath go too long. Some dyestuffs *do not* colour the water, but *do* colour the wool.
9. Water composition can make a difference; you may need to experiment with your tap water, rain water, or softened water.
10. Changing the pH of your water will affect colour (this is the usual dyer's practice of adding cream of tartar, or ammonia, or vinegar for example, to see what colour changes occur).

'Teaparty Bag' by Inga Hunter. indigosol dyes. Hand quilting and beading. Handmade bobbin lace.

'Punting Party'. Uses Indigosol and Naphthol dyes (painted on). Hand quilting and beading on silk. Inga Hunter.

Synthetic Dyes

Introduction

Eddie Voitkuns of Commission Dyers, South Australia starts off this section with a very comprehensive review of kinds of synthetic dyestuffs. As a quick reference and reminder, it is indispensable. Inga Hunter provides a closer look at a number of classes of dye: soga; indigosols; fibre reactives; naphthols; and disperse dyes for transfer printing on synthetic fabrics. Margaret Sandiford gives excellent detail on fibre reactive dyes for wool, going into industrial methods, and relating them to the home dye studio. And Wilmma Hollist and Roy Russell of Muswell Hill, England explain the uses of the pre-metallised dyes for wool.

These articles can be used as a starting place in dye research, for comparisons, and for learning what dyes can do and how they do it. It's a lot of information to absorb at once though. People who have tried to use dyes, or have done a short workshop, or examined dyed samples by other people will know that it is the power over colour which is usually the most exciting thing at first. Then technical knowledge becomes exciting because it gives you the power to really employ a skill, a craft — and the final gratification is once again the colour.

The people who contributed articles to this book all have in common a respect for the craft of dyeing. That is evident in their willingness to acquire technical knowledge, and to share it. A lighthearted approach is also possible, as the introductory article shows.

Synthetic Dye Korner

Meg King provided the following bit of nonsense (?) which appeared in the newsletter of the Queensland Group of Spinners, Weavers and Dyers.

Glug

A *glug* is a volume of liquid discharged from a vessel closed to the atmosphere during the time of discharge and is dependent in quantity on: (a) height of the surface of the liquid above the centre of the orifice through which it issues; (b) the hydraulic radius of that orifice; (c) the coefficient of rugosity of the material from which the orifice is made; (d) the specific gravity of the liquid; (e) the viscosity of the discharged liquid; (f) the surface tension of the discharging liquid; (g) the barometric pressure at the time of discharge; (h) the volume of air remaining in the containing vessel (i.e. the total volume of the vessel minus the volume of liquid contained).

As at any time all the factors enumerated above are capable of precise mathematical determination, the volume of *glug* may be regarded as a definitive volume. It is to be noted that where the discharging liquid does not completely fill the discharge orifice the *glug* reverts to a *flow* and the above factors no longer apply.

Slurp

A *slurp* is the volume of liquid issuing from a vessel of free surface through an orifice under negative pressure and is subject to the same conditions as for *glug* (q.v.). Basically *slurp* is the negative of *glug*.

Slop

A *slop* is the volume of liquid flowing over an edge from a vessel of free surface and the volume of discharge is dependent on: (a) height of liquid surface above discharge area; (b) length and shape of discharge edge; (c) specific gravity of liquid; (d) drag coefficient of discharge edge; (e) duration of slop. *Note:* any prolonged *slop* may be regarded as a *spill*.

For quantitative purposes a *slop* should be of very short duration only if it is to be regarded as a measurement.

Dollop

The *dollop* is a measure of volume applied to semi-plastic materials. There are two sizes known as (a) the passive dollop and (b) the kinetic dollop. Both are determined by the quantity of material adhering to and subsequently falling from a flattish container, e.g. spoon, spatula, etc. The parameters are: (a) viscosity of the material; (b) specific gravity of the material. In the case of (a) the 'passive dollop,' the material falls from a stationary position whereas in (b) centrifugal force is added, hence (b) is greater than (a).

Synthetic Dyestuffs and Their Use

Eduards Voitkuns

The discovery by an English chemist, William Henry Perkin, in 1856 that a mauve colouring matter that would dye silk and wool could be prepared by the oxidation of aniline, led to the discovery of the first synthetic dye. After aniline, a large number of brilliant dyes appeared, including magenta in 1859, aniline blue in 1860, the first water soluble acid dye in 1862 and then aniline black in 1863. The new understanding of basic chemistry, instead of the old hit-and-miss experimenting, enabled researchers to discover a large and ever extending range of dyestuffs. It has resulted in the production of approximately 8000 distinctively different dyestuffs all over the world, sold under 40 000 trade names.

In order to give the same dyes, marketed under different trade names, some common designation, colour index numbers as introduced by the Society of Dyers and Colourists in England have been adopted. Consequently a dye, regardless of the name given by the manufacturer, can be identified by its colour index number; for example, there are 59 known manufacturers and therefore 59 different names for a red wool dye now known as C.I. Acid Red 1.

Dye Designation

The commercial name of a dye consists usually of the following:

1. The brand name, which denotes the class of dye, and often is an indication of the manufacturer: Coomassie, Benzyl, Cyanine, Xylene, etc.

2. The hue name: red, green, blue, black, etc.

3. One or more suffix letters (often German in origin) and figures. They may indicate:

a.) The tone of the hue, referred to in colour (B for *blau* or blue, G for *gelb* or yellow, R for *rot* or red). For example, Benzyl Red G is a yellowish red, Coomassie Yellow R is a reddish yellow, Xylene Fast Violet B is a bluish violet.

b.) Blue hue might be described as R (reddish) or 2R (more reddish) or G (Yellowish) and so on. Similarly, reds may be described as bluish or yellowish in various degrees. The suffix G in yellows as well as in blues denotes greenness. Thus Coomassie Yellow 6G is greener than Coomassie Yellow G, and Carbolan Crimson BS is less blue than Carbolan Crimson 3B.

c.) Some special quality, for example, brilliant, fast (higher resistance to sunlight), milling (high washfastness, therefore suitable for milling). This special quality can also be expressed with letters: FF, very bright, L or LL, light fast, etc.

d.) Strength other than standard strength is denoted by figures, so that 200 indicates 200%, 150 indicates 150%, etc. Dyes of standard strength are denoted by S or the denotation is omitted altogether. Coomassie Brown GS is a yellowish brown of standard strength.

dyes singly or in pairs in varying amounts gives a complete colour circle of bright colours.

Taking all three colours in similar quantities, providing the dyes are of a similar strength, will produce a grey. If the quantity of dye taken is increased the grey shade will increase in darkness until a black dyeing is obtained. This brings us to the concept of dull or muted shades. Any two colour combinations can be made duller by the addition of the third colour. Stronger or weaker depth of any colour is obtained by using larger or smaller quantities of dye but maintaining the ratio of the three components.

The fundamental difference between dyeing with dyes and painting with paints is that dyes do not cover the fibre but rather colour it from within. Consequently re-dyeings can be carried out only to a darker colour or by making use of the colour already present in the fibre. Thus yellow wool can be dyed green by dyeing it with a blue dye, or orange by adding red. Yellow wool could not be dyed purple because adding red and blue to the existing yellow would produce grey: red + blue + yellow = grey. This applies to all complementary or opposing colours on the colour circle. This becomes evident when it is attempted to dye wool to a pale blue shade; because of the inherent yellowness of wool small amounts of blue will make it green. It will turn blue only as the amount of blue dye deposited increases.

Mixing

Almost all hues required in dyed textiles can be produced by mixing three individual dyes — red, blue and yellow. Of the colour mixing theories, the subtractive is the most applicable. Unfortunately pure red, blue and yellow are theoretical concepts. Despite the multitude of dyes manufactured, considering the fibre to be dyed, dye method used, colour required and fastness requirements of the end product, the choice in the number of dyes available is restricted. Therefore it has been found that instead of using three basic colours it is advantageous to use six. These six are two reds — a bluish (B) and a yellowish (G), two blues — a yellowish (G) or reddish (R), and two yellows — a reddish (R) and greenish (G). Mixing different amounts of these dyes gives a range of intermediate colours. Using these

Choice of Dye

In choosing a dyestuff, the conditions to which the finished dyeing will be exposed must be considered. Over 20 distinct and specific fastness requirements have been selected, and the performance of dyeings exposed to these conditions evaluated. The performance requirements of a dye on a swimsuit, for instance, is totally different from the dye on curtains or a pair of socks. Many textiles must withstand severe exposure to sunlight or repeated washing. Curtains, carpets, wall hangings and similar articles must be dyed with dyes that have a high light fastness. Washing fastness and possibly machine washability are important for materials used in making wearing apparel.

Fastness evaluations are frequently industry orientated and serve as a guide for the suitability for further treatment prior to garment manufacture. Consumer orientated fastness assessments help dyers to decide on the dye that will suit the end use of the article dyed or manufactured. Some of the consumer orientated fastness assessments are as follows: fading, machine washability, boiling, perspiration, dry cleaning (white spirit or perchloroethylene), hot pressing, steam pressing, chlorine resistance, salt water, gas fume fading (from oil heaters) and many others.

Nature of Dyeing

The nature of the dyeing process is also important in determining the choice of dye. In the dyeing of fabric or yarn, only the most level-dyeing dyes can be used because the slightest inequality in colour on different areas of the cloth or yarn would spoil the appearance. If loose fibre is being dyed, levelness is of less importance because any portion of uneven appearance will be evenly distributed when the fibre is spun.

Synthetic Dyes

Synthetic dyes used in the textile industry are broadly split into 11 groups:

1. Basic dyes	7. Mordant dyes
2. Direct dyes	8. Acid dyes
3. Vat dyes	9. Dispersed dyes
4. Fibre reactive dyes	10. Oxidation dyes
5. Azoic dyes	11. Mineral and
6. Sulphur dyes	pigment dyes

1. Basic Dyes

Mauvene, the first to be discovered by Perkin, was a basic dye and most of the dyes which followed, including Magenta, Malachite Green and Crystal Violet, were of the same type. Basic dyes dye wool and silk from a dye bath containing acid, but dye cotton fibres only in the presence of a mordant, usually a metallic salt that increases affinity of the fabric for the dye. Basic dyes include the most brilliant of all the synthetic dyes known, but unfortunately they have very poor light and wash fastness. Basic dyes are available in bright primary and secondary colours; these can be freely intermixed to produce compound shades.

Use: Basic dyes will dye wool and silk from an acid bath and are used where brightness is of prime consideration. With the introduction of cotton dyes possessing higher fastness properties their use for dyeing cotton has diminished.

Basic dyes are used extensively for dyeing cut flowers, as well as dried flowers, also in dyeing jute, sisal, raffia, coir and wood (toys). With the introduction of acrylic fibre, sold as 'Orlon' and 'Acrylan', modified basic dyes are manufactured to dye this material.

2. Direct Dyes

These are soluble in water and have a direct affinity for all cellulosic fibres. Some will also dye silk or wool. By continuous research, this group of dyes has been supplemented with dyes of good fastness to light and washing. As these dyes, when dyed without additives, do not exhaust well; an addition of salt is required to improve the yield of the dye and also to obtain deeper shades. Generally, the wash fastness of these dyes is inferior but there are a number of after-treatments available to improve the wash fastness of the dyeings done. Most direct dyes can be stripped by the use of stripping salts (sodium hydrosulphate) without harmful effects on the fibres.

Use: Direct dyes dye all cellulosic fibres, including viscose rayon, and most of them also dye wool and silk. They do not dye acetate rayon and synthetic fibres. Direct dyes can be applied well at low temperatures and therefore are suitable for tie-and-dye and batik work. Generally, these dyes are used where high wash fastness is not required.

3. Vat Dyes

Indigo, probably the oldest dye known to man, is one of the most important members of this group. Natural indigo extracted from the plant *Indigofera tinctoria*, was used by the Egyptians in 3000 B.C. The first synthetic indigo was introduced to the textile trade in 1897 and had the effect of completely replacing the natural product. Although the vat dyes may be divided into three chemical groups, they are similar in that they are insoluble in water and become water soluble when reduced in the presence of an alkali. After dyeing, the fabric is oxidised and the dye again becomes water insoluble. Because of the time consuming and costly procedure in reducing vat dye into a water soluble complex, dye manufacturers have produced a stabilised water soluble vat dye. This dye can be applied to cotton and viscose rayon by the methods used for applying direct cotton dyes. After the dyeing, a simple treatment restores the vat dye to its normal insoluble state. Solubilised vat dyes have an affinity for cellulosic and animal fibres.

Use: Vat dyes are used in cotton dyeing where high wash and boil fastness is required. Because of the high alkali concentration in the dye bath, pure vat dyes cannot be used on animal fibres (wool, various hairs and natural silk). Bright red is absent in the vat dye range. Solubilised vat dyes, not requiring the presence of alkali, are used on animal fibres as well. Because they are dyed at low temperatures, they are used in Indonesian batik dyeing for green, blue and pink shades.

4. Reactive Dyes

This is an entirely new class of dye, introduced to the market in 1956. They react chemically with the fibre being dyed, and if correctly applied, cannot be removed by washing or boiling. The main feature of the dyestuff is its low affinity to cellulose, therefore large amounts of salt are required to force its deposition on the fabric. After this has been achieved, addition of alkali causes the deposited dye to react with the fibre. Only a successfully concluded reaction guarantees a fast dyeing. Basically there are two types of reactive dyes — the cold dyeing (M) and the hot dyeing (H) type.

Use: Reactive dyes are used where bright dyeing with high light and wash fastness are required. Cold dyeing (M) type is used extensively in batik work.

While there are reactive dyestuffs that have been specially modified to dye wool, their main usage is in dyeing cotton, linen and viscose rayon.

5. Azoic Dyes

The word azoic is the distinguishing name given to insoluble azo dyes that are not applied directly as dyes, but are actually produced within the fibre itself. This is done by impregnating the fibre with one component, thus forming the dye within the fibre. The formation of this insoluble dye within the fabric makes it very fast to washing. Deposition of free pigment on the surface of the dyed fabric produces poor rub-fastness, but once the loose pigment is removed by boiling the fabric in soap, the dyeing becomes one of the fastest available.

Use: Azoic dyes are mostly used to produce yellow, orange, red, brown and sometimes black fast dyeing on cotton and viscose rayon. Contemporary Indonesian batiks are made almost exclusively with Azoic dyes. Since there are no useful greens and only a few blue shades in this range, Azoic dyes are combined with vat dyes to produce a full range of colours.

6. Sulphur Dyes

The first sulphur dye was discovered in France in 1873, and further work done by Raymond Videl enabled the manufacture of Videl Black. Its outstanding fastness to light, washing and boiling far surpassed any other cotton black known at that time. The general disadvantage of the sulphur dyes is that they produce dull shades and lack a red. The main advantage lies in their cheapness, ease of application and good wash fastness. In their normal state, sulphur dyes are insoluble in water but are readily soluble in a solution of sodium sulphide. In this form they have a high affinity to all cellulosic fibres.

Use: The use of sulphur dyes is restricted to dull brown, khaki and navy shades, where good wash but not boil fastness is required. Most khaki and navy overalls are dyed with sulphur dyes. An outstanding member of this family is sulphur black. It dyes all cellulose fibres, but particularly linen and jute, to a lustrous and deep black with excellent light and wash fastness. Sulphur dyes are dyed from a dye bath containing sodium sulphide, common or Glauber's salt, and are oxidised by airing or with some oxidising agents (sodium bichromate or hydrogen peroxide) in a fresh bath.

7. Mordant Dyes

Mordant dyes are so-called because, in applying them to textile materials, it is necessary to use a mordant. This group of dyes includes natural dyes: Logwood, Fustic and Madder (now replaced by synthetic Alizarine), together with a large group of synthetic dyes with a widely differing constitution. The mordant dyes can be applied to fibres by three different methods:

a). By mordanting the fibre with a suitable metallic salt and then applying the dye. This method is frequently used when dyeing with natural dyes.
b). By dyeing the fibre and subsequently after-treating it with a suitable metallic salt so as to form an insoluble lake. This is the basis of 'after-chrome' methods in their application to wool, particularly in dyeing fast black and brown colours.
c.) By the simultaneous application to the fibre of dye and mordant so that controlled lake formation occurs within the fibre. In wool dyeing it is known as the metachrome or monochrome process and is extensively used for the production of brown and khaki colours.

Use: The modern use of mordant dye is two-directional: the mordanting of cellulosic fibres so as to increase their affinity to natural dyes obtained from plants or their synthetic equivalents; the monochrome or afterchrome process in wool dyeing for high fastness chrome dyeings. Since the dyes used in this process vary widely not only in the methods of application but the dyeing of different fibres as well, reliable recipes and instructions are to be followed carefully.

8. Acid Dyes

These dyes comprise a large number of dyes used for the dyeing of wool. They vary considerably in their basic chemical structure, but have one common feature — they dye wool from an acid dye bath. All acid dyes can be grouped in three broad sub-groups:

a.) Level dyeing acid dyes These dyes produce bright dyeings. Their main feature is their good levelling properties. Usually dyed from a dye bath containing strong acids (sulphuric or formic acid), these dyes unfortunately possess low wash and light fastness.

b.) Acid milling dyes Selected because of their high wash and light fastness and are used extensively for dyeing woollen fabrics that are subsequently milled. These dyes require great care in application because uneven dyeings are difficult or impossible to rectify. The dye bath requires the presence of a weak acid (acetic acid) or acid releasing salts (ammonium sulphate or ammonium acetate) from which acid is liberated during dyeing.

c.) Pre-metallised dyes These dyes represent an extension of the mordant dyes discussed in (7) above. In the case of pre-metallised dyes the metal components, in special form, are incorporated in the dye under conditions where the dye lake remains water soluble.

Use: The family of acid dyes is very large and diverse, varying widely in their method of dyeings, application and the end use of the fabric dyed. A choice of dyes should be made considering the following, sometimes incompatible, factors: level dyeing, fastness, brightness, and ease of application. Care must be taken to use the appropriate dyeing method as prescribed for a given dye.

9. Dispersed Dyes

The introduction of a new, regenerated cellulose acetate fibre in 1920 led to the necessity to develop an entirely new range of dyes. It was found that cellulose acetate (or Celanese) fibre had scarcely any affinity for water soluble dyes. A new dyeing principle was introduced — dyeing with water dispersed coloured organic substances. These finely coloured particles could be applied through aqueous dispersions to the acetate material and actually dissolved in the fibres, effecting satisfactory dyeings.

Use: Whilst basically developed for dyeing of acetate fibres, dispersed dyes are also used in dyeing polyamide (nylon) and acrylic (orlon and acrylan) fibres. With the addition of 'carriers', or swelling agents, these dyes are also used to dye polyester fibres (terylene, tetron, dacron, etc.). As these dyes do not dye cellulosic fibres, single bath combination dyeings can be done by introducing direct dyes in the same dye bath.

10. Oxidation Dyes

These are not dyestuffs in the same sense as other soluble or dispersed dyestuffs, but because of their excellent fastness to light and washing, are of great importance. The most important member of this group is a dyestuff produced by the oxidation of aniline. The method of oxidising various organic substances to give brown to black shades is much used in the dyeing of fur and leather goods.

Use: In addition to fur and leather dyeing, aniline black was almost exclusively used to produce a highly lustred black umbrella fabric.

11. Mineral and Pigment Dyes

It is preferred to use water soluble dyes in textile dyeing mainly for two reasons — ease of application and greater softness of the fabric. There are two processes where pigment colouration is used:

a.) Mineral khaki Cotton army equipment is being dyed with a 'Mineral Khaki' process because of the cheapness of the process, suitable fastness properties, and also because it renders the fabric resistant to rotting and attack by bacteria and insects in damp conditions. The dyeing is done by the formation of iron and chromium salts on the fabric.

b.) Synthetic resin printing The introduction of heat-setting synthetic resins has opened new fields of textile printing. Mineral and organic pigments, as used in paint manufacture, can now be applied to any fabric and after heat treatment rendered washfast.

Use: Whilst the formation of mineral pigment on a fabric is used less and less as a dyeing process, the use of pigment printing is increasing continuously. The key to this is the development and availability of soft and flexible synthetic resins, available as binders (or adhesives) to secure the pigments to the fabric without including a harsh or stiff finish.

Calculation of Quantities of Dyes and Chemicals

Since dyes colour fibres from within and are transparent, depth of shade or darkness of the dyeing depends on the amount of dye deposited in the fibre. Thus a direct relationship is established between the depth of the dyeing, amount of dye used, and the weight of the fibre to be dyed. This relationship is usually expressed as a percentage of dye as against the weight of the fibre. It is only a generalisation, but it can be assumed that:

Pastel shades require approximately 0.5—1% of dye or 5—10 gm for 1 kg of fibre.
Medium shades require approximately 3% of dye or 30 gm for 1 kg of fibre.
Brown and Navy Blue require approximately 5% of dye or 50 gm for 1 kg of fibre.
Black shades require approximately up to 8% of dye or 80 gm for 1 kg of fibre.

These percentages will be valid only if the dye has penetrated well, depth of shade is evenly distributed on and in the material dyed, and the dye bath is completely exhausted at the conclusion of the dyeing.

The calculation for the correct amount of dye to be taken can be made as follows:

$$\frac{\text{weight of fibre} \times \text{depth of shade required}}{100} = \text{weight of dye to be taken}$$

This formula applies to all dyes and chemicals on all fibres, regardless of whether the weight is expressed in grams or ounces. If fibre or fabric is weighed in ounces the weight should be multiplied by 28.35 to convert same to grams. The amount of water used should be adequate to allow fibre or fabric to be moved in the dye bath. The usual proportion is 1 part of material or fibre to 50 parts of water and it is called a goods-to-liquor ratio of 1:50.

Some Technical Terms Used in Dyeing

The fibre is usually said to be 'entered' when first placed in the 'dye bath' (or dye-liquor) which when prepared is said to be 'set'. When all dye is taken up by the fibre, the 'dye-bath' is 'exhausted'. The amount of dye on the fibre determines the depth of the dyeing, sometimes called 'depth of shade'.

A dyeing is 'level' when it is of the same depth all over the yarn or fabric and when it shows complete penetration of the material. Both types of levelness are ensured by good agitation during the whole dyeing time and by the control of the rate of dyeing (too fast rate of dyeing usually results in poor penetration) and allowing sufficient time in the dye bath. A third type of unevenness in wool dyeing is caused by exposure to the atmosphere of the wool fibre whilst on the sheep's back. This is manifested in difference in colour between the root portion of the fibre and the outer parts of the same fibre. This 'skitteriness' is more difficult to avoid than other forms of unlevelness and is more dependent on choice of the dyes used. It can be assumed that at the beginning of the dye cycle some uneven dyeing occurs that is levelled out during the dyeing process. The transfer of dye from heavily dyed to lightly dyed portions during dyeing is called 'migration'.

Since the most important component in dyeing is the dye, some attention is required in dissolving it. Dye is best 'pasted' with a small amount of water to which a drop of detergent is added. Hot water is then added and the dye is dissolved to make sure it is free of lumps and undissolved particles.

Synthetic dyes give professional as well as amateur dyers a wide range of choice, the ability to fulfil the most exacting fastness requirements, combined with ease of application, reasonable repeatability of colour and immediate availability. We hope that this brief summary will help in the evaluation, comparison and consequent use of synthetic dyes in home use.

Methods for the application of many of the dyes described in Mr Voitkun's article are to be found in this book. Commission Dyers supplies instructions with all the dyes they sell. This information is taken from those instructions sheets. These dyestuffs were chosen because their use is not described elsewhere in this book.

Direct Dyes

To dye with direct dyes, paste the required amount of dye with cold water, then dissolve in an adequate amount of hot water until a clear solution is obtained.

Start dyeing hot, and if possible bring the dyebath to the boil. Add 3-5% of common salt or Glauber's salt. Pale shades do not require the addition of salt. Allow to cool for 20-30 minutes until the dyebath is reasonably exhausted. Dyeings interrupted before the dyebath is exhausted result in poor wash fastness.

Remove fabric from the dyebath, rinse in cold water until all loose dye is removed, and dry.

If increased wash fastness is required, after-treat the dry fabric in 3-5% of liquid fixing agent. Use lukewarm water and run the fabric for fifteen minutes. Then dry it again.

Note: Formulas for calculating dye quantities and the amount of additives also occur throughout this book. Percentages are based on the dry weight of fibre or material. With direct dyes you use 3% of dye to the dry weight of fabric to get a medium shade. Thus, if your fabric weighs 100 gm, you need 3 gm of dye powder. Use less dye for pastel shades and more for dark shades. Similarly, if you add 5% salt, this would be 5 gm salt for 100 gm fabric.

Vat Dyes

Vat dyes don't dissolve in water so the way you prepare them is very important. For dyeing 100 gm cotton fabric use 5 gm dye; 10 gm caustic soda; and 10 gm sodium hydrosulphite.

Note: Blue dye requires twice the amount of chemicals given above, including dye quantity. And black dye needs four times the amount.

Paste the required amount of weighed dye with a small amount of methylated spirits. Firstly, add 200 ml soft, hot water and half of the dissolved caustic soda, then sprinkle half of the sodium hydrosulphite into the solution, stir and leave to stand for ten minutes. The caustic soda should be dissolved in *cold* water only. Handle caustic with great care and always add it *to* water (not the reverse).

Prepare your dyebath with the required amount of soft water, which should be warm. You need enough water to cover the fabric. Add the remaining half of the dissolved caustic soda and sodium hydrosulphite, along with the prepared dye stock, and immerse the fabric. Dye the fabric by agitating it slowly and keeping it under the surface of the dye all the time. After ten to fifteen minutes remove the fabric, rinse it, and air the fabric to oxidise the dye. The colour will change to the shade you are-dyeing. Wash the fabric in mild detergent, and dry.

The Pre-Metallised Dyes

Wilmma Hollist and Roy Russell

The pre-metallised dyes form a small group of dyestuffs, about forty in all, which are classified in the colour index, and by manufacturers, as acid dyes. Although they have some similarities they differ significantly both in properties and in application methods. They are included in the acid group because the physical and chemical bonds which hold the dye to the fibre are similar. They are principally intended for dyeing wool and the following application methods are for use on this fibre. Pre-metallised dyes also bear some similarities to synthetic chrome dyes and natural dyes on a chrome mordant, differing in that the chromium dye complex is formed prior to dyeing. Pre-metallised dyes are chromium, and occasionally cobalt, co-ordinated complexes of azo dyes. They divide into two major groups:

1:1 Pre-metallised or acid pre-metallised dyes
1:2 Pre-metallised or neutral dyeing pre-metallised

Group 1:1 Pre-Metallised Dyes

The 1:1 group of pre-metallised dyestuffs are not recommended for craft use. They are marketed under such names as Neolan and Palatine. They are applied from a strongly acid dyebath, 8% sulphuric acid, and the health hazard present in using such a strong acid, in the home, studio or college is considerable. They give moderately bright colours with similar fastness to light, but slightly inferior wash-fastness, compared to the 1:2 group.

Group 1:2 Pre-Metallised Dyes

The 1:2 group of pre-metallised dyestuffs is by far the most important from the craft dyers point of view. They are marketed under such names as Cibalan, Irgalan, and Isolan. These dyestuffs provide colours of limited brightness but with very high fastness properties. An important feature of the 1:2 pre-metallised group is that they retain their high fastness properties when dyed to pale shades, a property not generally found in the acid dyestuffs. They do not provide a tri-chromatic set as there is not red, blue or yellow suitable for matching the spectrum. The colours are compatible and can be mixed to make a wide range of shades. The 1:2 group of pre-metallised dyes are compatible with only a few of the acid dyes of the type which exhaust reasonably under neutral or weakly acid dyeing conditions. They can be safely mixed with a range of acid dyes marketed under the name of Irganol, which gives a brighter range of colours.

Volumetric Solutions

The most convenient way to handle the dyes is to make them into volumetric solutions. If a known quantity of dyestuff is dissolved in a known quantity of water and measured portions of the dye solution are used to dye (or to mix with other colours before dyeing) then control over the strength and the composition of the colour itself is easy. If a solution of a red, a blue and a yellow are made, then literally thousands of colours can be produced by mixing the colours in an endless permutation of proportions. Add to the three 'primaries' a brown, a black and a purple, and the range will be extended still further.

Measurements

It is much easier to work in metric measurements when dyeing. It makes all the mathematics so easy that they can be done mentally, although we do advise that you note down your answers for future reference, you will find that no long division will be required. Can you work out 1% of 3 ounces in two seconds? Try 1% of 85 grams. The answer to both is 0.85 grams and we are not going to try to convert 0.85 grams to Imperial. The following table gives a few of the main conversions between Imperial and metric measurements, and a more detailed conversion table can be referred to if necessary.

1 ounce	=	28.45 gm
1 pound	=	454 gm
1 pint	=	566 ml
1 fluid oz	=	28 ml
100 grams	=	3½ ounces
1 litre	=	1.76 pints
1 kilo	=	2 lb 3¼ ozs

Safety

The 1:2 pre-metallised dyestuffs are harmless if handled with care. Avoid breathing in the dye powder. Wipe up spillages immediately. Use rubber gloves to avoid staining the hands. Keep out of reach of young children. Wash hands when finished.

To Make Volumetric Solutions

The standard strength of dyestuffs is 100% and this figure is taken for granted unless otherwise stated. If a dyestuff is specified as being 200%, 250% or 300% they are twice as strong, two and a half times as strong, and thrice as strong, respectively, as the standard strength dye.

The strength of a colour is described as the percentage dye applied. For a 1% depth of colour 1 gm of dyestuff is used to dye 100 gm of fibre, and for a 3% depth, 3 gm of dye. Weighing small amounts of dyestuff requires a chemical balance and a lot of patience. It is easier to prepare volumetric solutions and use measured amounts as required. A 1% volumetric solution, 10 gm of dye per one litre of water, used at the rate of 1 ml per 1 gm of fibre will give a 1% depth dyeing, 2 ml per 1 gm a 2% depth, 5 ml per 1 gm a 5% depth and ½ ml per 1 gm a ½% depth, etc. The final amount of dye solution for any dyeing can be composed of varying amounts of different colours.

A 2% dye solution, 20 gm of dye per litre of water, can be used for processing large amounts of material (in this case for a 2% dyeing use at the rate of 2 ml per 1 gm of fibre). We do not recommend making the solutions stronger than 20 gm per litre because of the poor solubility of these dyestuffs.

Stir Your Dye Not Your Yarn!

It is of *utmost* importance to stir dye solutions and assistants very thoroughly into the dyebath before entering the fibre. Inadequate mixing at this point is often the cause of uneven dyeing. It is necessary to move the yarn in the dyebath during dyeing. This is to maintain a uniform temperature. We recommend gently 'turning over the material'. Most hand dyeing pots tend to have a higher temperature at the bottom, nearer the source of heat, than at the top and this difference in temperature will cause uneven results with this type of dyestuff.

Chemical Assistant

To obtain the neutral condition in the dyebath necessary for level dyeing ammonium acetate is used. Ammonium acetate provides a 'buffer' and neutralises small residues of acid or alkali left in the fibre from previous processes. Furthermore, due to slow release and evaporation of the ammonium part of the compound, the dyebath becomes slowly and increasingly mildly acid, due to the presence of acetic acid. This slow release of acid as the dyebath comes to the boil promotes the slow and even absorption of the dye. The final amount of acid in the dyebath is very small, pH about 6.

Ammonium Acetate Ammonium acetate can be purchased as a white crystalline solid which readily absorbs water from the air and should be kept in an airtight container. Use at the rate of 4 gm per 100 gm of fibre. A solution prepared by dissolving 40 gm of ammonium acetate in a litre of water provides an easy working solution and is used at the rate of 1 ml to 1 gm of fibre.

Home Made Ammonium Acetate Ammonium acetate can be made by adding approximately 2 litres of white vinegar to 1 litre of 5% domestic ammonia (Scrubbs Ammonia). The accuracy of the preparation depends on the relative strengths of the ingredients but a good guide is to add the vinegar to the ammonia until the characteristic smell of the ammonia changes to a sharp sweet smell. The smell is difficult to describe but easily recognised when tried. If indicator paper is available the pH can be taken and should read 7 to 7.3. This recipe will give an approximate 4% solution of ammonium acetate and should be used at the rate of 1 ml per 1 gm of fibre (1 fluid ounce per 1 ounce of fibre).

Ammonium Sulphate Ammonium sulphate may be used as a substitute for ammonium acetate. It is a white crystalline solid used as an agricultural fertiliser, in which form it is slightly impure. Working solutions can be made by dissolving 40 gm of ammonium sulphate in a litre of water and filtering off the insoluble impurities by pouring the solution through a filter paper or fine muslin. Use the solution at the rate of 1 ml per 1 gm of fibre.

Method

1. Measure out the dye powder.
2. Add a little cold water to the powder and stir well to make a paste.
3. Add 500 ml of boiling water to the paste, stir thoroughly to dissolve the dye.
4. Make the solution up to 1 litre with cold water.
5. Decant the dye solution into a clearly labelled screw top bottle with a plastic cap. Shake well before use.

Liquor Ratio

The ratio of liquor in the dye bath to the weight of fibre being dyed is termed the liquor ratio or L/R. The liquor ratio used for the 1:2 pre-metallised is 30:1, that is for every 100 gm of yarn being dyed 3000 ml of liquor is required in the dyebath, or for every 2 ounces 60 fluid ounces of liquor. Liquor = water + assistant + dye formula. When dyeing fleece or bulky yarns it is sometimes necessary to increase the liquor ratio a little, say to 35:1.

Temperature and the Problem of Migration

The pre-metallised dyes have poor 'migration' properties so an essential feature of dyeing with these dyestuffs is very careful control of the temperature throughout the dyeing process. The temperature at the various stages of the dyeing is an intrinsic part of the process. The migration properties of these dyes is poor which means that the movement of the dye from place to place on the fibre is restricted especially at temperatures above 50° to 60°C (120° to 140°F). It is therefore important to allow time for good migration to occur below this temperature. The property of non-migration shows itself to advantage when dyeing fleece, as the dye does not show an inclination to gravitate to the tippy ends of the fleece as with some other dyestuffs, and a uniform dyeing is obtained.

Pre-Dyeing Preparation

The yarn or fibre to be dyed must be clean and well 'wetted out'. Wetting out can best be achieved by washing the material but do not leave it 'lying about' to drain before entering the dyebath, this tempts uneven dyeing. It is best handled by leaving it to soak in the last rinse water and then transferring it directly to the dyebath. If the yarn or fibre is clean but dry, it can be wetted out in warm water to which a few drops of wetting agent or liquid detergent have been added. We cannot express strongly enough how important adequate wetting out is prior to dyeing.

Method of Applying the Dyes

1. Wet out the fibre.
2. Put enough water into the dyebath to give a final liquor ratio of 30:1 and heat to 30°C (86°F). Add the required amount of ammonium acetate, stir well.
3. Enter the wetted out fibre and soak for 15 minutes.

In the meantime prepare the dye formula by placing the measured amounts of colour or colours in a mixing bowl, add a little water and *mix well*.

4. Remove the fibre from the bath and add the prepared dye, *stir very well*.
5. Replace fibre. Raise slowly and steadily to the boil taking about 45 minutes or longer. Turn the fibre over occasionally to keep the dyebath temperature uniform.
6. When the dyebath reaches boiling point allow

to boil 'gently' for 15 to 20 minutes. This short boil fixes the dye.

7. Allow the fibre to cool in the dyebath to about 60°C, 140°F.

8. Remove fibre and rinse, wash, rinse in warm water.

9. Dry away from direct sunlight or heat.

Additional Information

Absorption   These dyestuffs are absorbed onto the fibre as the temperature in the dyebath rises, unlike most acid dyes which are absorbed at the boil. The absorption of pre-metallised dyes is very good and the dyebath should be almost clear at the end of a dyeing.

Water   Your water supply may exert an influence on the quality and colour of your dyed material. Soft water is fine, if you have a soft water supply you are lucky, except if it contains iron. Some iron is usually found in water which has been stored in corrugated iron tanks. The presence of iron in the dyebath dulls or 'saddens' the colour.

We did some tests with water from different sources with the Weavers Group in Roma, Queensland, and found that the dulling of the colour caused by the iron present in the tank water was only significant on bright yellow. Our water supply is extremely hard and we use it untreated for almost all our dyeing. Soft water will give slightly better results but we do not feel that the expense and hassle involved in softening the water is cost effective for the craftsman.

Fibre, yarn and material   For the purpose of this article the words fibre, yarn and material or cloth are interchangable. The same application methods apply to all. As already mentioned fibre may require a slightly higher liquor ratio. When dyeing cloth take care over the wetting out process and during dyeing hold the temperature at between 40° and 50°C (104° and 122°F) for some time to ensure good migration and penetration of the dye.

Mix and match   The volumetric solution technique enables the dyer to sample dye a weighed or measured amount of fibre, yarn or material and then to process a much larger quantity by increasing proportionally the amount of water, assistant dyestuff and material.

Name of dye powder	Grams of powder per litre of water for 2% stock solution
Irgalan Yellow 2GL 200%	10 gm/L
Irgalan Red 2GL 200%	10 gm/L
Irgalan Bordeaux EL	20 gm/L
Irgalan Blue FBL 200%	10 gm/L
Irgalan Navy Blue B	20 gm/L
Irgalan Brown 2RL 200%	10 gm/L
Irgalan Black BGL 200%	10 gm/L
Irganol Brill. Yellow 3GL	20 gm/L
Irganol Brill. Red BL	10 gm/L
Irganol Brill. Blue RLS 200%	10 gm/L
Irganol Brill. Blue 7GS 200% (Turquoise)	10 gm/L

Dyeing silk

Wilmma and Roy give instructions for using these dyes on silk. Bring the bath to just *below* the boil over 30 minutes. Keep at this temperature for another 30 minutes — avoid boiling! To restore lustre and liveliness of silk, rinse first, then steep the silk in a solution of water and tartaric acid (at 15% of the dry weight of the silk). Let it soak 1 hour, then let the silk dry without rinsing.

Fibre Reactive Dyes

Inga Hunter

Fibre reactive dyes were first introduced on the commercial market in 1956 by ICI, under the brand name of Procion. Since then many different brands have been developed for many specialised purposes. The two brands most readily available to craftsmen at present in Australia are Procion and Drimarene K.

Fibre reactive dyes are so called because they undergo a chemical reaction with cellulose fibres (e.g. cotton, linen, rayon) under alkaline conditions, to produce a range of brilliant colours with good washing fastness. Reaction with wool and silk is also possible. None is cheap. It costs roughly $2 000 000 to launch a dye colour on the market, so you must expect to pay for the complex technology used to develop a good cold water dyestuff.

There are two sorts of fibre reactive dyes (always excluding those dyes which have been developed for the special dyeing of wool, etc.):

Hot water dye (e.g. Procion H) (less reactive) which has only one reactive chlorine atom, and is the dye most generally used for hot water dyeing and for printing methods where the cloth is baked or steamed to help fix the dye.

Cold water dye (e.g. Procion M, Drimarene K) (more reactive) which has two reactive chlorine atoms, and is capable of being applied in cool conditions. This is the dyestuff which is generally used for cold water batik dyeing.

With Procion M and Drimarene K under alkaline conditions, the two chlorine atoms will react with hydroxyl groups on the molecular chains of cellulose fibres, i.e. the chemical composition of the fibre actually changes to form a dye/cellulose compound which can no longer leave the surface of the cellulose.

Without alkali (soda ash, washing soda, bicarbonate of soda) *no reaction will take place.* The reaction is what fixes the dye; if the reaction does not occur the dye will wash out of the cloth. *Reaction, that is, fixation, will only occur in the presence of alkali over a suitable period of time.*

Because the dye must be applied in an aqueous solution (water), another factor must be considered in the reaction process; the dyestuff atoms will also react with water, as well as with the cellulose. Consequently, the dyebath will not last indefinitely because the dye is being used up in the water. This process is called hydrolysis.

A dyebath will therefore last only 2-3 hours once the reaction process begins. Speed of decomposition will depend on the type of alkali used to start the reaction, i.e. a bath made with bicarb soda lasts longer than one made with soda ash, but fixation time is correspondingly longer as well.

You can keep the dye for some time in solution (out of light and air) without adding the alkali, but as soon as this is added, hydrolysis is accelerated and the dyebath gradually loses its strength. Pale dyeings can be obtained with partly decomposed dyebaths.

Recipe for Dip Dyeing (courtesy of Batik Oetero)

Dyeing Procedure (for quantities of dye, water, etc. see chart below).
1. Mix dye with a small amount of water to form smooth paste. Add required amount of water.
2. Immerse cloth and agitate to ensure even penetration of the dye. Leave for ten minutes.
Dissolve kitchen salt in a little hot water, then add it to the dyebath. Slowly agitate for ten minutes.
3. Dissolve soda ash (*not* washing soda) in a little hot water, then add it to the dyebath. This will start a chemical reaction which will fix the colour to the material. Leave for 60-90 minutes, depending on the depth of shade required. The material should be periodically agitated during the dyeing period.
4. Rinse the material under cold running water for 5-10 minutes to remove any unfixed dye.

After-Treatment
After all dyeing is completed, boil material in water containing 2 grams per litre of pure soap (Lux); and ½ gram per litre of water softener (Calgon).

The following chart sets out the amounts of dye and other chemicals required for successful dyeing, and is fool-proof if followed accurately. It must be remembered that *weight of material* pre-determines the quantities of water, dye and fixing agents. (One metre of cotton lawn weighs approximately 100 gm.)

Weight of fabric	50 gm		100 gm		150 gm		200 gm	
Amount of water	1 litre		1 litre		1 litre		1 litre	
	shade		shade		shade		shade	
	med	dark	med	dark	med	dark	med	dark
Amount of dye	1.5 gm	3 gm	3 gm	6 gm	4.5 gm	9 gm	6 gm	12 gm
Amount of Salt**	40 gm	50 gm	80 gm	100 gm	120 gm	150 gm	160 gm	200 gm
Amount of soda ash	15 gm	20 gm	30 gm	40 gm	45 gm	60 gm	60 gm	80 gm
Fixing time	60 min	90 min	60 min	90 min	60 min	90 min	60 min	90 min

**Note:* For Scarlet, Turquoise and Green you must use sodium sulphate instead of kitchen salt.

After dyeing your cloth, the dyebath is completely exhausted and cannot be used again. The remaining liquid should be disposed of.

A Faster Dip Dyeing Method: Caustic Soda Shock

You can speed up the dipping process by adding a small amount of a much stronger alkali to your dyebath halfway through the fixation process.

Proceed with your normal dipping bath, first adding dye, then salt, then half the usual quantity of soda ash. After the soda ash has been in the bath for 15-30 minutes add 1-2 ml per litre caustic soda solution (38%). Loog solution used in naphthol dyeing is ideal (ie 441 gm caustic soda flakes carefully added to 1 litre cold water, allowed to cool and bottled). Leave the fabric in the dyebath for a further five minutes, then rinse in a weak bath of vinegar and water to neutralise the strength of the alkali.

Fibre Reactive Dyes for Wool

Margaret Sandiford

Dye Chemistry

All dyeing involves a chemical reaction if the colour imparted is to be permanent and not fugitive. A typical dye-fibre reaction is the result of a chemical attraction between certain reactive groups on the dye molecule and reactive groups on the fibre molecule. Each textile fibre differs in its chemical structure and the nature and number of sites for dye attachment. As these features are unique for each fibre type, different dyes and dyeing techniques have been developed.

The wool fibre is composed of the protein *keratin*, a complex molecule made up of 18 different amino acids combined to form a chain. These chains are joined together at different points with amino acids by both ionic and covalent bonds. The dye molecule can attach at these bridges. Strong alkalis, especially at high temperatures, can damage the covalent bonds, thus damaging the wool fibre and impairing dye attachment. It is this covalent bond that sunlight damages — hence tippy fleece.

The protective cuticle of the wool fibre, with its overlapping scales, is susceptible to heat, moisture, and friction. The scales can become locked creating a physical barrier to the dye molecule. So avoid unnecessary agitation of the dyebath.

Wool should be prepared for dyeing by prescouring to remove any lanolin or spinning oil. The fibre should be immersed in soft water for at least 20 minutes before entering in the dye bath to allow even penetration of the water molecules with the fibre interstices.

Fibre Reactive Dyes

Fibre reactive dyes are used to produce bright shades when better wash fastness properties are required than can be obtained with acid wool dyes — e.g. carpet fibres, machine washable wool fabrics, felt. With fibre reactive dyes the dye molecule bonding takes place at the covalent bond site and special dyeing procedure is required if levelling is to be even. Reactive dyes for wool are used under near acid to neutral conditions and do not hydrolyse. Covalent bonding occurs at temperatures over 185°F. Very slow heating is important, for once the required temperature at which covalent bonding occurs is reached, levelling is no longer possible.

Reactive dyes are very sensitive to variations in the nature of the fibre surface. Dye fibre reaction occurs as soon as the dye has been absorbed by the fibre; no further movement of the dye is possible once the dye fibre reaction has taken place. So initially skittery dyeings do not become level with prolonged heating. Gentle agitation during dyeing is important if levelness is to be achieved.

Fibre Reactive Dyes for Wool — Dye Houses and Brand Names

Bayer: Verofix   Ciba Geigy: Lanasol, Cibacrolan

Sandoz: Drimalan   Hoechst: Hostalan

ICI: Procilan   Dylon

The *Colour Index* is a joint publication of the Society of Dyers and Colourists of Great Britain and the American Association of Textile Chemists and Colourists in the USA. It provides a dual classification of all dyes, grouping them according to their classes and to their chemical structure. Each dye has a C.I. (Colour Index) Number. With the fibre reactive class of dyes, code letters are used after the brand name indicating the conditions under which the chemical reaction takes place with the reactive groups involved. Different companies may use identical dyes under different names, in which case these dyes can be substituted for a particular dyeing technique — each company develops a particular dyeing technique! But if the dyes are not identical, they cannot be substituted.

e.g. Hostalan YEG is interchangable with (=) Lanasol Y4G

Dyes recommended for 3-component combinations

company	brandname	red	blue	yellow
Ciba Geigy:	Lanasol	Red 6G	Blue 3G	Yellow 4G
Hoechst:	Hostalan	Red E-G	Blue E-FB	Brill.Yellow E-G

Using the three primary colours — red, blue and yellow — the artist dyer can create any hue, tint or tone.

Dyeing Instructions and Details for 'Lanasol' Fibre Reactive Dyes for Wool

1. L.R. — the liquor ratio Water is an excellent solvent. Chemical compounds break up into their component parts in water. Fibre reactive dyes for wool do not hydrolyse in the dyebath under the recommended conditions of dyeing. Only a small proportion of the dye on the fibre at the end of the dyeing remains uncombined. The quantity of water used in the dyebath is critical. If too little is used, the fibre will not be completely immersed, if too large a volume is used the reaction time will be slowed down. For fibre reactive dyes, the L.R. is 20:1; pale shades require 40:1. As 1 ml of water weighs 1 gm and occupies 1 cc of space, the volume of water used in the dyebath (in mls) = fibre weight (in gms) × dye liquor ratio.

Soft water must be used.

2. Albegal B The auxilliary Albegal B is used to improve dyeing. Its functions are to (1) promote level dyeing (2) increase the rate of dyeing. It is amphoteric (having both acidic and basic properties) and highly substantive to the fibre.

3. Glauber's salt (sodium sulphate) This is added to ensure the maximum effectiveness of Albegal B.

4. Acidity (pH) Dye fibre combination is controlled by

i.   the time of dyeing

ii.   the pH

iii.   the temperature of dyeing

Initial dye reaction takes place at neutral to near neutral pH — add acetic acid. But greater wet fastness is achieved by raising the pH and prolonging the dyeing at the end of the dyeing process. Thus the dye on the fibre which is not yet chemically combined with the fibre, but is still fibre reactive (still capable of attaching to the fibre), can be made to combine with the fibre by raising the pH to 8-8.5 by adding ammonia and boiling for 10-15 minutes, or by continuing dyeing at 105°C. This should be done to ensure no subsequent bleeding.

Dye Calculations

Calculating the correct amounts of dye and dyeing auxilliaries is made easier if 10% solutions are made of all chemicals used. That is, 10 gm (or 10 ml) of the solid (liquid) chemical is weighed (measured) out and made up to 100 ml with water — it is essential that weight and volume be accurate if colours are to be replicated later! Heat may be required to dissolve the chemical. Then the following formula is used to calculate the amount of dye or chemical auxilliary needed for a specific weight of yarn:

volume of solution required (in mls) =

$$\frac{\text{percentage}}{100} \times \frac{\text{weight of material (gms)}}{1} \times \frac{100}{\text{solution strength}}$$

e.g. 1% of 80% acetic acid is required for 10 gm of wool

$$\frac{1}{100} \times \frac{10}{1} \times \frac{100}{80} = 0.1 \text{ ml}$$

Extrapolating from Table 1, Table 2 below represents a dye concentration series (Lanasol dye for wool) where the quantities in mls have been estimated for:

• 10 gm yarn using

• 10% solutions of amm. sulphate, Glauber's salts,

• 80% acetic acid   Albegal B, dye

• 25% ammonia

Table 1
Standard dyeing process for Ciba Geigy 'Lanasol' dyes for wool.

Table 1 and the accompanying graph contain all the relevant information for the dyeing process. The graph indicates time and temperature at which chemicals and yarns are introduced to the dyebath, and the table gives the percentage of chemicals used for the desired dye concentration.

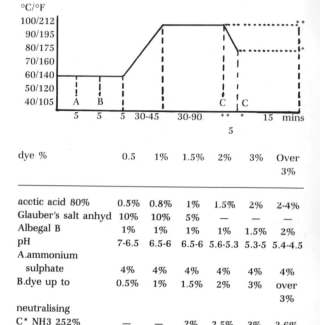

dye %	0.5	1%	1.5%	2%	3%	Over 3%
acetic acid 80%	0.5%	0.8%	1%	1.5%	2%	2-4%
Glauber's salt anhyd	10%	10%	5%	—	—	—
Albegal B	1%	1%	1%	1%	1.5%	2%
pH	7-6.5	6.5-6	6.5-6	5.6-5.3	5.3-5	5.4-4.5
A.ammonium sulphate	4%	4%	4%	4%	4%	4%
B.dye up to	0.5%	1%	1.5%	2%	3%	over 3%
neutralising C* NH3 252%	—	—	2%	2.5%	3%	3-6%
pH about			8.5	8.5	8.5	8.5

Colour value expressed as % shade

very pale	0.25%
pale-light	0.5
light-medium	1
medium	2
medium-dark	3
dark	4

Table 2 Dye concentration series — Lanasol for 10 gm of yarn

dye concentration	0.5%	1%	1.5%	2%	3%	4%
acetic acid	0.06	0.1	0.125	0.19	0.25	0.5
Glauber's salt	10	10	5	—	—	—
Albegal B	1	1	1	1	1.5	2.0
pH	7-6.5	6.5-6	6.5-6	5.6-5.3	5.3-5	5.4-4.5
amm. sulphate	4	4	4	4	4	4
dye	0.5	1	1.5	2	3	4
ammonia	—	—	0.8	1	1.2	2.4

A silk sash by Lise Cruickshank. The warp yarn has been dyed by Lise ('ikat' resist dyeing).

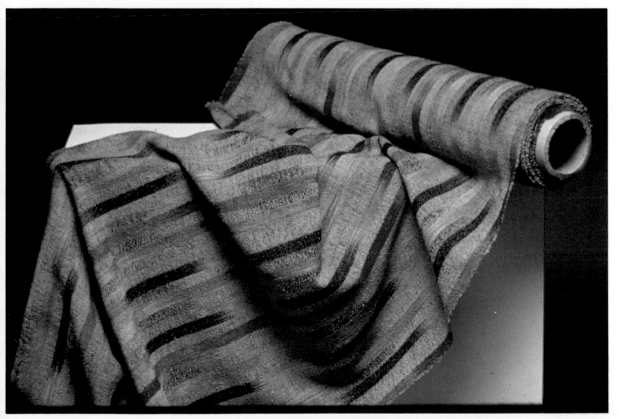

Fabric dyed and woven by Lise Cruickshank, of silk noil. 'Ikat' resist dyeing.

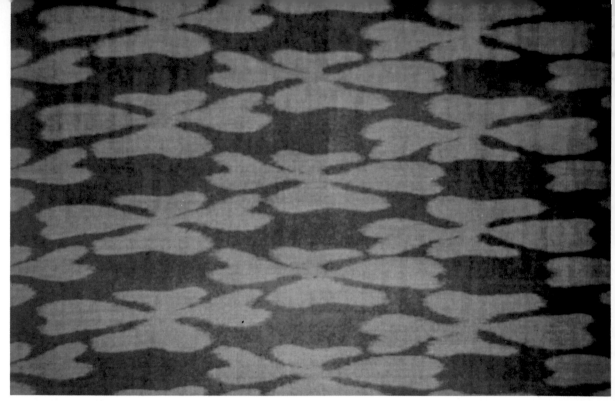

'Clovers Blue', detail of fabric by Lyn Waring, purchased by the Queensland Art Gallery. Woven from 2/30s woollen yarn. 'Weft Kasuri' (weft threads resist dyed before weaving).

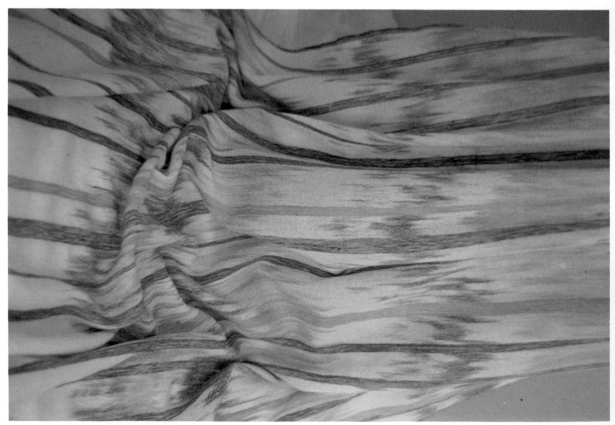

Detail of cloth by Lyn Waring, entitled 'Sea'. Tie-dyed warp (acid dyes). Warp of 2/36s worsted wool; solid stripes of silk yarn. Weft of 2/30s woollen yarn, 4 colours (including white).

Method (for 3% dye concentration)
1. add 200 ml water at 40-60°C (105-140°F)
   0.25 ml 80% acetic acid
   1.5 ml of 10% solution Albegal B ... to dyebath
2. add wetted (20 mins minimum wetting) wool
   (10 gm)
3. stand for 5 mins
4*. add 4 ml ammonium sulphate (10% solution)
5. stand for 5 mins — pH should be 5.0-5.3
6*. add dye solution (composite 3 ml of 10% dye
   solution)
7. raise temperature to boiling over 45 mins — stir
   gently
8. boil 30 mins
9. cool to 80°C (175°F)
10*. add 1.2 ml of 25% ammonia — pH 8.5

*wool should be removed from bath whilst auxil-
iaries are added.

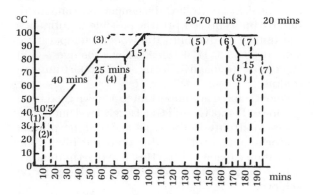

Dyebath Procedure

(1) ×% acetic acid 60%   (7) rinsing
    1.5% Remol GES   (8) NH₃ treatment pH 8-8.5
    2% ammonium acetate
(2) dye, pH check
(3) with deep shades
(4) with pale shades
(5) acetic acid replenishment
    with deep shades
(6) 5% Hostalan Salt K

Note: 10' means 10 minutes, etc.

Standard dyeing process for Hoechst 'Hostalan' dyes for wool

Additions to the bath and the treatment time in the dyeing of wool with Hostalan dyes can be ascertained from the following table:

Table 3

Hostalan dyes in %	up to 1	up to 2	up to 3	over 3
Remol GES in %	1.5	1.5	1.5	1.5
Ammonium acetate in %	2	2	2	2
×% acetic acid, pH of dyebath	5.5	5.2	5	4.7
dyeing time at 100°C in mins	20-45	60	70	up to 90
Hostalan Salt K in %	—	5	5	5
Addition of Host. Salt K to the dyebath takes place after stated number of mins dyeing time at the boil (obviates treatment with ammonia) or	—	40	50	60-70
Treatment with NH₃ 25% for 15 mins at 80°C takes place at the stated pH	—	8-8.5	8-8.5	8-8.5

Dyeing Instructions for Hoechst's 'Hostalan' Fibre Reactive Dyes for Wool

The levelness of dyeings produced with Hostalan dyes is governed by four factors:
a. the behaviour of the dye itself
b. control of temperature
c. adjustment of the necessary pH
d. the use of Remol GE or Remol GES (S – defoaming agent)

With Hostalan dyes, the attachment point is via the vinyl sulphone group which is present initially in an inactive form. Only at a relatively high temperature does this slowly change to the reactive form and then react with the fibre if the pH is maintained within a certain range. The dye in its inactive form first establishes a salt-like linkage with the wool and is thus still capable of migration until it forms an additive linkage with the wool after transition to its reactive form.

Surface levelness can also be affected by points a,b, and c. By controlling the temperature and maintaining the required pH it is possible to influence the uptake of dye onto the wool. A temperature stop at 80-85°C (176-185°F) allows the dye — still largely in its inactive form — an opportunity to migrate.

Points a and d are important to achieve good fibre levelness. Remol GE and GES largely level out differences in affinity in the wool material, permitting uniform uptake of the dye onto the fibre. The migration capacity of the Hostalan dyes in their inactive form enables good fibre levelness to be achieved.

In dyeing, care should be taken to ensure that the prescribed dyeing times at the boil are maintained, for only in this way can an optimum degree of fastness be achieved.

The dyes recommended for 3-component combinations are:

Hostalan Brilliant Yellow E-G
Hostalan Red E-G
Hostalan Blue E-FB

These dyes all have very similar uptake. For bright navy shades, Hostalan Red EG may be replaced by Hostalan Red 4B.

Auxilliaries Remol GE and Remol GES

Remol GE is a weakly cationic auxilliary with affinity for both dye and fibre. Remol GES contains foam inhibitors in addition and should be used wherever froth is likely to occur.

Remol GE and GES largely level out differences in the affinity of the wool. Most of the auxilliary moves onto the wool during the dyeing and changes the uptake of the Hostalan dyes in such a way they hardly react to differences in affinity of the wool. The quantity added is 1.5% relative to the weight of goods to be dyed.

Remol GE and GES are highly stable in the presence of water hardness compounds, metal salts, alkalis, and acids. They are miscible in any proportion with cold or hot water.

pH Value

Maintenance of constant pH during dyeing promotes levelness, and is best achieved by adding acetic acid and ammonium acetate to the dyebath as a buffer. With deep shades, the dyebath can be further exhausted after 30-45 mins boiling by adding 0.5-1% acetic acid 60%.

Glauber's Salt

Glauber's salt would impair the levelness of the dyeing and should not be added. It slows the uptake of Hostalan dyes below the boil. When boiling is reached, the dye moves onto the fibre very rapidly, and since it is converted to its reactive form at the same time, there is a risk of unlevelness.

Prescouring

This consists of a 15 minute treatment at 50°C (122°F) in a liquor containing a nonionic detergent — e.g. 0.25% Hostapal — followed by a thorough rinse.

Dissolving Hostalan Dyes

The dyes are pasted up with cold water, covered with 10-20 times their quantity of hot water, boiled for 1-2 mins. The temperature must reach 80-85°C (176-185°F). The dye is then added to the dyebath in which the auxilliary and chemicals are already present.

Hostalan K Salt

This is used to obtain the best possible wet fastness when over 1% dyes are used. 5% Hostalan K Salt is added at the boil to remove the small proportion of dye not linked completely to the fibre. Hostalan K Salt changes the pH of the dyebath and dispenses with an alkaline (ammonia) treatment, thus obviating the risk of wool damage and reducing the dyeing time.

It is dissolved in warm water (50°C) and is resistant to acids, alkalis and electrolytes under the conditions of the dyeing process.

Treatment with Ammonia

A 15 minute ammonia treatment at pH 8-8.5 can be carried out in the cooled dyebath (80°C) if Hostalan K Salt is unavailable. The goods should then be rinsed with water and, ideally, scoured off with acetic or formic acid.

Substitute Chemicals

Homemade ammonium acetate

Made by adding approximately 2 litres of white vinegar to 1 litre of 5% domestic ammonia. The accuracy of the preparation depends on the relative strengths of the ingredients but a good guide is to add the vinegar to the ammonia until the characteristic smell of ammonia changes to a sharp sweet smell. The pH can be taken with indicator paper and should read 7 to 7.3. This recipe gives an approximate 4% solution of ammonium acetate.

Ammonia

Scrubbs Ammonia from the supermarket indicates 9% ammonia concentration. Hunter's cloudy ammonia indicates 5% concentration. Calculate adjustments and use accordingly.

Acetic acid

Household vinegar is usually about 3% acetic acid. Industrial acetic acid comes as 80%, 60%, or glacial (100%).

Prescouring

Wool should be prepared for dyeing. A simple home recipe is to soak the wool in a bath containing a small amount of ammonia. This removes any lanolin or spinning oil. This ammonia bath should contain 250-500 ml of clear ammonia per 20 litres of soft water (1 cup/5 gals).

Disperse Dyes for Transfer Printing

Inga Hunter

Transfer, or as it is sometimes called, sublistatic printing, is an inexpensive, simple technique for the graphic decoration of fabric.

The design is first painted with dyes onto paper. Then it is transferred to fabric by ironing. Whatever is put on the printing paper is accurately reproduced on the cloth, from finest pen lines or brush strokes, to textures, washes, etc. The dye is both light- and wash-fast to a high degree, and can therefore be used for all sorts of clothing, wallhangings, panels, furnishings, soft sculpture, quilting, patchwork — in fact, anything you like.

The dyes used are *disperse dyes* i.e., those which are specially designed for use on synthetic fibres.

Disperse dyes do not dissolve in water, but are dissolved in the textile fibre itself under conditions of heat and pressure. The colour is suspended in the water, which is only used as a vehicle to get the dye onto the printing paper. With the application of heat the dyes turn into a vapour (sublimation — hence sublistatic) which is forced by pressure into the fibres of the materials, such as polyester, nylon, and rayon acetate (not viscose rayon, which is made from regenerated cellulose and needs dyes intended for cotton, linen etc.). On cooling, the dyes re-condense in the fibres and cannot escape. This sublimation of disperse dyes was originally considered to be a defect in the normal dip-dyeing process, because colours would cross from one cloth to another in drying chambers and cause spotting and other problems. However, in 1960 the possibilities of printing the dyes by transfer from paper to cloth was first explored by a European Consortium, leading to the enormous business that sublistatic printing is today. Disperse dyes available to artists come in various forms, all of which sublime at temperatures of approximately 180 degrees Centrigade (400 degrees Fahrenheit).

Transfer dyes are not widely available in Australia because the process is still largely uncommon. Batik Oetero sells 100 gm jars of Polysol dyes in powder form, all colours including a good deep black. Many shops sell a Deka brand transfer dye, marketed in tiny jars. This is dye thickened to the consistency of poster colours. There is also available a form of transfer crayon (not to be confused with those crayons which you use directly on the fabric, like Pentel). Crayola have a box of crayons which you use on paper and heat transfer to cloth. They come in a red, white and blue pack and are very cheap — ideally suited to work with children. Polysol dyes are most economical because they will last for months mixed in water. They don't dissolve and don't deteriorate. You will find that you use all your dye instead of having to throw it out after use (like fibre reactives). Powdered transfer dyes are mixed with cold water and behave like inks, but can be thickened for use in screen and relief printing. Liquid dye needs to be stirred before use because it tends to settle in the jar.

The paper used in transfer printing should be smooth and non-absorbent. Lay-out paper gives very good prints and also comes in extremely large sizes, but good quality typing or duplicating paper is sufficient. There is a balance to be achieved between using a liquid as paint and needing a smooth paper. Very shiny litho papers for instance, are good for printing because the dye comes off them easily, but are bad for painting. The biggest problem with using liquid dyes on smooth papers is usually crackling (buckling). The unevenness does not usually show in the first print, but will on subsequent ones.

The tools you use to paint your print papers can be anything you want. The dye will not harm good brushes but might clog up an airbrush because the particles of dye don't dissolve. Pens should be of the kind that you can dip into the dye. Speedball calligraphy pens come with a variety of interesting nib shapes which are ideal for transfer designs. Once completed, your print papers must be allowed to dry before printing, otherwise the design will smudge. Print papers can be stored indefinitely before using.

You must use synthetic fabrics for transfer printing. You will get an image on other fabrics but it will be paler and will not be washfast. It might be light-fast — you would have to do proper tests. You can use blends of natural and synthetic fibres providing the synthetic dominates (i.e. T-shirts, 65% polyester; 35% cotton).

A simple test will give you a rough guideline for identifying fabrics for transfer printing. Take a few threads from the fabric, bring them slowly to a flame and observe the results. Synthetics behave in a variety of ways from burning freely to shrinking and melting in long black drops, but they will all leave a hard or gritty ash behind. If fibres burn to an ash which can be crushed like powder, you have a fabric unsuited to transfer printing. Many people sneer at synthetic fabrics but when it comes to the test are unable to distinguish them from natural fibres. If you begin to be aware of synthetics, you will see that there are many interesting and beautiful fabrics ideally suited to heat transfer.

The Process

The process of printing is not a complicated one, but does need to be learned. Most of the problems encountered by beginners are caused by inefficient printing. Dyes need heat and pressure to transfer to fabric, and there are three possible tools for the job.
1) A professional sublistatic press. These come in all sizes, the smallest being the machine used to transfer designs onto T-shirts in shops. They are all expensive. A small press runs to about $1000.
2) A domestic ironing press (e.g., Elna or Singer). The print area is small but will suffice.
3) A domestic iron. Steam is *not* required; the necessaries are 180 degrees C in heat (cotton); pressure; and time. The heat sublimes the dye into vapour. The pressure forces the vapour into the fibres. And time is needed for this to take place. With an iron and the correct technique you can successfully transfer very large designs. The best iron is one without steam holes. With a steam iron you need to move it around to avoid a pattern of steam holes in your print. This necessitates anchoring down print paper and cloth to prevent movement of the

design during printing. You also need to press down hard to print, ordinary ironing technique is not good enough — you are being a substitute for a printing press. Each dye colour requires a different time for sublimation, only experience will help you. However, a 60 second printing time over the whole area (which means longer, unless you use an iron-sized print) is suitable for most colours.

For printing you need a padded surface protected from dye with brown paper, which will need to be changed after each printing to avoid pick-up from earlier prints. On this surface you lay your (ironed) fabric and over this, face-down is the print paper. On top of the paper is another sheet of brown paper which protects the synthetic fabric from the hot iron and stops it from being burned or melted during the printing process. Polyesters stand up to this better than other fibres.

To estimate the progress of printing you hold down one side of the sandwich and carefully lift the other so that you can see the print. You will need to check each side of the print — right-handed people characteristically neglect the right side and vice versa for left handers. Do not separate the layers fully until you are satisfied with the print. Beginners are always impatient and rarely press for long enough. You will find that if you use an ironing board for printing it will need to be set at a lower height than is usually used for ironing. This will help you to *press* rather than to smooth. If your print is too pale, either your iron is not hot enough or you have not allowed sufficient time for sublimation. Prints on fabrics other than synthetics tend to be pale also.

Transfer

Theoretically, transfer printing is a monoprint technique because there is a fixed amount of dye on your paper and it will be used up in printing. In practice however the number of prints you can get from one paper seems to vary widely with different individuals. Some people can print many times with one paper. To get a long print run of course, you either screen or block print a series of papers. Extremely thick areas of dye can cause problems with the print because the dye sublimes into itself instead of the paper, and very dilute dye will generally print only once. Experience will help you judge what you want.

The major disadvantage of transfer colours is the change of colour from print paper to printed cloth. The dyes (and crayons) look dull and muted on paper, then change into brilliant clear colours once they are printed. This makes things difficult for everyone and especially for those not experienced in colour mixing. The answer lies in pre-testing your colours. All polysol dyes are intermixable. You can mix your colours and try them out on small samples of your cloth. The dyes do not deteriorate, so that you can keep known colour mixtures indefinitely. It is wise to use a standard strength of mixture (perhaps 3 gm dye in 100 ml water) so that you can control your colours more easily. If all else fails, try printing on pale grey fabric to dull down the colours. Polysol colours are transparent and can be overprinted. You won't need to be reminded that transfer printing gives a reversed image and lettering will need to be reversed. Some of the most interesting results can be had by using resists between print paper and cloth. Print papers can be cut, torn, woven, crumpled etc. before printing. The most complex collages can be made with print papers which can then be transferred in a single printing onto your fabric. A polycell and wallpaper paste is helpful to anchor down and separate units onto a background for ease of printing, but you must be wary of other glues which can leave a pale area on your print.

Transfer printing is such a simple process that you could fall into the trap of thinking that the results have to be trite, but it is in fact a process which has enormous scope for the surface designer, and combines extremely well with other fibre and fabric techniques.

Suggested Approaches

Make a series of colour charts of your available dyes and test them on different fabrics. Do the same thing for tints (dye diluted with water) and for the basic secondary mixtures.

Try making crayon rubbings as print paper.

Try printing onto stitched fabric and then undoing the stitching.

Make print papers by using dyes as a wash over crayon.

Make print papers to tear and cut up, and use as collage.

Try printing pleated and folded material.

Print over a series of leaves, meshes, threads, lace, edges of fabrics, vilene cut-outs.

Print through lace, then print the lace, then print the paper alone.

Wash several layers of colours onto your paper — say blue over orange, and print several times.

Try over-printing.

Soga Discharge Dyeing

Inga Hunter

Soga 2391 is a brown dye which can be discharged (bleached) in successively lighter shades back to white. Australian batikers use it for positive dark lines which are otherwise difficult and time-consuming to achieve.

Our soga is a synthetic version of an old Indonesian vegetable dye, which was widely used for the characteristic brown colours of traditional batik cloths. Indonesians now use the synthetic soga because of its reliability and speed of use. The way in which we use the dye was brought to us by Karen Edin, who had learned it from a well-known Indonesian artist called Saad Ibny Sudachmir.

Soga is not a widely-known technique in the Western world, and is full of problems that we will have to live with, since no one lays claim to great expertise in its use. Dyeing in general is an art always fraught with pitfalls, especially for the artist who is stretching technique to its limits, and soga in particular seems to have more pitfalls than other dyes, despite its apparent simplicity. — I am regularly besieged with phone calls and letters from people whose soga dyeing has produced strange results, and I can't really help them very much. You might ask why we use the technique if it is so unreliable. I suppose the answer would be, 'Because it is there'.

Most discharge techniques use hot bleaching baths unsuitable for batik. Cold discharge methods (chlorine) work only with fibre reactive dyes, not naphthols, and fibre reactives are well-known as difficult dyes for really dark colours. At least, dark colours take a long time in the dyebath. Soga, on the other hand, is very quick to apply (just like any naphthol dye) and goes a very, very dark brown. The discharge process can result in beautiful gradations of this brown, down to pure white. It is one of those processes you either love or hate: a totally subjective decision on your part. Should you decide you want to try the soga process, I will outline it for you. It is not the sum total of all knowledge about soga, but a reasonably tried recipe which works well, given a degree of dyeing skill and commonsense, and providing you don't introduce too many new variables.

I don't recommend its use on anything but cotton or linen. I have used it successfully on silk and know others who have done so as well, but the fibre is definitely weakened in the process, and on occasions I have produced something akin to silk porridge! Some people find that repeated bleaching turns their silk coal black first and then disintegrates it. All discharge methods are rough on fibres, so I suggest that you do a little research on the effects of acids and alkalines on your favourite cloth before you start experimenting.

Soga Dyeing Method

First you must dye your cloth brown. You make the soga dye in two baths. The first contains soga and the second diazo salts.

5 gm soga to 7.5 gm Red B plus 7.5 gm Black B. This will give you a good dark brown.

For the first bath, the 5 gm of soga is pasted with a small quantity of hot water and then made up to 1 litre with cold water. For a larger quantity multiply both dye and litres of water. That is, 10 gm : 2 litres; 15 gm : 3 litres, etc. It is a good idea to label your baths, they look alike (brownish liquid).

For the second bath, measure out 15 gm diazo salt powder (7.5 gm Red B; 7.5 gm Black B). Use scales rather than teaspoons. Paste the dye with a little cold water and top up with cold water to form a litre. Keep both baths equal in water volume. As you can see this dye is heavy on diazo salts, which makes it too expensive for straight brown dyeings. The combination of the two salts gives not only a good deep bright brown, but what is most important, a tonally believable scale of browns down to white. Other diazos often show a change in tone which rather ruins the gradation.

To Dye

Treat the baths as if they were a naphthol dye. Immerse your cloth for 3-5 minutes in the soga bath and then hang till the drips subside. The colour at this stage is orange.

Immerse the orange cloth into the diazo salt bath for 3-5 minutes. Make sure that the dye reaches every part of the cloth. Rinse. Needless to say, you should wear rubber gloves for all this.

For a very dark brown repeat the two dips several times. Once the cloth is dry you can start the bleaching process. Batikers should note that the brown colour seems to tender the cloth impervious to wax. It is very difficult to get the wax to penetrate a soga-dyed cloth, so that waxing on the reverse side is always necessary.

The Bleaching Process

Again this is in the form of two baths. The bleaching is carried out as a two-part process using potassium permanganate and sodium hydrosulphite (hydros). The potassium permanganate liberates oxygen from the dyed cloth and leaves a brown stain, which is further bleached with the hydrosulphite. Hydrosulphite is a reducing agent, sometimes known as sodium dithionite. The bleaching of silk and wool is quite safe with this chemical alone used in a hot bath. In this soga process both baths are used cold. Sometimes hydrochloric acid is added to bath 1 for total bleaching.

2 gm per litre potassium permanganate (and 3 ml concentrated hydrochloric acid if desired). BATH 1.

2.6 gm hydros per litre. BATH 2. (Use B.P. chemicals rather than laboratory tested.)

Bath One   It is important to dissolve the Condys crystals properly in hot water before adding cold water to 1 litre, otherwise dark spots will appear on your bleached cloth and nothing will move them. Don't add the acid unless you want to bleach it white.

The cloth is immersed in the Condys bath until the desired effect is achieved. This can be gauged only by practice, because you can't really see anything much. Your cloth will go a purple colour and you must take it out and let it oxidise a little before immersing in Bath 2. Only experience will tell you how long you need to leave it in the first bath.

Bath Two   Add the hydros to the cold water (to avoid premature decomposition) and immerse your cloth. The purple will disappear. You will have to decide how long to leave it in this bath (by experience, again). The fumes are pretty disgusting and are not really very good for you. I recommend that you wear a mask. If you have chronic bronchitis you may decide not to use this process at this point — it usually feels as if you have scoured your lungs with a wire brush.

Control of colour depends on time spent in the two baths. You can repeat the process several times, rinsing well in between. It is difficult to assess the colour change because cloth looks much darker when it is wet. I can only stress that experience is crucial.

You must rinse very well after bleaching to remove the various solutions.

When you want to bleach back to white, add the hydrochloric acid carefully in a thin stream to Bath 1. Don't forget to wear rubber gloves and to replace the lid on the acid bottle. It is not dangerous in the dyebath, the concentration is too weak.

Common Problems

These are my guesses.

1. Dark spots on bleached cloth: these are formed by undissolved Condys crystals. They tend to come just where you don't want them, the equivalent of white spots in dyed cloth. I suspect that grease and dust on the cloth may prevent the bleaching solution from penetrating and result in dark patches too. I should wet the cloth in cold water and detergent before bleaching, if I were you. If iron or copper are present in the dyebath they will also cause dark spots, i.e. rust.

2. Grainy appearance: dark lines along the warp and weft of the cloth. I think the solution may be too weak. Hydros doesn't keep well. If it goes hard and stops smelling, it won't work. The disgusting fumes are an indication of strength of solution. Insufficient penetration of cloth can also result in this effect. Wet the cloth before bleaching. Different fabrics behave differently depending on weave, thickness, fibre content, etc.

3. Silk not bleaching back to white. It doesn't. Silk is a protein fibre and always bleaches to yellow. If you decide to use silk for soga batik, *do not boil out the wax*. The action of alkali in the boiling bath will combine with the effects of the acids in the bleaching bath and you will get mush. Sometimes the silk will not bleach at all. There are more problems with silk than anything else. I would avoid it. Use spirits for wax removal, if you must.

4. Uneven gradation: skill in the bleaching process tells here. You should be able to get a total of 7 grades from brown to white. If the colour itself changes in the middle of your scale, it may be the particular dyes. Black ANS and Black K give different colours from Black B. Different water supplies also affect dyeings.

To sum up, if it goes wrong, no one will be able to tell you why, and if it goes right it is a beautiful process. In batik successful use of soga gives effects something like the sepia tones of old photographs.

Bibliography and Supplies

Soga 2391 may be bought from Batik Oetero, 201 Avoca St, Randwick, NSW. It is not cheap because it has to be purchased retail in Indonesia and resold here. The firm who make it have an agreement not to sell anywhere other than Indonesia.

I suggest that you will learn more about soga by learning about your fibres and discharge methods in general, so I have listed some books in this category:

Textile Scouring and Bleaching, E.R. Trotman, Chas. Griffin and Co., Ltd. London
Textile Science, E.P.G. Gohl and L.D. Vilensky, Longman Cheshire, Australia, 1980
Fabrics for Needlework, R.P. Giles, Methuen, paperback
Slide kits: Craft Resource Productions, 'Soga Discharge Dyeing' by Inga Hunter (available for purchase only, or by rental from organisations owning the kit)

Indigosol Dyes

Eve Vonwiller et al.

The following information is taken in part from an article written by Eve Vonwiller in the newsletter of the Batik and Surface Design Association of Australia (P.O. Box 85, Coogee, 2034). It also includes excerpts from a leaflet produced by Batik Oetero 203 Avoca St., Randwick, NSW. Inga Hunter assisted as well in the preparation of this information.

Indigosols are derived from vat dyes. They are cold water soluble vat dyes and are well known for their excellent fastness to light and boiling. Application is easy and rapid. Colours in the range are warm pastel shades (if applied by the immersion method) although strong colours are obtained by painting the dye directly onto the fabric. They are particularly suitable for batiking on cotton. Unfortunately, they aren't cheap, but there is no waste because the dyes last for a long time in solution.

Indigosols do have the advantage over many other dyes (such as fibre reactive dyes) in that once prepared they can be used for many dyeings over a period of 4-5 hours. You can also store the dissolved dye for up to four weeks in a tightly sealed bottle, placed in a dark cupboard.

Materials suitable for dyeing are cotton, silk, viscose rayon and polyester. Wool is difficult to use, and there is a colour change as well.

Application is by way of two baths. The first contains Indigosol dye, and the second is a developing (or oxidising) bath. The developing bath consists of a very weak solution of hydrochloric acid (HCl) and a small amount of sodium nitrite ($NaNO_2$) — see the table that follows this article. Indigisols can be used as a dip dye, spray dye or paint-on dye.

Rules to Follow

1. Keep powders covered at all times.
2. Keep all equipment washed clean of dyes at all times.

3. *Never use a wet spoon* when measuring dye powder.
4. Weigh everything very carefully.
5. Check the group number of dye to make sure you use the correct chemical (see the table below).
6. Weigh powder into paper patty cup papers, and destroy them after use. The smallest trace of a previous dye powder may spoil the following batch.

Timing is very important when dipping. Leave the material in the dye for five minutes. But, for good penetration, it is probably better to leave the material in for fifteen minutes.

Lay *painted* or *dipped* material flat on a clean cloth to dry.

The material needs to be placed in the sun for two minutes on each side to bring out the rich colour of the dye through oxidation; if you are batiking be sure the sun is not so hot it will melt your wax. (Some of the colours reach their full strength only from exposure to the sun; others can be applied without this step.)

The Dyebath

1. Dissolve dye in a little hot water (about 60°C) and then add the required amount of cold water. Use 3 gm dye per litre for a dip dye, and 3 gm dye in 100 ml water for a painting solution (this is a good basic concentration).
2. Immerse the material and make sure it is well covered with the dye solution.
3. Lift the material from the dyebath and either expose it to the sun, or leave it for a few minutes before immersing the material in another bath containing the developing solution.

The Developing Bath

The chemicals used are sulphuric acid (H_2SO_4), or hydrochloric acid (HCl). Hydrochloric acid is also known as muriatic acid. All these acids are extremely dangerous to use. Acid is used at 20 ml per litre of water. *Always add acid to water* and not the reverse.

Sodium nitrite is also used, at 6 gm per litre. Notice that this is *nitrite*, and not nitrate. The designation for sodium nitrite is $NaNO_2$.

The first step is to put your water in a container and then add the chemicals. The two chemicals (an acid, plus sodium nitrite) are required in development for oxidising and for fixing the indigosol dyestuff. Some indigosol dyes also require soda ash (indicated below). Soda ash is added as an alkali to stabilise the dye liquor against acid action.

Measure the acid into a millilitre measuring glass and carefully add it to the cup of water, one drop at a time, *being very careful not to breathe any fumes*.

Immerse the material, and when the colour has fully developed, wash the material well under cold running water until *all* the smell of acid has gone. You can repeat the whole process again to obtain greater penetration and depth of colour.

Caution: Work in the open. *Do not breathe the acid fumes.* And use rubber gloves. Never use hot water in the development bath, because it will give off highly toxic fumes.

Once all the dyeing is complete, rinse well. If you don't, the acid will rot the fabric.

The Charts

Note: the required amount of water depends on the size of the fabric, not its weight. Also dyes in Group 3 must be exposed to strong daylight until full colour is developed, *before* immersion in the developing bath.

	Indigosol bath	Developing bath
Red AB	3 gm of dye	20 cc (8 drops) of
Brown 1BR	per litre	hydrochloric
Grey IBL	of water	acid & 1 gm of sodium
Grey IBZ		nitrite per litre of water
Group 2		
Yellow I2G	3 gm of dye	20 cc (8 drops) of
Violet I4R	& 1 gm of	hydrochloric
Green IB	soda ash per	acid & 1 gm of sodium
Olive Green IBU	litre of water	nitrite per litre of water
Group 3*		
Pink IR extra	3 gm of dye	20 cc (8 drops) of
Blue O4B	& 1 gm of	hydrochloric
Red Violet IRH	sodium nitrite per litre water	acid per litre of water

*Note: Dyes in Group 3 must be exposed to strong daylight until full colour is developed *before* immersion in developing bath.

Painting

Painting directly onto the fabric produces strong colours and permits the application of as many colours as you want in a single dyeing operation.

The method is: dissolve 3 gm of Indigosol (and chemicals as per the table) in 100 ml water. Apply each colour with a separate brush. Develop as usual. The remaining liquid can be kept and reused for up to four weeks if kept in a small lightproof and airtight container.

The Use of Naphthol Dyes

Inga Hunter

Naphthol dyes belong to the class of azoic dyes; they are made from coal tars in the same way as all present day commercial dyestuffs. They are fast to boiling and to light to a high degree, and they are not difficult to apply once you have learnt the process. Store your dyes properly, out of the light, in airtight containers and away from acid fumes. Tins, freezer jars, painted jars, anything opaque and fully air-tight will keep your dyes active for as long as you need them.

Naphthol dyes are applied by means of two baths. The first bath impregnates the cloth with a chemical, which penetrates the fibre and reacts with the dyestuff in the second bath to form an insoluble compound (the colour), both inside and on the surface of the fibre. The first, or impregnation bath, is called the naphthol. The second is called the diazo salt bath.

Naphthol plus diazo salt equals colour. No colour results from either bath used alone. The aim of naphthol dyeing is to fill the hollow centre of the cotton fibre with naphthol solution. Then we make the naphthol inside the fibre react with the diazo salt solution to form an insoluble colour which cannot escape — like catching a fish in a trap.

The reaction in the diazo salt bath is instantaneous (with minor variations for some colours, e.g. Blue BB and Violet B). Depth of colour is *not* obtained by leaving the cloth in the dyebath for long periods, but by repeating the dipping process and rinsing in between dips. You must dip first in the naphthol and then in the diazo bath every time. Three times will give a strong colour. The colour obtained is instantly fast and needs no hanging, drying or steaming, although it is recommended that an after-treatment of boiling in a soapy bath be carried out, to make the dye achieve its proper colour and fastness.

The dyes are not listed under their colour names but under code letters, though the diazo salts do have a colour coding. What you have to do is learn which naphthols combine with which salts to give you your desired colour.

All naphthols react with all diazo salts to give variations of colour. There are however some basic principles which you can apply to help you use the dyes. Some naphthols are specialised and some are general. For instance, naphthol (AS) G is a specialised naphthol which will give a yellow with all salts. Each salt will result in a different yellow. For example:

"G" plus Red B = bright golden yellow
"G" plus Blue BB = brownish yellow
"G" plus Violet B = acid yellow, and so on.

Naphthol LB is a brown naphthol; all salts used with this will give browns. Naphthol SR is a grey to black naphthol.

Naphthols D, OL, TR, RS and BO are generalised naphthols. That is, they will give colours ranging from orange through red and wine to blue, according to which diazo salts you use with them.

Fairly generally, Orange RD, Red KB and Scarlet G will give lighter oranges/reds than Red B, which is a crimson red.

Red AL gives a brownish red generally.

Bordeaux GP and BD give wine colours. Violet B gives violet and purples.

Blue BB and Blue B give various blues. Green BB gives blue-green.

Black B, and ANS give deep blue to black. The actual shade depends on which naphthol you use with which salt, how strong the dyebath, how many times you dip, and what cloth you are using. So it is difficult to generalise any further than this.

Naphthol dyes were originally intended for use on cellulosic fibres (cotton, linen, and viscose rayon). However they can also be used on silk and wool with care.

There is a colour change on silk because the protein fibre of silk itself reacts with the diazo bath to alter colours slightly. Yellows, oranges, reds and browns are all vivid on silk. It is more difficult to get blues and greens and violets because this reaction leads to a slight yellowing of colours. This can be counteracted to a certain extent (read further on), but you will never achieve the same colours on silk as you do on cotton; they will be as bright, but different.

43

Two or more naphthols and two or more salts can also be mixed to produce additional differences in colours. Indonesian batik painters mix colours as a matter of course. Each artist collects his own special recipes which are often guarded carefully and handed down from generation to generation within his family.

Mixture formulas are necessarily matters for individual experimentation, but at the end of this article some basic principles and examples may help you with your own recipes.

A Simple Basic Recipe for One Litre of Dye in a Medium Strength Colour, Naphthol Dye

Naphthol solution
(1) Measure out 2 gm naphthol powder.
(2) Paste with either TRO or a little boiling water.
(3) Add really boiling water — ¼ litre, stirring.
(4) Add 'loog', drop by drop until mixture clears. (Important: add loog as soon as you can after adding the boiling water. Don't let it cool while you search for the loog.)
(5) Add cold water to make the mixture up to 1 litre.

Diazo solution
(1) Measure out 4 gm diazo salt powder.
(2) Paste with a little cold water.
(3) Add cold water up to 1 litre.

To dye
(1) Wet cloth thoroughly before dyeing.
(2) Immerse cloth in naphthol solution, making sure it is thoroughly impregnated.
(3) Hang or hold until all the drips subside.
(4) Immerse cloth in diazo salt solution until colour is fully developed.
(5) Rinse well in cold water.

This may seem complex at first reading, but once you master the general process you can make up the dyes in a matter of minutes.

What you will need   You will need your dyebaths in pairs. Two is minimum. These should not be metal; plastic baby baths are cheap and good to use. Shallow baths are best.

You will need two measuring jugs, spoons and a source of boiling water. One thing you should have is a set of scales. The dyes work on the basis of a 1:2 gm proportion *by weight*. Until you know the differences in weight of the various dyepowders (and they vary considerably) you will need to have a fairly exact measure. A set of spring balanced letter scales with a double scale (0-50 gm; and 0-500 gm) will serve you for both dyes and waxes, etc. Teaspoons will *not* work. You will only waste money and dye powder. Naphthol dyes are extremely economical providing you measure them carefully.

The only chemical you really need is *caustic soda*, which is most easily used in solution. The way to make the caustic solution or *'loog'* as it is called in Indonesia, is to measure out 441 gm caustic soda flakes and add them *very carefully* to one litre of *cold* water, avoiding splashes. (*Note: never* add water to caustic soda. Add the caustic soda flakes carefully and slowly to the water.) Stir gently and *leave to cool*. Bottle in a dark bottle with a plastic (or cork) stopper — metal will corrode. Label the bottle as a corrosive poison and *keep it away from children*. This solution *is* caustic, and will burn. If it comes in contact with the skin, wash it off with plenty of cold water. The amount used in dyebaths is so dilute that the danger here is negligible (much less than hot wax, for example) — especially as you will wear rubber gloves to keep the dye off your hands.

Another chemical which may be of use is TRO or turkey red oil (sulphonated castor oil). This is pasted with the naphthol, and acts as a wetting agent and an emulsifier. It is useful if you are dyeing very thick cloth, or cloth which has been drip-dry treated and will not wet out easily.

How much dye to use   The dyes work by using a basic proportion by weight of naphthols to diazo salts per litre of water. The basic proportion is one part of naphthol to two parts of diazo salt. For example:

Bath One = 1 gm of naphthol to 1 litre of water
Bath Two = 2 gm of diazo salt to 1 litre of water.
You should always use equal quantities of water in each bath. Whatever you do with naphthol dyes, this proportion should be observed. You can multiply this to make it stronger, so long as there is approximately *twice as much diazo salts* (by weight) *as naphthols*. A good working rule goes like this:
Light shades = use 1 gm naphthol to 2 gm diazo salt to one litre water in each bath (1:2).

Very pale, pastel shades = dilute the 1:2 proportion by using 5-6 litres of water in each bath.

Medium shades = double the 1:2 ratio to 2:4 (2 gm naphthol to 1 litre of water in the first bath; and 4 gm diazo salt to one litre of water in the second bath.

Dark shades = Use a proportion of 3:4 or a proportion of 4:8. (*Note:* the 3:4 is a departure from the general rule, but it *will work* and is economical).

Dyeing procedure Let us suppose we want to dye a piece of cotton yellow to a medium shade in 1 litre of water. Always wet the cloth out first, making sure the fibre is wet through. Look on your chart to find out which naphthol combines with which salt to give yellow (say "G" + "Red B" in a proportion of 2:4). There is a rough guide to colours at the end of this article.

Measure out 2 gm Naphthol G and put it into a plastic jug. Boil some water (it must be *really* boiling), and paste the dye to a nice, smooth consistency. You may use TRO for this pasting instead.

Add more boiling water until you have ¼ litre. While the mixture is very hot, add your loog. (You will have poured out a little loog into a medicine measure first — allow about 1.5-2 ml to each gram of naphthol powder.) You may not use all the loog; add it a little at a time, stirring the solution. You will see the solution change until it becomes clear. (*Note:* the Naphthol SR is an exception; it will not become clear.) Stop adding loog; the mixture is now activated. The loog and boiling water render the naphthol soluble.

If your naphthol solution will not clear, add more caustic solution — up to 8 ml per gram of naphthol powder. If it still won't clear, heat up the solution in a pan on the stove, as the mix may have cooled off too much to be activated. If nothing happens then, you have a dye which has gone off. All you can do is throw it away and check on your storage methods. *Don't overdo the loog.* It will destroy your wax resist in batik if you use too much.

Leave your mixture to cool a little. Do *not* do this in sunlight; sunlight will decompose your dyes. Always keep naphthol dyebaths in the shade.

When the mixture has cooled enough (a couple of minutes is ample), add sufficient cold water to make the bath up to a full litre (this will be ¾ litre cold water). Your first dyebath is now ready.

To make the diazo salt bath, measure out 4 gm diazo salt (in this case, Red B), place in a plastic jug, and paste with a little cold water. Then add enough cold water to make up to 1 litre, and your bath is ready.

Never mix the two dyebaths — keep them apart and use separate utensils. You will need to remember which bath is which. Naphthol dyebaths have no definite colour; they are usually clear or yellowish. Labelling the baths as you make them will help you avoid confusion until you are experienced.

To dye Pass the cloth through the naphthol bath, making sure that the whole cloth is impregnated (3-5 minutes). It will turn a yellowy-grey at this stage, if coloured at all. Lift the cloth and allow it to drip until all drips have subsided — about five minutes. You don't want to get any more naphthol solution into your second bath then you can help. It will become exhausted too soon if you do.

Remember that the naphthol reacts with the diazo salts *anywhere*. You want it to react inside the fibre — *not* on your hands, *not* on the surface of the cloth where it will later fall off, and *not* in the water, where it will be wasted. Every drop of naphthol solution in the diazo bath uses up valuable colour, which is then not available to your cloth. Dripping is most important.

An exhausted diazo salt bath is coloured, and looks curdled because of the suspended particles of insoluble colour.

To increase the depth of colour, you repeat the whole process. However, *you must rinse* in between, and you must dip into the naphthol bath *before you dip in the diazo salt bath* — each time.

The naphthol dyes will reach their full colours and fastness after a boiling in an alkaline, soapy bath. The dye solutions will last for about six hours at full strength and fastness. The dyes will work quite adequately after 24 hours, but full fastness cannot be guaranteed.

You can *counteract the colour change on silk* to some degree by the use of vinegar in the diazo salt bath. You must use only a tiny amount, or you can destroy the acid/alkali balance, and you will get no colour at all.

You will need no more than 8 ml vinegar to 4 litres of water, maybe less. The amount will be determined best by experiment. You must be careful not to wipe out the colour completely.

Mixing Colours

You can mix colours with naphthol dyes providing you remember four things:

(1) never mix naphthols and diazos together;

(2) observe the general rules for proportions;

(3) remember which colours result from whichever naphthols and salts you use;

(4) measurement must be accurate.

Here is an example which will help you. To get a brown in the 2:4 proportion, use 0.5 gm "D" + 1.5 gm "G" with 4 gm of the diazo salt Bordeaux GP. "D" with Bordeaux GP gives wine; "G" with Bordeaux GP gives yellow. Yellow and wine will make a brown.

Only experiment will make you familiar with mixing colours. However, there is enormous scope for anyone keen enough to try.

Dyeing Hints

The action of dipping cloth into dye varies in naphthol dyeing from the methods used with other dyes. There is no need to cover the cloth with water. There is no need to stir the dyebath. There is no need to have the cloth in the dye for long periods of time. The dye action is a 'passing through' the bath.

Shallow dye containers are best. Take your cloth in one hand and gently pass it through the dye solution with the other, bringing it out the other side once it is thoroughly wetted. For batik a soft brush may be used to work the dye in between the areas of wax and aid penetration.

Evenness of colour depends on dexterity with naphthol dyes. The colour comes so quickly that the dyeing action is most important. Patchy colour is the result of:

(1) poor wetting of cloth prior to dyeing;

(2) poor dyeing technique;

(3) exhausted diazo salt bath

What to do if your dyes won't work   Check that:

(1) your loog is effective and not too cold;

(2) you have correctly made up your dyes;

(3) you are dipping into the correct dyes (i.e. naphthol first; diazo second);

(4) you have suitable cloth — not drip-dry or synthetic;

(5) you have washed the dressing from the cloth;

(6) the cloth is properly wetted out before dyeing;

(7) that your dyes have been stored correctly and are still fresh.

To remove resin drip-dry treatment from cloth   Wash in 5 ml hydrochloric acid per litre of water at 50-60°C for 20 minutes. Neutralise in water and soda ash at 60°C.

Note: 5 ml hydrochloric acid is safe for cotton, and will not damage the fibre. *Always* add the acid *to* the water and avoid splashing. Wear rubber gloves.

Colour Guide

Here is a rough guide to the colours to help you get started. You will need to make your own colour charts according to your own needs, but this should help.

Naphthol G will give yellow with all salts *except* Black B and Green BB.

Naphthol D will give orange with Orange Rd, Orange GC

Naphthol D will give reds with Scarlet G or Scarlet GG

Naphthol D will give reds with Red A1, Red 3 GL

Naphthol D will give reds with Red KB, Scarlet R

Naphthol D will give reds with Red B

Naphthol D will give clarets with Bordeaux GP, BD

Naphthol D will give blues with Blue BB, B

Naphthol D will give violets with Violet B

Naphthol D will give deep blue to black with Black B and Black ANS

Naphthol D will give blue-green with Green BB

Naphthols TR, OL, RS, BS and BO give a similar range. They vary slightly. 'BO' is the strongest naphthol.

The strongest salts are Red B, Blue B, and Black B.

Naphthol LB gives brown with all salts.

Naphthol GR gives green with Blue BB, Blue B, and Black B.

Naphthol GR gives pink/violet with other salts.

Naphthol SR gives grey to black on cotton; and khaki to brown to black on silk.

Blue BB, B and Violet B develop more slowly than the other salts. Leave your cloth longer in the diazo salt bath than for the other colours. If possible, hang without rinsing for a while so the colours will oxidise.

Naphthol dyes do not give either bright greens or turquoise; you must use fibre reactive dyes for that. Their great strength however, is in the areas of yellows, reds, and browns; and they give a good strong black if you make a mixture of naphthols BO and D, used with Black B in a proportion of 3:4.

Methods of Dye Application

Introduction

Knowing the kinds of dye available and the basic steps in their use can be just a beginning. How about thickening those dyes and painting them on cloth? Can fabric be 'marbled' just like paper, with the same vibrant results? Can some dyes be made to 'take' without heating when they are applied to wool or silk? What is this strange thing called 'cyanotype'? And where do you get heat if not from the top of a stove?

Janet De Boer reviews experiments with the microwave oven as a heat source for dyeing, along with the sun (solar dyeing). Elizabeth Simm of New Zealand tells spinners how to approach their fleeces with synthetic dyes; and Rhonda O'Meara tells weavers how to approach their warps. The Cold Batch Process she describes is carried through in Elizabeth Lindsay's article on the Earth Palette Dyes. And Inga Hunter gives an excellent survey on directly applying dyes — what thickeners and agents you will need and how to go about it. The art of marbling fabric is also reviewed, including a practical 'Australian' recipe. And Alvena Hall of South Australia details how she uses cyanotype to enhance her imagery. Finally, Marie-France Frater gives an overview of how silk painting is done.

Readers will benefit from the enormous amount of research, and trial and error, that these authors have done, condensing many hours of frustration and success alike into a sound methodology. Normally you would turn to many books, articles, and workshop notes to even have a starting place for using these methods. Here, a big part of the work has been done for you, leaving you the freedom to express your ideas through the controlled application of colour.

I mixed red and violet but I don't seem to get brown.

Eeny meeny, miney, mo

Synthetic Dyes for Spinners

Elizabeth Simm

Most beginner spinners are horrified at the thought of immersing their precious product in hot water and *colouring* it. At first the range of fleece breeds and natural fleece colours seems quite sufficient; then comes the excitement of plant dyes. These seem magical, and satisfy a lot of people. But if the family start complaining about funny smells; you get fed up with fading colours; or you have problems getting enough of a particular plant, then synthetic industrial dyes are the logical next step.

Some spinners condemn synthetic or 'chemical' dyes as harsh and factory looking, but with a little bit of practice lovely subtle 'hand-made' colours appear, which are far more appropriate to hand-spun yarns.

Rule No. 1 — *read the instructions*

Rule No.2 — better too little than too much. The strength of the colour is decided by the *weight* of *dye-powder* to *weight* of *wool*. i.e. water doesn't dilute the dye strength, merely provides a medium for the dyeing to take place in.

If you see your wool is already as dark as you want, but it has only been simmering for a few minutes, then take it out of the dye-pot, and put it in fresh hot water and continue simmering for the required time — usually at *least* 20 minutes or until all dye is absorbed.

To obtain 'plant-type' colours, start with a basic primary colour and deepen with either black or brown. Dissolve each dye colour in warm water in a jam jar, then mix the liquids in another jar to the desired colour.

The addition of black deepens to a cold tone; brown to a warmer tone.

e.g. red plus black = purply/grape
       red plus brown = brick/burgundy

A similar effect comes from dyeing oatmeal or silver-grey fleeces with just one colour — the white fibres pick up the colour, the dark fibres resist dye; so a pale grey fleece dyed with red ends up a soft old-rose colour.

Dyeing in the fleece gives even more variety and different breeds of fleece take up the dye in different ways. A Perendale with dry chalky tips will absorb a lot of dye at the tips, then fade down to a pastel butt. When carded and spun lovely heather shades are the result of just one dye-bath. For more interest, try dyeing ⅓ pink, ⅓ lavender; then carding together with the remaining ⅓ left its natural white. Or 2 shades of green plus yellow; or red, yellow, orange — the possibilities are endless. A high lustre Border Leicester, worsted spun, then dyed, ends up resembling embroidery silks.

Another advantage — industrial dyes are not too fussy about the dye-pot they are in, so you can use something like an old metal baby-bath on an outside barbecue to dye a big quantity of wool.

No poisonous mordants to be added either, which is safer if small children are in the house. Just remember the hazards of gallons of simmering water, and if using acid dyes (the most suitable for wool, mohair and silk), then don't use acetic acid stronger than 30%. The woollen mills use 100% strength but it is not necessary for home dyeing and the fumes from this strength can cause blindness. Many people just use white vinegar, which is about 5% acetic acid, and far safer.

As with plant dyeing, the wool needs to be clean and grease-free for even take-up. Tie skeins loosely but securely to prevent tangles, and bring the temperature of the dye-pot slowly up to simmering point, and keep it there for the required time, then rinse in hot water and lower the temperature slowly. If the wool is boiled hard, or moved straight from hot to cold, it will felt.

Synthetic dyes can rescue most plant-dyed 'disasters'. One friend recently dyed a whole warp and weft for a knee-rug in a bark dye. The result was a sad grey/brown. Instead of abandoning all the wool we over-dyed it with a soft coral-red and managed to bring it up to a warm mahogany. When some soft hand-spun singles, dyed with the same coral red, were added to the weft, a beautiful warm knee-rug arose like a phoenix from the ashes of potential disaster!

So next time you get out the dye-pot add a few inches of any colour yarn you have around and see what some of the unlikeliest combinations will give.

Small rugs, 60 cm × 90 cm. Woven in 1986 by Diana Conroy and Jenny Gifkins. Designer, Diana Conroy. Fleeces: Border Leicester and/or Tukidale. Mostly white, sometimes light grey. Also white mill-spun rug wool is used.

Rug, 'Flame Tree', 90 cm × 165 cm. Designer, Diana Conroy. Weaver, Ann Streckfuss ('Tapalinga Rugs').

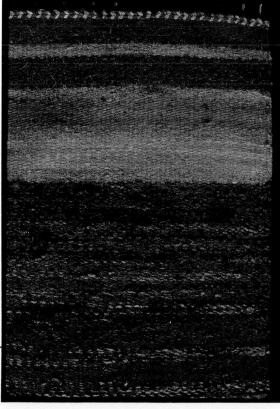

Detail of 'Flame Tree' rug, which shows the dyed weft more clearly.

Workshop. Painted hank demonstration, Rhonda O'Meara (see article starting page 59).

Warp painted — ready to be rolled after removing old sheet.

Production length. Painted warps — varying widths and fibres.

Direct Dyeing with Cold Water Dyes

Inga Hunter

Traditionally dyeing is known as a process whereby fibre or fabric is dipped into a bath of dye to come out evenly coloured. What we call the 'hand' or 'direct' application of dye does none of these. The dye is applied directly by hand, using a variety of tools and techniques, and the result is fabric or fibre coloured evenly or unevenly, according to the dyer's wishes: a process much more like painting than traditional dyeing. With this method of application we can break all the rules of traditional dyeing — except one. *The process must ensure the normal dye fastness appropriate to the dyestuffs, fabrics used, and the purpose for which they are intended.* Bearing this in mind it is easy to see that certain dyestuffs lend themselves better to direct application methods than others. Dyes which depend upon heat for fixation cannot always be applied by hand without substituting some other fixation method (usually steaming, after the dye has been applied). However, cold dyes which are fixed in some other way than simmering over heat are ideally suited to direct application.

The three dyes I am going to treat here are (a) azoic (naphthol); (b) fibre reactive (Procion, Drimarene); (c) soluble vat (Indigosol).

In order to keep this article to its original intent, and to stop it from turning into a book, I shall have to assume a basic knowledge of these dyestuffs. For those who do not have the basics I refer you to the bibliography at the end of this article. This is also an appropriate time to give you some basic points on dye safety.

1. Protect yourself from breathing dye powder. Manufacturers test dyes carefully for general safety but it is not wise to ingest dyes or chemicals through the lungs or skin. Wear rubber gloves and a mask when mixing dyes. Always work in a well-ventilated area.
2. Protect others. Keep dye utensils away from food preparation areas. Don't store dyes and chemicals in the fridge, or anywhere children can reach them. Don't leave loose powder lying around. Clean up well after you have finished dyeing. Don't store toxic solutions in food or drink containers unless they are clearly marked as dangerous. You should look at a good reference on safety for the artist, such as the papers put out by Monona Rossel, available from your state Crafts Council; or consult M.McCann's *Artist Beware* (Watson-Guptill).

All three of the dyes I am going to discuss are specifically designed for cellulosic fibres but all three are successfully being used on protein fibres by craftsmen in Australia. Wherever possible I will include special recipes for use on silk and wool, but must stress that you will have to do considerable individual research if your needs are very different from already well established methods. Hand application methods have potential for use in all surface design fields (batik, quilting, screenprinting, embroidery, stamping, shibori) and some weaving (ikat or kasuri).

Naphthol Dyes

For dipping, naphthol dyes traditionally use two dyebaths. The first (the 'naphthol bath') impregnates the fabric with naphthol solution which reacts with the diazo salt solution in the second bath (the 'diazo salt bath') to give colour. The colour is actually formed in the fibre, the baths being colourless, and the whole process takes about 20 minutes from beginning to end. For direct application, naphthols are bewilderingly versatile because you can vary what you do with each bath and still maintain good wash and light fastness. All you have to do is to make sure that the properly mixed naphthol and diazo salts come into contact with one another inside your fibre. For instance you can dip your fabric in the naphthol first and then apply the diazo salts by painting, spraying, stamping. Or you can spatter dry diazo salts onto the naphthol impregnated cloth. Or you can thicken the diazo salts with printing thickener DR33, and apply them in any way you desire, including screenprinting. You can conversely do all that to your naphthol solution as well, i.e. spray on naphthol and stamp or paint or spray diazo salts, or paint on naphthol, etc. To thicken naphthol solutions, Printing Thickener MX15 must be used.

A rinse in water containing 5 gm/litre sodium bisulphite will prevent any uncoupled diazo reacting with the naphthol in uncoloured areas. For some results in the hand application of diazo salts it is desirable to dry the naphthol impregnated cloth first. Use a hair dryer or fan, but keep the cloth out of sunlight and do the drying as quickly as possible, because some naphthols react to carbon dioxide in the atmosphere. This method is ideally suited to screen printing, or any technique where you want precise images.

Depending on thickness and weave of fabric (or twist in fibre) you will have less penetration of dyestuff when you directly apply naphthol than when you dip-dye it. Naphthol dyes do not have the same penetrating quality that fibre reactive dyes have. Those who want to experiment with direct application of naphthols to warps would do well to remember this. However, on the good side, you do not have the problem of the dyes spreading during fixation that you have with fibre reactives. One by-product of the fixation of naphthols is the complete separation of colours that you can achieve when you paint or spray several different diazo salts onto a cloth impregnated with one naphthol. Each diazo salt reacts with the naphthol in its own way and its own colour — there is no blending.

To Mix Naphthols for Direct Application

Mix naphthol solution normally if you are going to dip the cloth first, and hand apply diazo salts. If you hand apply naphthols use the normal mixture for a one-litre dyebath but reduce the amount of water.

For example: 1 gram naphthol pasted with a little Turkey Red Oil; add ¼ litre boiling water and stir. Add caustic soda solution (38%) drop by drop until the mixture clears, cool and use. Dilute with cold water if you wish. Always use acrylic brushes with this mixture, as bristles will dissolve if left in naphthol baths. If you hand apply diazo salts, make them up in a concentrated form — i.e. 3 gm in ¼ litre cold water, or however much you feel you need.

To Make up MX15 and DR33 Printing Thickeners

The thickeners are based on natural vegetable gums which will give prints with sharp definition. The pastes are flexible and stable during printing, dyeing and steaming.

MX15 is used for naphthol Indigosol, vat and direct dyes on all fibres. DR33 is used for diazo salts, fibre reactive, disperse, metal complex and acid dyes on all fibres.

Stock thickeners   Paste 3 teaspoons thickener with methylated spirits in a screw top jar. Add 250 ml cold water and shake vigorously. Add 2 drops Dettol and leave overnight to swell. This should be thinned as needed to desired consistency.

For diazo salts merely add pasted diazo powder to thickener and use at whatever consistency you need.

For naphthol make up by pasting naphthol powder with a little methylated spirits and Turkey Red Oil. Add caustic soda solution till mixture clears. Add two parts stock thickeners to one part water and mix with naphthol, diluting with water if necessary.

For a sheet of standard printing recipes for use with all these dyes contact Batik Oetero (see bibliography).

To apply naphthols to wool you should make up the naphthol with methylated spirits (hot caustic soda damages wool fibre). Penetration is usually the main problem so you might try soaking the fibre overnight in Lissapol (non-ionic detergent) before hand applying naphthols. The same applies to cotton yarns of any bulk. Prechlorination of wool yarn before dyeing increases the colour yield with naphthol dyes, and I refer you to the Wool Corporation's paper on 'Printing Wool' by H.D. Pleasance, as well as to the section in this book on 'Adapting Wool to the Batik Industry'. The sort of colours that naphthols give on unchlorinated wool are muted and very like those obtained from natural sources, but it is an area where considerable experiment is needed for the crafts.

Here is a simple basic recipe to mix a naphthol dye. Readers are referred for more extensive information to the Batik Association of Australia's leaflet on 'Naphthol Dyeing' and the Craft Council Resource Centre's slide kit on 'Naphthol Dyeing for Craftsmen'.

Recipe for 1 litre dye
First bath
1. Measure out 1 gm naphthol powder.
2. Paste this with a little boiling water.
3. Add boiling water up to ¼ litre. Stir well.
4. Quickly add loog drop by drop until the mixture clears, stirring.
5. Add *cold* water to make up to 1 litre.
Second bath
6. Measure out 2 gm diazo salt powder.
7. Paste with a little cold water.
8. Add (up to) 1 litre of cold water.
Note: Both baths contain equal amounts of water.

Dyeing Procedure
The nature of the dye makes this very different from other dye techniques.
1. Wet your cloth thoroughly.
2. *Pass the cloth through* the naphthol bath making sure that it is thoroughly and evenly impregnated (3-5 mins).
3. *Most important.* Hang the cloth to allow all the drips to subside. Naphthol solution entering the second bath will react to form colour in the water and will ruin the bath (5 mins). Keep cloth out of direct sunlight which will decompose the dye at this stage.
4. Pass the thoroughly dripped cloth through the diazo salt bath until the colour has developed (3-5 mins).
Uneven dyeing is usually the result of either
  a. Improperly wetted cloth.
  b. Poor dyeing technique.
  c. Exhausted diazo salt bath.
5. Rinse under cold running water till the water runs clear.
Repeat whole process up to two times more for stronger colours. If you want an even stronger colour repeat the process up to three times. For really strong colours you may double the amount of dye per litre water in the two baths i.e. 2 gm naphthol/litre to 4 gm diazo salt/litre. For very pale colours simply dilute your 1:2 proportion with 4 or 5 more litres cold water in each bath. The amount of liquid in each bath should be even. As you will have gathered, dyeing with naphthol dyes is usually done by passing your cloth or fibre through quite shallow, small baths. If you want to dye fibres for macrame or weaving, you should add more time in the pre-wetting time and the dyebaths, so that the dye can penetrate the twisted fibres. A good wetting agent is a desirable assistant for this sort of dyeing.
Once you have mastered the basics, you can experiment with variations in dyeing and in mixing colours. The scope for experiment is enormous.

(The above recipe is printed by permission from *Craft Australia*)

FIXATION PROCEDURES must be observed.
Fixing Fibre Reactive dyes takes **time**.

Fibre Reactive Dyes

These are marketed in Australia under the brand names of Procion (ICI) Remazol (Hoechst) and Drimarene K (Sandoz). The particular dye you want is the *cold* dye, i.e. Procion M (not 'H' which is for hot water dyeing). Fibre reactive dyes are normally fixed in a dyebath containing water, salt and an alkali. The fabric floats in the bath with the water and dyestuff. The salt is added to push the dye into the fibre. The alkali is added to start the fixation process. And the whole thing is left for a period of time for fixation to take place. In direct application, the dyestuff is dissolved in a small amount of water, and urea is added to this mixture to increase the solubility of dyestuff in the meagre liquid. Alkali is added to start off the chemical reaction with the fibre and the mixture is painted, sprayed or stamped onto the cloth or fibre. Time is needed for fixation to take place. The cloth is not rinsed, but laid flat in a cool place for 24 hours. The urea in the dye mixture will open up the fibres and act as a hygroscopic agent to help delay drying so that the alkali can fix the dyestuff to the cellulose fibres. There is a considerable amount of spreading of dye during the fixation process if the mixture is not thickened. Fibre reactive dyes are thickened in two-ways with DR33 or with Manutex RS.

A Basic Recipe for Hand Application of Fibre Reactive Dyes

This makes a 250 ml solution.
Dissolve 2 teaspoons urea.

Dissolve 1/8 teaspoon Resist Salt L (Matexil PAL) in a little hot water (this prevents decomposition by reduction, in printing and painting mixtures).

Dissolve in a separate container 1 teaspoon soda ash (or 2-3 teaspoons washing soda if soda ash not available); plus ¼ teaspoon bicarb. soda in a little hot water.

Paste required amount of dye in a little hot water. Use a stiff brush to dissolve dye particles. *Note:* In all direct application methods it is difficult to calculate dye on the basis of weight of fibre, because the process is more akin to painting. Experience helps you tell how much dye to use.

Combine the 3 mixtures and use within two hours. You can make up the amount with cold water to 250 ml if desired, or use a concentrated solution. Apply dye to cloth and allow it to lie flat for 24 hours. Fixation is improved if the cloth is steam ironed afterwards, before washing off surplus unreacted dye in a hot soap bath. You can rinse your cloth in a cool bath containing a little Sandopan DKA *or* sodium hydrosulphite, *or* 2% acetic acid prior to wash-off. This is to neutralise the action of the alkali and to prevent the unreacted dye from staining undyed areas. Lay the cloth flat to dry after rinsing and washing-off.

If you wish, you can make your urea/soda ash chemical solution in bulk (steps 1 & 2) and store it, using only enough for each dye mixture. You cannot store dye in solution because of hydrolysis. The dye reacts with hydrogen and oxygen groups in the fibre — and with the water. A fibre reactive dye never *looks* exhausted, but what you end up with can be coloured water with no available dye.

All cold dyes should be made up as needed, and discarded afterwards.

To Thicken Painting Solution with Manutex

1. Measure out 30 grams Manutex RS and paste with a little methylated spirits.
2. Add chemical solution (steps 1 & 2), mix well till desired consistency (use a mixer, blender, or shake in a jar) and add a few drops of disinfectant. This is your stock solution.
3. Use a little at a time and mix dye with stock solution. Once mixed with dye, the paste is active for only a few hours.

To Make 1000 gm Printing Paste with DR33 (Batik Oetero's Recipe)

20 gm dye
100 gm urea
10 gm resist salt
280 ml hot water
565 gm stock solution
25 gm bicarb soda

Mix dye, urea, and resist salt, and dissolve in hot water; mix with thickener. Add bicarb soda at the last moment before printing. Steam to fix, or press with steam iron (5-7 minutes *at least*). Rinse in water with vinegar or sodium hydrosulphite to prevent staining of unprinted areas.

Note: Creative embroiderers may omit final rinse, depending on objects dyed, i.e. wallhangings not designed to be washed, but only if dye has not been thickened.

Screenprinting Paste with Manutex (David Green's Recipe)

Stock solution:
Sprinkle 50 gm Manutex RS into 950 ml water. Beat well.
To 350 gm of stock paste add —
    100 gm urea (opens up fibres to help penetration)
     10 gm Matexil PAL (resist salt)
     25 gm bicarb soda (12 gm for silk).
Dilute if necessary to correct consistency for screenprinting.

The above mixtures are suitable for polychromatic screen printing of fibre reactive dyes. The screen is painted with fibre reactive dyes mixed with water only, allowed to dry, and the thickened chemical solution is squeegeed through the dyed screen onto the fabric. Because screens are covered with synthetic fabrics, the dye will not have any effect on the material and will transfer through the screen to the cloth beneath, where it will be fixed in the normal way by baking or steaming. This process is virtually a monoprint technique in the hands of a beginner, but experienced craftsmen can use it successfully for small print runs, using several colours without having to prepare a number of screens. The screened prints give distinctly dyed effects because of the nature of the technique.

Fibre Reactive Dyes on Wool (Australian Wool Corporation Recipe for Urea Pad Batch Printing of Wool)

Dyes used in experiments have been Procion. Some fibre reactives cannot be used with sodium bisulphite.

  3 gm dye
30 gm urea
24 ml water
40 gm thickener (Manutex, or whatever you like)
  2 ml wetting agent
  1 gm sodium bisulphite (if chlorinated wool, omit this)
Urea fixes the dye in this recipe. It is the solubilising agent and must be fixed with the dry dyestuff and then pasted with hot water. This mixture should then be heated till the dye is fully dissolved. This is added gradually to thickener and stirred. This recipe will only work on wool, and not on cotton or rayon or synthetics.

    The dye paste is screened onto the fabric, which is then kept moist for 24 hours by covering with plastic sheeting. No steaming is required. Wash off is carried out in 4 stages to avoid felting:
1. Cold water with 2 ml/litre ammonia + 0.5 gm/litre detergent — for 10 minutes.
2. Warm water 55°C with 1 ml/litre ammonia + 0.5 gm/litre detergent — for 10 minutes.
3. Hot water, 75°C with 0.5 gm/litre detergent — 10 minutes.
4. Cold water with 1 ml/litre acetic acid for 5 minutes. Dry immediately.

    For further information, readers are referred to *Dyeing with Fibre Reactive Dyes* by I. Hunter; and *Cotton Dyeing, a guide to Using Fibre Reactive Dyes* by Margaret Ainscow.

Soluble Vat Dyes

Soluble vat dyes (Indigosol, Anthrosol) are dip-dyed in two baths. The first contains dyestuff and sodium nitrite ($NaNO_2$). The second contains a weak solution of HCl (hydrochloric acid). The fibre or fabric is immersed in bath one, removed and laid flat in the sun for 10 minutes, or until dry. The colour is developed and fixed in the second bath, where the dye is hydrolised by the acid in the presence of an oxidising agent. We lay the fabric in the sun as a substitute for heat. It is not safe to heat the development bath because it gives off highly toxic fumes. Not all colours need the sun to develop full colours.

    For direct application, we mix the dye powder with a little hot water (60-80°C) and dilute to whatever concentration is desired. This is applied by brush, spray, stamp, etc. to the fabric or fibre, and is then developed in the acid bath which now contains the sodium nitrite. The laying in the sun can be carried out or not as desired, depending on the colours expected. The developing solution may also be hand applied if desired. *However at no time can this solution be left on the cloth.* The fabric or fibre, once it has been in contact with the acid bath, must be thoroughly rinsed. Rinsing for painted-on fibre reactive dyes can be judiciously omitted under certain circumstances, but never for these dyes, because the fibres will disintegrate on contact with heat (ironing).

Recipe for Direct Application of Indigosol Dye

Measure out 3 gm dye powder
Dissolve in 50 ml hot water
For light colour dilute to equal 300 ml
  Medium colour: 100 ml
  Strong colour: 50 ml
Some colours require a few grams of soda ash to help them dissolve and to keep the dye alkaline before development. These mixed dyes can be stored for several days in sealed containers in a dark place. Paint, spray or stamp dye onto the cloth and expose to sunlight for strong colours.
Develop in a bath containing.
  10 ml HCl/litre water (add acid to water *very* carefully)
  2-6 gm/litre $NaNO_2$.
Rinse well in cold water. If desired, neutralise acid with a little soda ash added to rinse. Indigosol dyes paint well. The colours can be blended into one another easily with a high degree of control, because the blending process can be stopped at any point by immersion in the development bath. Unique effects can be obtained by painting dyes onto crumpled cloth and drying in the sun before

developing colours. Indigosol dyes can be thickened for printing with MX15, in which case the cloth must be left in the development bath for a little longer than the normal 30-60 seconds, especially if the paste has dried.

For further information readers are referred to *Modern Techniques in Batik Art* by P. Kitley; and *Batik* by Miep Spee.

Mixing Colours

Colours can be mixed with varying degrees of difficulty with all three dyestuffs. With naphthols you have to know your dyestuff before attempting to create dye mixtures of different naphthols. You can begin by mixing diazo salts together; it is easier to see what sort of colour you are likely to get. Mixing naphthols is definitely advanced work. You must remember that with dyestuffs you can obtain mixtures by overdyeing as well. A whole lifetime of colour work could be devoted to overdyeing.

Fibre reactives on the other hand mix easily, a bit like watercolours. You can use primary colours to create whatever you need in the way of secondaries or tertiaries. Fibre reactives have the only turquoise, but black is really a dark blue.

Indigosol dyes mix easily but are hard to learn because there is a colour change between application of dye and development in the acid bath. For example, Green 1B applies as red-brown and develops in the acid bath as blue-green. Blue applies colourless, goes blue-grey in the sun, and bright blue in the acid bath. You have to learn how the dyes behave, and will need to mix colours by means of that knowledge.

Dyeing is a complex art. Successful dyeing demands a great deal of care and skill as well as recipes, and some of the areas of craft dyeing need careful experimentation and documentation by those who are creating new ground.

Craftsmen can take dyestuffs and stretch them at the edges providing they obey the central core of rules concerning fixation. Where you stretch the rules to depends a great deal on your own standards and needs, and on the purpose to which your work will be put. Clothing demands more rigid rules than wallhangings. It is really up to you to decide which corners you can cut, where you can be innovative, and where not.

Bibliography

Textile Science, E.P.G. Gohl and L.D. Vilensky, Longman, Cheshire, Melbourne
Dyeing With Naphthol Dyes, booklet, Batik Oetero. Slide kit by Inga Hunter. Crafts Council Resource Productions
Dyeing With Fibre Reactive Dyes, booklet by Inga Hunter, from Batik Oetero
Adapting Wool to the Batik Industry, H.D. Pleasance, Australian Wool Corporation
Printing on Wool, H.D. Pleasance, Australian Wool Corporation
Fabric Printing by Hand, Stephen Russ, Studio Vista
Batik with Noel Dyrenforth, J. Houston, Orbis
An Introduction to Textile Printing, W.C. Clarke, Butterworths ICI Dyestuffs Division
Fibre Reactive Dyes, W.F. Beech, Logos
Design on Fabrics, Meda Parker Johnston, Van Nostrand Reinhold
Traditional & Modern Batik, Miep Spee, Kangaroo Press
Dyes and Fabrics, Joyce Storey, Thames & Hudson
Surface Design on Fabrics, Proctor & Lew, University of Washington Press, USA
'Dyeline' articles from *Fibre Forum* magazine, by I. Hunter (*Fibre Forum*, P.O. Box 77, University of Queensland, St Lucia, Q4067):
  'How to Choose a Dyestuff', Vol. 4, Issue 1, No. 12, 1984
  'Learning to Use a Dyestuff', Vol. 4, Issue 3, No. 14, 1985
  'Extending the Boundaries of Your Dyestuff', Vol. 5, Issue 1, No. 15, 1986
  'Setting up a Dye Studio', Vol. 5, Issue 3, No. 16, 1986
  'Failure', Vol. 6, Issue 2, No. 19, 1987
Artist Beware, M. McCann, Watson Guptill
Polychromatic Screen Printing, Joy Stockdale, Oregon Street Press, USA
The New Dyer, S. Vinroot and J. Crowder, Interweave Press, USA
Dyes and Dyeing, Max Simmons, Van Nostrand Reinhold
Japanese Stencil Dyeing, E. Nakano and B. Stephan, Weatherhill
Modern Techniques in Batik Art, P. Kitley, Darling Downs Institute Press
Light and Pigments, Ray Osborne, John Murray. Also *Colour Principles for Artists*

Adapting Wool for the Indonesian Batik Industry

For the purpose of this paper, I shall continually refer to Wax Resist Batik Effects (abbreviated WRBE) to differentiate from screen printed batik effects. The design is created by wax resists, but the definition permits the use of synthetic dyestuffs, and any fibres which will accept a cold dyeing process.

The study has been carried out in three areas of Indonesia, namely Jogjakata, Solo (Surakarta) and Jakarta.

Fabric Considerations

The traditional fabric for batik is pure cotton, and this remains today as the mainstay of the industry.

The cellulosic-chemistry of rayon allows the production of true wax resist batik effects, and the fabric has good counter appeal in western markets. Rayon is a cheap fibre with low abrasion resistance, low wet strength and generally poor appearance retention.

It is almost impossible to produce genuine WRBE on pure synthetic fibres. In the market place you may encounter many skilfully screen printed batik _designs_ on pure synthetics.

Some highly specialised exponents of batik are producing exclusive designs on pure silk.

In Indonesia the base fabrics are woven in mills which are very modern, and highly productive by any measure. The market size is 100 million metres per annum, with a 10% increase each year.

The fabrics are woven to four set fabric specifications:

Prima   Biru
Premissima   Voilissima.

The fabrics vary in quality, weight and cost, all of which is supervised by the GKBI co-operative.

The fabrics are scoured, sized and callandered ready for marketing.

The movement of 100 million metres of fabric from 15 weavers to 200 000-300 000 cottage craftsmen is a problem we must be aware of, even if we do not fully understand the machinations.

Wax Resist Batik Effects

The following operations are carried out sequentially:
1. Apply wax to the fabric in a patterned form.
2. Crack the wax if this effect is desired. Reinforce the wax where white resist is required.
3. Immerse in first cold dyeing bath.
4. Remove the wax — partially by scraping _or_ completely by boiling in water. Dry the fabric.
5. Apply wax to protect the first colour, and create second colour design.
6. Immerse in second cold dyeing bath.
7. Boil in water to remove the wax.
8. Wash in soap.
9. Dry.
10. Flatten the fabric.

Each sequence will be described in greater detail.

Apply wax to the fabric in patterned form. Traditionally, the molten wax is 'drawn' onto the fabric using a 'canting' by artists who draw the designs from memory. Designs are repeated time and time again, but each is an individual creation, and no two are identical.

When the wax design has been created on one side of the fabric, the whole process is painstakingly repeated on the reverse side of the fabric prior to the application of the first colour.

This ensures an equal colouring effect on both sides of the fabric, which is the hallmark of genuine WRBE. Hand drawn patterns are called _batik tulis_.

Many designs employ complex motifs which repeat frequently. In order to speed the process, these motifs are reproduced in shaped copper 'chiaps'. The operator places the 'chiap' in molten wax, then transfers this wax onto the fabric by a pressing and tapping action. Motifs may be joined by using many varying chiaps, or by the use of cantings and hand created designs.

The wax used in this operation is made from a variety of raw materials:
Paraffin wax — white and yellow with differing hardness and melting point.
Resin — both sticky and plain.
Beeswax, and tallow.

These products are mixed according to the effects required.
Normal outline wax, called *klowong*
Cracking wax
Capping wax, called *tembok*.

Cracking wax An attractive effect can be produced by applying a brittle wax in patterned areas, and squeezing the fabric in a manner which cracks, or crazes the wax in a random pattern.

The cracks permit the entry of small amounts of colour, which attaches to the fabric in the crazed pattern.

Authentic WRBE can be recognised by its equal two-sided effect which is always different on a piece to piece basis. Mock batiks may have a printed crazed effect, which can be recognised by its repeatability and one-sided effect.

Immerse in first cold dyeing bath The WRBE relies on cold dyeing techniques, because high temperature dyeing would melt the wax resist. Historically, batik designs were confined to blue, using natural Indigo, and brown using soga or logwood. Each colour takes approximately a one month immersion to build up to the required depth of shade.

A range of synthetic dyestuffs known as 'naphthols' has found complete acceptance in todays WRBE industry for the following reasons.
The dyeing process is carried out in cold water. Dyeing time is of the order of minutes.
The colours produced simulate the natural blues and browns, as well as opening up the pallette to include yellow, orange, red, violet, blue and black.
The dyestuffs are comparatively cheap.
The fastness properties are good. The colours, for example, must withstand boiling water for ten minutes whilst the wax is being removed.
The colours can be made and applied using unsophisticated techniques.

Dyeing with Naphthols is a two stage process:
Impregnate with naphthol,
Develop in Fast Salt (*see* naphthol recipe by Inga Hunter).

Remove wax If the design combines two colours plus a white resist, it can be economical to physically scrape the wax from selected areas with a blunt knife whilst the capping wax is allowed to remain intact.

Fresh wax is then applied over colour 1 prior to the application of colour 2, which dyes the areas where wax has been scraped away.

Complex multicolour designs utilise painted-on solubilised vat dyes to create the colour novelty, and the wax is removed completely by boiling, rather than scraping off.

Re-wax for second colour The second wax application has two functions. The first colour applied must be covered with wax to prevent any unwanted interference from the second colour.

A wax pattern is applied in the remaining white areas to further contribute to the design effect.

The same principles outlined earlier apply to the application of the wax, and subsequent cracking.

Immerse in second colour The same principles apply as outlined previously.

Boil in water to remove wax The completed waxed and dyed fabric is dropped into a vessel of boiling water and agitated for about 5 minutes. During this time the wax melts and rises to the surface of the water, allowing it to be decanted off for re-use.

The resin is not completely removed by the boiling water, so the fabric is dropped suddenly into cold water, where it becomes brittle and is easily rubbed off.

Wash in soap Where white resists are important the fabric may be re-washed in soap at the boil.

The fabric can also be sized and/or softened at this part of the sequence.

Dry The fabric is hung over poles, where the natural, abundantly available hot air quickly dries the fabric without tension, and without contributing to the energy crisis.

Flatten fabric When a flat surface is required, the fabric is laid on a large teak log and hammered with a huge wooden mallet.

At this stage, we have a dress length of fabric ready to be made into a garment.

Modifications Required for Wool

After study, the process was found to be unsuitable for wool. The caustic soda used in naphthol colours is a cause of severe chemical damage to wool fibres, and the naphthol colours have very little affinity for unmodified wool.

The situation was researched with the understanding that any solution must be appropriate to a cottage industry.

A solution to the problem has been achieved by a combination of three modifications.

1. The wool is chlorinated in order to make it receptive to the naphthol colours.

This is a sophisticated chemical treatment which is incorporated into the fabric finishing process where technologists are available.

2. The amount of caustic soda used in the naphthol colours is reduced marginally.

3. The fabric is neutralised with acetic acid prior to boiling off the wax.

The wool is not damaged by the lower concentrations of *cold* caustic soda, and neutralisation ensures that there is no build up of caustic soda in the *boiling* water.

These minor modifications have been found acceptable to the Indonesian batik industry, and the results on wool/cotton blend fabrics have been of excellent fastness, handle and appearance, whilst the fabric has retained its strength and durability.

Recipe for Chlorination of Wool

Bath 1

40:1 liquor ratio, cold water.
60% acetic acid used at 2% of the dry weight of material.
(or use white vinegar at 10% of the dry weight).
Immerse wool till thoroughly wet. Stir gently. Remove wool and add: Nobolaine DS (supplied by Croda Chemicals) or Basilan DC (supplied by BASF Chemical Suppliers). These products are used at the rate of 3% based on the dry weight of wool.
Reintroduce wool to the bath and stir gently for 45-60 minutes.

Bath 2

Final treatment is with 1-2% sodium bisulphite. This neutralises residual chlorine after the reaction is complete.

Chlorination is achieved by adding an organic chlorine-containing compound to a mild acid solution. The Nobolaine DS and Basilan DC are such products.

To chlorinate a 50:50 wool/cotton blend, add half as much of the Nobolaine DS or Basilan DC as the above recipe suggests. Viyella is a good blend to use.

Hand Dyeing Wool and Silk with Earth Palette Cold Dyes

Barry Bassett and Elizabeth Lindsay

The cold dyeing of wool or silk, more correctly known as the Cold Pad Batch method, can be one of the most useful and versatile dyeing techniques available to the serious craftsperson.

'Earth Palette' have developed a cold dye system in which the necessary dyes and chemicals are incorporated into one mixture ready to be stirred into a measured volume of hot water.

The 'Earth Palette' system uses reactive dyestuffs which actually react with the fibre forming extremely fast covalent bonds, giving a dyeing which is fast to light, washing, perspiration, rubbing, etc.

One of the most exciting discoveries made during initial work was the ability to successfully dye greasy fleece wool and unscoured handspun yarn by the addition of Fixing Agent 'A.' Without Fixing Agent 'A,' the system dyes well on commercially prepared fibre, yarn and fabric, but has limited success on greasy or handspun wool. This is due to the very little amount of damage done to the surface of the wool fibre by hand scouring as compared to commercially prepared wool. The use of Fixing Agent 'A' is therefore a breakthrough for handspinners who wish to use the Cold Pad Batch method of dyeing.

The standard dye solutions can be mixed to obtain a wide range of shades. Dye solutions are measured out by volume, and are mixed in plastic containers. It is, therefore, easy to keep records of dye recipes. e.g. 50 ml red + 50 ml blue.

When using the cold dye system, it is also possible to dye many shades very quickly. This is of particular advantage to handspinners who want to card and blend many shades into rainbow or heather mixtures; or for tapestry weavers who combine multiple shades of yarn on their bobbins.

To fully develop the fastness of the dyes it is necessary to remove any unfixed dyes and chemicals from the dyed article. Rinse well in warm water (30°C).

On greasy wool some of the dye will complex with the wool grease and this grease/dye complex will wash off, giving some colour to the washing water — continue washing until no other colour comes off.

The beauty of using this method of dyeing greasy wool is that some of the grease is retained by the fibres thus enhancing the spinning characteristics.

Dyeing Yarn

A similar technique is used as for the greasy wool — multiple colours can be applied to the one hank, creating a space-dyed or variegated appearance. One of the features of this system is that you can see immediately the colour and effects you are getting — whatever you paint or apply to the fibre will be the final appearance of the dyeing. Once again, fixation of the dye is similar to that on greasy wool.

Dyeing Fabric

When dyeing fabric you can really let your imagination run riot! There are limitless ideas for designs, colour-ways and dye application. Once the dye has been applied the best method of fixing is to lay a sheet of plastic over the fabric and roll the whole lot up. The plastic stops the dye from marking off. Allow it to stand for a minimum of 24 hours. Then wash off.

Some Dye Techniques

Dyeing Greasy Fleece Wool

When dyeing wool, whether fibre, yarn, or fabric, a good 'pick-up' (amount of dye liquor to add) is between 100-150%. For every 100 gm of wool, measure out 100-150 ml of dye liquor. Work the dye into the wool by slowly adding the dye and gently squeezing it into the wool (using rubber gloves) until the dye has been applied to your satisfaction. Store the dyed goods in a plastic bag for a minimum of 24 hours at room temperature (20-25°C). To check the degree of fixation of the dye, squeeze a small amount of dye liquor out. If the liquor is clear, the dyes are fixed and the material can be washed off. If there is still colour left in the liquor, leave for a further 12 hours or until fixed.

The rate of fixation is dependant on temperature. At low temperatures, the fixation period may be longer.

Creative Dye Techniques

The 'Earth Palette' dye solution may be applied by many techniques:
1) Dip dyeing (squeeze out excess dye)
2) Paint brush or roller
3) Spray gun
4) Screenprinting or block printing
5) Warp painting on loom
6) Tie-dyeing.

There will be other methods you may devise which will give you the creative effects you are after.

There are also several ways to rapidly fix the dye other than the normal system of allowing to stand for 24 hours. The following techniques can be used for small amounts of wool:
1) Pre-set oven at 100 degrees C. Put the dyed wool in an oven bag and place in oven for 10-15 minutes.
2) Pre-dry the dyed fabric using a hair dryer, then iron with a steam iron until fixed.
3) Put in a plastic bag and place in a sunny spot.

Cold Pad Batch Dye Process Applied to Wool Warps

Rhonda Omeara
Diagrams — Graham Willoughby

Boiling, steaming, pressing, spraying, wrapping, dipping, printing — I tried them all in pursuit of a dye technique appropriate for individually designed weaving. Hampered by limited facilities and funds to purchase expensive equipment, and acknowledging that the labour intensive methods of most dye techniques added to the final pricing of the products, I intensified my research into dyes and dyeing. I discovered the cold batch print process, and through the application of this method to warps and skeins, I was able to develop gentle colour merges which penetrated the yarn, simply and cheaply.

Cold Pad Batch Process

Dyes are placed in a thickened solution and applied to the material in the fibre, yarn or piece goods stage, and wet batched at room temperature for 24-48 hours. The process yields bright colours, fast to rubbing, light and washing; no heat setting is required and basic equipment is used. These features are a bonus in small scale production.

Regular use of the cold batch method will enable the user to exert greater control over colour and merges of colour. However, while gaining experience with this process, one's efforts may produce results which may not only be unexpected, but which may also extend one's knowledge of colour theory and dyes.

This article is an account of the procedures I have adopted as a weaver designer. Thus it concentrates upon warps and featured weft shots, and begins with a brief design component before explaining the actual dye technique.

Design

The appeal of this dye method is its freedom and simplicity as it lacks the precision of percentage dye methods; the results can be a mystery until the final rinse. Unlike hank or piece dyeing, precise calculations of the weight of the yarn related to the quantity of dye are not possible. Experience with the technique helps to avoid the use of excessive dyes and to reduce dye wastage. While preparing the batik print processes, the applicator has direct visual contact. However, with the cold pad process, changes can and do occur during the batching time.

Design Ideas

1. Warp movement   Instead of using the warp movement box as in 'Kasuri' dyeing, prepare small groups of warps. Position them in order whilst painting. Use strong colour contrasts, and leave a gap between the colours. They will merge to link the blocks. For example. Block 1, Red B; Block 2, Blue B — the merge will be purple.

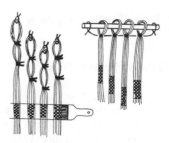

2. Reverse of colour blocks   Commence with alternate ends of the warp, paint across them. When beamed, the colours will be reversed.

Example: for six 2-metre scarves. Prepare 3 warps: 2 of 100 ends, and 1 of 160 ends; all to 13 metres. The centre band is to be reversed, and the outer bands moved. Tape the dye cartoon beside the warps and repeat the design 6 times.

The colours and movement in the painted warps are the major design elements. Carefully consider the dried, finished result and combine this with supplementary warp colours, ground warps, weave structures, weft colours and supplementary colour bands to enhance the painted warps. The process can be used for scarves, sashes, shawls, meterages, cushions, featured wall lengths and rugs.

Equipment

For cold batch you will need measuring equipment for liquids (0-1 litre); powder (0-300 gm); plastic containers: buckets; old sheets and towels; strips of medium to heavy weight plastic; cardboard cylinders; brushes; protective clothing and gloves; and a long, sturdy workbench at a good working height.

Facilities

You need a wet area suitable for dyeing. The ideal would consist of a paved area with hot/cold running water, sinks, wringer and a drying rack. These may be adapted to existing facilities and scale of operation.

Materials

Wool Yarn for Warps

As weavers do not always have access to the ideal range of wool yarns, this section only offers general guidelines as to initial yarn selection. The yarn construction, degree of twist, method of spinning (eg. worsted or woollen) and fibre blends (eg. wool and nylon) all influence the end result. Excellent results are obtained using yarn spun on the woollen system, using fine to medium wools with a soft, balanced spin.

For even dye penetration remove lanolin, dressings and spinning oils by soaking the yarn in 2% ammonia solution. As ammonia is an alkali, prolonged soaking will damage the wool fibre. Rinse the yarn well to remove the alkali, as it neutralises the acid base of the stock solution. Soaking swells the fibres and facilitates the actions of the dye solutions. The percentage of moisture in the yarn can vary the dye strength, and encourage dye migration or merging. If the yarn is too wet, the excess moisture bleeds out during the wet batching and can cause excessive blurring of colours (eg. 'greying'), especially if long warps or thick yarns are being dyed. To minimise this problem, chained warps can be firmly squeezed or run through a wringer with light pressure. As well you can use old sheeting under the warps during painting, to absorb excessive dye/stock solution. If the yarn is too dry or the stock solution too thick, less migration occurs.

Warp Preparation

To avoid weaving problems it is vital that the original warp tension is retained and that warps are not tangled during the dyeing process. Careful warp preparation is important; use a wall mounted warping board, or warping mill to prepare multi-warp ends using a paddle. Avoid using large numbers of warp ends in each warp. Divide the total warp ends into smaller groups; this will aid penetration of dye. Before chaining the warp from the warping equipment, firmly tie a single and group cross at each end of the warp. Additional lease ties to be applied at 1-2 metre intervals along the warp. Ties to secure the warp must be short to avoid tangling. Use masking tape and a water-proof pen to record the warp details (ie. length of warp, paddle group, number of ends and warp sequence) and attach them to the end of the warp. When calculating the warp ends, add an extra 2-4 ends for repairs. These repair ends are beamed, and as the weaving progresses they are rolled onto a spool unless they are needed to repair broken warp ends.

Dyes

Reactive dyes form a permanent bond with the fibre, which gives good wash and lightfast qualities, making them ideal for woven products. The dye yields will vary. Test dyes and yarns before commencing the project.

A range of reactive dyes are produced:

    Drimarine — Sandoz
    Procion — ICI
    Lanasol — Ciba Geigy
    Remazol — Hoechst

Reactive dyes are stable if stored in airtight containers away from light and heat, but they hydrolyse (ie. react with water) and therefore are not stable in the stock solution. Be prepared, and work quickly to avoid colour variations.

A wide range of colours can be mixed using a basic set of dyes. A basic set in the Lanasol range is: Yellow 4G, Red 6G, Scarlet 3G, Blue 3G and Blue 3R. To broaden the spectrum, include Orange GR, Navy and Cibacrolan Blue 8G.

Recipe for Stock Paste: to make 1 litre

300 gm — Urea
8-12 gm — Manutex
10 gm — wetting agent
10-20 gm — resist salt
10 gm — acetic acid
(water up to 1 litre)

Dissolve the urea in 500 ml of hot water and add the wetting agent, resist salt and acetic acid. Mix the Manutex with methylated spirits and stir rapidly into the stock solution. Make up to 1 litre using cold water. Allow to stand for 1-2 hours.

Divide the stock solution into 4-6 containers. Using the range of basic dyes, paste the dye powder with water and add the stock solution; mix well. Develop the range of colours using the dye/stock solution according to design. A chemical resist can be used to preserve the original warp colour by preparing a stock solution with an alkali base instead of acid. The chemical resist is painted on the yarn to resist dye penetration.

Urea A hygroscopic agent, which facilitates the transfer of dye into the fibre, aids in the dissolving of the dyestuff and acts as a swelling agent. Supplier — fertiliser suppliers for cheaper grades.
Manutex A thickening agent (sodium alginate) which controls the location of the stock solution. (Wall paper paste — not with fungicide — can be used as a substitute.)
Wetting agent Select an agent with low frothing characteristics; it can affect the rate/degree of fixation. Eg. Lissapol N; ICI, Wetter OT.
Resist Salt Mild oxidising agent (use if available).
Acetic Acid pH value of stock paste 5.5 to 5.

c) strips of plastic
d) cardboard cylinder
e) spare sheeting and plastic
f) bucket for used sheets
g) dye cartoon.
3. Make up stock solution and prepare the range of colours to be used.
4. Tape dye cartoon beside warps.
5. Use paint brushes to apply the colours according to design, repeat for the length of the warp.
6. Remove the sheeting before rolling warps between layers of plastic.

Batching

To fix the colours, the warps are batched in a wet condition at room temperature. The batching time varies with depth, yarn and class of dyes. Allow 24-48 hours for heavier shades. Suspend the roller to allow excess moisture to drip out.

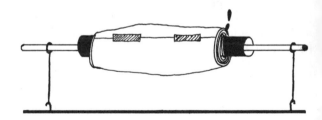

Warp Painting: Technique

1. Scour, rinse and soak the warps; squeeze to remove excess water. For direct colour control the warps need to be unchained and painted flat; to marble the warps paint the warps chained. The chained warps are quicker to dye and easier to rinse, but the results are random.
2. Prepare the work area as in diagram.
a) chained warps in bucket
b) strips of old sheeting

Washing Off

During the batching as much dye as possible has bonded with the fibre; the washing off is to remove the unfixed dye and auxiliaries. To ensure good wash fastness, all unfixed dye must be removed. The painted warps are rinsed in diluted ammonia (pH = 8.5-9) to discourage back staining and to assist with fixation. Sudden temperature changes when rinsing the wool yarn will cause felting and will damage the yarn.

Method:

1st bath — cold water 10-15 minutes, ammonia pH 8.5-9.

2nd bath — cold water overflow until no further colour is removed.

3rd bath — hot water 45°C and detergent, 10 minutes.

4th bath — hot water 75°C, 10 minutes.

5th bath — warm rinse 5 minutes, weakly acetic. Between each rinse run the warps through a wringer; to avoid tangling hang the start over the sink.

An excellent product, Mesitol NBS, available from Kraft Kolour, Melbourne, avoids back staining and assists in the removal of unfixed dye.

Arrange the warps on the drying rack.

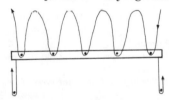

When dry, secure one end of the warp firmly and chain the warp under tension.

During the dyeing process all spinning oils have been removed; with some wool yarn it may be necessary to recondition the warp with oil.

As mentioned in the introduction to this article, I have concentrated on the application of the cold batch process to wool warps. Other fibre workers may wish to explore further possibilities for applying this technique in their work. What follows is a brief outline introducing the technique at different stages of production.

Application to Fibre, Skein or Piece of Wool

Fibre preparation   Gently wash in detergent to remove impurities, soak in 2% ammonia solution and rinse well.

To dye   Arrange staples of fibre on a plastic sheet. Paint or dribble dyes/stock solution over the fibres. Batch in plastic. Rinse in 2% ammonia solution; final rinse, weakly acetic. Take care to avoid felting at each stage of preparation.

Industrially, the process is termed Vigoureux printing or Melange. When combed and spun the partially dyed, carded fibres blend to produce subtle marbled yarns. Beautiful effects can be produced when dyeing silk bonnets.

Skein preparation   Careful preparation is important to avoid tangling the skeins. Prepare long hanks (100-300 gm), and if possible wind by traversing the yarn on a vertically mounted swift. Tie the two ends of the skein together with a double knot to indicate the starting end (ie. where to start balling the skein). Tie 3-4 loose leases using figure-of-8 ties, leaving space for the yarn to swell.

To dye   Lay skeins on large plastic sheets. Paint or pour the dye/stock solution on the skein. Batch and rinse as per warps. Skeins can be prepared for featured weft shots or prepared prior to warping for random warps. A similar industrial print process is termed Chine or Chene.

Piece preparation   Scour the woven or knitted product. Avoid using the process for large applications; it is suitable for small featured panels or highlights. The painted area should be stretched under slight tension to simplify the dye application. Paint, batch and wash as per instructions. The use of a chemical resist will help localise the design: omit the wetting agent in the stock paste to minimise seepage of dye.

Brief guidelines for the application of the cold batch process to cellulose-cotton and viscose rayon   As this is only a brief introduction, I would recommend further research. The characteristic properties of cotton and rayon need variations to the process; for example, the stock solution is alkali. The alkali pad can be applied at varying stages of the process.

Method 1: alkali pad prior to dye application   Scour the yarn, bleach to remove all dressings and rinse well. Dip in strong alkali solution (washing soda or soda ash); dry the yarn. Paste the dye with water and paint onto the yarn. If the dye solution seeps out, add dye to thin paste of Manutex. Batch and rinse thoroughly to remove unfixed dye.

Method 2: dye/fix with alkali pad   Paste the

reactive dye with water and then add thin paste of Manutex with wetting agent. Paint onto soaked yarn. Dry the yarn. Fix with alkali pad.

To make 1 litre of fixing agent
    10 mg Manutex
    10 gm soda ash
    10 gm urea.

Dissolve Manutex by sifting into 250 ml of hot water. Allow to thicken. Dissolve soda ash and urea in 750 ml of warm water: add Manutex and blend into smooth paste. Make up to 1 litre. Pad for 2-4 hours. Rinse well to remove unfixed dye. Product available from Batik Oetero called Drimafix — a fixing agent for Drimarine dyes.

Method 3: cold batch process using direct dyes

To make 1 litre of stock solution.
    50 gm urea
    2 gm wetting agent
    2 gm ammonium sulphate
    5 gm manutex
    3 gm methylated spirits

Dissolve urea in 500 ml of hot water; add ammonium sulphate and fixing agent. Mix Manutex with methylated spirits and add to urea. Stir well. Make up to 1 litre.

Paste direct dyes with water and add stock solution; use as required and batch for a minimum of 4 hours. Rinse well to remove unfixed dye.

It is emphasised that the material in this section on cellulose has been rigorously condensed. As with all developmental work the processes involve building blocks of knowledge. Use the above as initial guidelines, be observant, keep records and samples; evaluate the results and continue to build on the experience gained with each dye session. The processes are simple and cheap, but with broad scope for experimentation, free from the constraints of precision dye techniques (eg. Ikat, warp printing).

This article has only touched upon the field of cold batch process and can do little justice to the extensive possibilities inherent within the technique. But through further research, trial and error, and experience the weaver/dyer may achieve the versatility and richness of colour and design that this technique offers.

References

Dyes and Dyeing, M. Simmons, Van Nostrand Reinhold, Australia
Dyes and Fabrics, J. Storey, Thames and Hudson, Manual
Handloom Technology, A. Fannin, Van Nostrand Reinhold, U.S.
Synthetic Dyes for Natural Fibres, L. Knutson, Madrona (republished, Interweave Press, 1986)
Textiles for Modern Living, E. Gohl, L. Vilensky, Longman, Cheshire
The New Dyer, S. Vinroot and J. Crowder, Interweave Press.

Technical Papers
'The Application of IWS Print Batch Cold Process to the printing of wool knitwear', J. Mills
'Urea Pad Batch Printing Technique for Wool', D. Pleasance. Aust. Wool Corp.

Lanasol Dye Manual, Ciba Geigy.

keins of yarn space dyed using Earth Palette dyes,

Elizabeth Lindsay wearing a coat she wove and made. Yarns dyed from Earth Palette dyes.

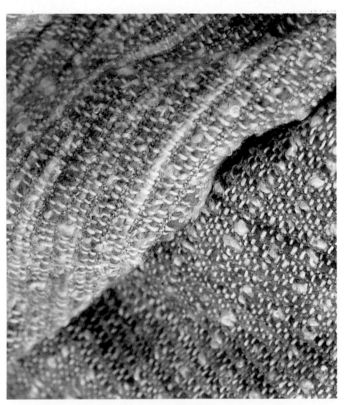

Close-up of the woven fabric by Elizabeth Lindsay, Earth Palette dyes.

'Kimono' by Inga Hunter. Approximately 20 cm square. Polyester cloth, heat transfer printed. Mounted on handmade paper (shibori-dyed in indigo).

'Kimono' by Inga Hunter. Mounted on handmade paper

Miniature kimono, indigo dyed by Inga Hunter.

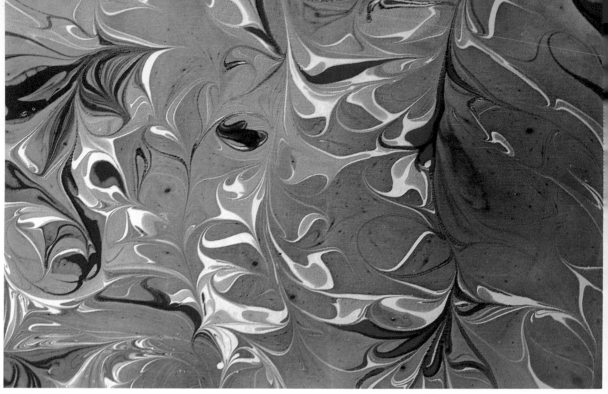

Marbled fabric.

'Let the Red Poppies Dance'. Hand-quilted marbled silk purse, by Alison Snepp. In collection of the Embroiders' Guild, NSW.

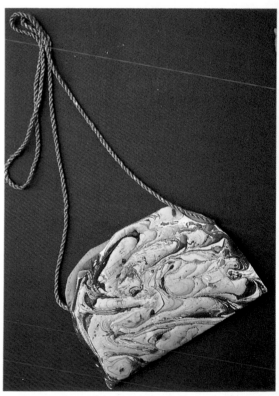

Marbled fabric purse by Alison Snepp.

Marbling Cloth

A number of American textile publications have run articles on marbling fabric in recent years. The term 'marbling' is usually familiar to people through the marbled end papers often found in older books. Paints are swirled in colourful patterns, with traditional names and traditional formations. Being able to control or truly 'craft' the materials takes a craftsperson's skills. This article surveys what has appeared in print, both in the USA and in *Textile— Fibre Forum* magazine in Australia (article by Alison Snepp, 1987/1). Bear in mind that marbled fabric can be an end in itself. But it can also be combined as a technique with quilting, stitchery, batik and so on.

The Ingredients

Colouring Matter

Perma-Set paints like the ones used in silkscreening cloth are satisfactory. Water-based acrylic paints such as 'Chromacryl' or 'Derivan' will work on fabric too. Some respond better than others to marbling, so be prepared to test for variations. Fabric paints such as 'Harlequin' can also be used.

Don Blake advises that 'colors for marbling . . . can be made from most any water soluble color. Although they work technically, many of the prepared water colors on the market come out very pale in application. Pelikan ink is one that works satisfactorily. Dry pigments can be used by grinding, first with pestle and mortar, then mixing with water . . .' The printing paints listed above are also diluted with water for marbling; and distilled water is used if the mixture is kept any length of time. To get pale colours, mix them by using white paint. Also, each successive dip into the marbling bath gives a paler shade.

(Don Blake wrote for *The Textile Artists' Newsletter* or 'TAN', Vol. II,-No. 2. Alas, the newsletter is no longer in print.)

Some recipes mention adding ox gall to make colours disperse over the surface of the sized water and still remain floating. Ox gall comes in liquid form, unless you find ox bile pills! Blake suggests adding 4-6 drops of the liquid to 1 oz. of colour. *Note:* ox gall may be difficult to purchase locally.

Size

It was mentioned above that colours float on a sized surface. Carragheen moss, or Irish moss is suggested as a traditional size. I followed the tip that it could be found at home brewing suppliers and/or health food shops. While I eventually found some in both places it was in limited and irregular supply, needed quite a bit of processing and was rather expensive if you want to do a lot of marbling. It came in 'moss-like' form (it is a red algae or seaweed), though it was dried of course. I boiled it up according to directions from Blake and strained it, then guessed from there as to proportions to mix in water. Blake's recipe is: 1 oz Irish Moss boiled four minutes in two quarts of water. Then add one pint cold water and let it stand till cool; strain. If you are going to keep it very long he suggests formaldehyde as a preservative.

After trying dried Irish moss I located Colophon Book Bindery in the USA (1902 No. 44th St, Seattle, WA 98103, USA) and ordered processed carragheen powder from them. One tablespoon of this powder, blended one minute in agitating water gets me through a whole day's experimenting in marbling. The powder is now available in Australia from Batik Oetero, Randwick, Sydney.

As a general rule, I prepare the size, and cover the bottom of my marbling tub with a very thin coating of it. Next I add water to the height of my index finger, when marbling in the large 'Namco' brand plastic tubs. The bath should sit overnight, and then be skimmed before use. (Single sheets of newspaper work well for this. Just lay them on the bath, pick them up, and throw them away. Repeat several times.)

Other sizes mentioned in articles: gum tragacanth (½ cup in 2 quarts water, aged 24 hours, put in blender and strained); cornstarch/water mixture; liquid starch used full strength. And there's tapioca size, wallpaper size and gelatine, which all work.

Marbling Tub

A baby's bath works well, or flat tray such as a photographic tray, gardener's tub, or baking sheet. For making large pieces it is important to be able to marble all in one go if possible. So a bathtub could be used, or a child's wading pool. Or a large bath could be devised by draping a plastic sheet over a wooden frame. Consider pre-cutting pattern pieces for a garment and marbling these units. An inert surface (enamel or plastic) is desirable for marbling with paints, but it is not essential. A pale coloured tub lets you see the surface colours better.

Fabrics

Any type can be used depending on what fabrics are suitable for your paints. Usually cotton is easiest to use, but rayon works with many paints. Silk gives beautiful results. The cloth should be pre-washed to remove any size in it, just as you would do before dyeing or painting on it. Heavier fabrics need a longer time to absorb the dye from the bath's surface. Leave the cloth in till you can see wet coming through to the back. With a lightweight cotton lawn, it saturates immediately. Satin and hard surface fabrics give clearest designs. Pile fabrics need lots of colour to show the design. Even black cloth can be marbled beautifully, says Blake! I've found lots of variation with different fabrics so be prepared for some revelations.

Preparing the fabric: pre-wash and dry. Some instructions say to treat the cloth with alum water, as the alum helps absorb and maintain a sharp edge to colours. Blake says to dissolve 1 oz alum crystals in a pint of hot water. Stir to dissolve, cool, and coat fabric with a sponge or brush. Marble the fabric after about 10 minutes, while it is still damp, or you can mix one tablespoon alum with one quart room temperature distilled water, apply it to the fabric, and let the fabric dry flat. The fabric should not be ironed till after dyeing, once the alum is ap-

plied. It is possible to marble without the alum of course, so experiment to see what suits your needs.

Miscellaneous

Work near a sink or hose. Have cups or jars for mixing, and one plastic spoon per container. Use rubber gloves to keep dyes or paints off your skin. Newspaper is needed to skim the surface of excess size or old paints. Protect the work area adequately and do not work in the kitchen. The laundry is ideal if you have a laundry tub, or outside will do, by a tap. Forks, combs, toothbrushes, basting whisks, straws — many 'found' objects can be used to distribute the colours in patterns. Once used with paints, do not use these objects for anything else.

Procedure

Prepare size, according to type. Skim the surface with newspaper to remove the scum which develops easily, and prevents colour spreading. You can also marble sheets of paper while preparing a bath for cloth marbling.

Add the thinned paints by whisking or flicking colour on — or drop it from a spoon (work close to the surface). You can try many ways of putting in colour — eyedroppers for example. A single drop should rapidly expand to 8-12 cm diameter. Colour which doesn't spread may need more thinning. But when it is too thin it will disperse too far. You will notice some amount of colour does sink to the bottom. Within reason, that's all right. Size which is too thick or scummy or cold will let paints sink.

You can start with just one or two colours and progress from there. A comb can be used to gently move and swirl and pattern colours.

Finally, place your cloth gently on the surface. It helps eliminate air bubbles if you let it droop in the middle as it touches the bath — then let the rest of the cloth go, from the middle outwards. Don't drag it or prod it. When you see the design through the back (with thin fabric this can be instantaneous) it's as 'done' as it will ever be. Lift by two corners, remove, and rinse. It may help to have an inclined board by the sink or tap. Lay the cloth on this and run water over until all excess size and paint is removed. Don't skip this step! Then dry the cloth and heat-set the paints if they require it, by pressing on the wrong side of the dry fabric with a hot iron for about three minutes. Test fabric pieces for their washability after all this — some may be machine washable, with other paints you may want to recommend hand washing.

Variations and Hints

Handmade magazine suggests using 'sprinkling water' to create negative areas in a design. This is made from a mild dish detergent (1/8 teaspoon) in ½ cup cold water. Wherever the sprinkling water touches the bath it pushes paints away from each other. Some colours also are 'expanders' like the irridescent ones.

If you don't like the fabric you can't re-marble it while it is wet. Let it dry and then do an overprint. Experiment with fabric scraps and with paper until you gain some control and predictability. I usually marble quite a bit of paper when starting a marbling bath until I feel it's getting under control. (Again, the relative absorbency of papers varies.)

After the first piece of fabric has been marbled, a paler piece will be the next result if you don't add fresh paints. Remember to skim the surface when you want to get rid of old or excess paint.

There is a noticeable break line if a section is dipped, raised, and then the section next to it is lowered for marbling. I'd suggest cutting out pattern pieces ahead of time if a garment is planned. Try to create a bath larger than the biggest pattern piece. Prepare colours and marble piece by piece, when you feel secure enough to judge what results your colour preparation will give.

If you have air bubbles, they leave a white place in your pattern. You can dip these areas again, but a variation will be noticeable.

Some colours just don't adhere to fabric. It could be that they sat on the size too long before being picked up, so they sank just enough to keep them from adhering to the fabric.

Don't mess with the bath more than is necessary. And don't stir size or colours that have fallen to the bottom.

But *do* enjoy yourself!

Having given you all those preliminaries, I'll finish with a recipe devised in Australia by Alison Snepp. 'In a blender, mix 1 tablespoon *carragem* with 300 ml hot water. Blend for two minutes. While the blades are still running, add 1 litre hot water and blend for three minutes. Leave to stand overnight. (Marbling inks, 'carragem' and marbling combs are available from Batik Oetero, 201 Avoca St, Randwick, NSW.)

'The carragem solution is poured into a 10 cm deep tray to a depth of approximately 4-5 cm. The tray size determines the size of the pieces of fabric for marbling (fabric is cut slightly larger than the size of the tray). The fabric should be well washed, dried, and then mordanted by immersing it in a solution of 30 gm of alum dissolved in 600 ml hot water. (Alum is potassium aluminium sulphate, available from the chemist; it is often used as a mordant with vegetable dyes on wool.)

'Allow the fabric to dry, and iron it carefully with a moderate heat setting on your iron. The fabric marbling inks are thinned with white spirit, added a few drops at a time. When the ink and white spirit are well mixed (use a bamboo 'sate' stick) to the consistency of runny cream, they are dropped in single drops onto the surface of the carrageen solution. The ink should spread evenly. The ink may then be combed into patterns, or the patterns may be made with a fine stick, or by blowing through a straw. The fabric is then carefully lowered onto the pattern of ink in the tray. After about half a minute or so the fabric is gently lifted out of the tray and rinsed by pouring water over it. The fabric must be kept flat until it dries. After it is dry, the fabric should be ironed between paper towels. The surface of the solution is skimmed with paper, and then it is ready to use again.'

Be prepared for some disappointments. Things can go well one day and fail on you the next. The marbling inks were decided upon by Alison, and Michel Kostavik of Batik Oetero. Alison Snepp and Karma Bains have produced a range of marbled needlepoint tapestry canvases which were released onto the market in 1986.

Bibliography

Handmade, Vol. 1, No. 1, April-June, 1981. Lark Communications, 50 College St, Asheville, NC 28801, USA

Textile Artists' Newsletter, Vol. II, No. 2. TAN, 3006 San Pablo Ave, Berkeley, CA 94702, USA. Article by Don Blake

Handwoven, Vol. IV., No. 3, 1983. Interweave Press, 306 No. Washington, Loveland, CO 80537, USA. Article by Anne Bliss

Textile—Fibre Forum, Vol. VI, Issue 1, No. 18, 1987. AFTA, P.O. Box 77, University of Queensland, St Lucia, Q4067, Australia. Article, 'Marbling Cloth' by Alison Snepp

Prussian Blues: Blueprinting for Textile Artists

Alvena Hall

Cyanotype, as blueprinting is properly called, is but one of a number of related processes available to the textile artist. What follows is just one way to make prints using sunlight. Cyanotype must be one of the simplest, least expensive, and most seductive of all the photographic methods. It requires very little special equipment, because the prints are made by direct contact between the thing printed, and the light sensitive surface, in sunlight.

However, the chemicals are *extremely toxic,* and great care must be taken with them. Protective clothing must include gloves, overalls, and face-mask. Don't tear open packets, but carefully undo them on a sheet of white paper, so that any spills can be seen and taken care of. Use a paper liner on the scales when measuring out. Make a paper funnel to transfer the powdered chemicals to the water, and use fresh paper for each chemical. Carefully fold up the discards so that no powder escapes. The chemicals should be stored in a cool dark place, preferably under lock and key. *Never* store acids like tannic acid or acetic acid in the same place. Keep a damp sponge handy for any spills of liquid or powder. I keep all the equipment for handling blueprint chemicals separate from other things, and scrupulously clean.

The main items of equipment needed are a glass or plastic jug; and a small 40 ml plastic measure from the chemist (for measuring liquids); two large glass or plastic bottles with plastic lids; a plastic stirring rod or spatula, white newsprint paper, scales, distilled water, heaps of newspaper, and for exposing the prints, a board covered with wadding, or felt, or thin foam sheeting, and a sheet of glass about the same size.

First, prepare your textiles. The best prints are made on pure cotton that has had any dressing removed. Cotton calico, headcloth or lawn are suitable, and so is pure linen. Blended fibres like cotton-polyester will give paler prints, depending on the amount of synthetic fiber in the cloth. The textiles should be thoroughly washed, rinsed and ironed.

Next, prepare the sensitiser. This is made up in two parts, called A and B. These are kept in separate, labelled bottles. To make up solution A, measure out 250 gm of ferric ammonium citrate (green gritty powder). Put 1 litre of distilled water into one of the bottles, make a paper funnel, and carefully transfer the powder into the bottle. Screw down the lid and shake to make the powder dissolve. Label the bottle 'Solution A'. To make up solution B, measure out 200 gm of potassium ferricyanide (rust coloured crystals), and add it to 1 litre of water as before. Label this bottle 'Solution B'. These can be stored until needed.

The sensitiser is light sensitive, so work in conditions of subdued light. It is made by mixing equal amounts of A and B together. Measure out 40 ml of solution A, and pour it through a piece of pantyhose to filter it, or you can use a coffee filter. Measure out 40 ml of B in the same way. You may notice that solution B tends to have a mould growing on it if it has been made up in advance. Filtering will remove it, and it does not seem to affect the prints. Ordinary household light is fine, but put down the blinds if it is a bright day. Only mix up enough sensitiser for the work in hand, because it will not keep for more than a few hours.

I usually use a large brush to apply the sensitiser to the cloth. Put down a stack of newspaper, and spead out the cloth out smoothly. Mark the top surface in some way. Systematically paint the sensitiser down the cloth, and check to make sure the whole is covered. For really intense results you might want to coat both sides; and very lightweight textiles — like silk — are best soaked in the sensitiser in a tray for 5 minutes or so. For a gradual fade-out effect, work on dampened cloth. Some lovely results can be got by progressively diluting the sensitiser, like a watercolour wash. Since the mixture is a greenish yellow it is not easy to judge dilution just by the colour.

The textile must now be dried in the dark. This is most easily done by sensitising the cloth at night, and pegging it out in the dark to dry. But be sure to collect it well before dawn, and watch out for dew! I use an old cabinet style clothes dryer, with a bundle of newspapers to catch the drips. Very light textiles can be blow-dried with a hand held hairdrier. It is fairly easy to rig up a drying box by using a blow-heater, a cardboard box, some black garden plastic, some string and pegs. Line the box with the plastic. Cut a hole near the bottom for the heater. Cut a pair of slits near the top on the opposite sides for the exhaust. Make little clotheslines across the top with some string, remembering to allow room for the pegs. Put newspapers in the bottom, peg out the cloth, clamp down the lid, and turn the heater to a low setting. Things should be dry in no time. Most cardboard boxes will collapse, so this equipment can be stored flat.

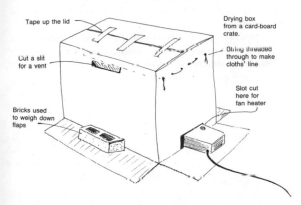

Tape up the lid

Drying box from a card-board crate.

Cut a slit for a vent

String threaded through to make cloths' line

Slot cut here for fan heater

Bricks used to weigh down flaps

Before exposure the cloth can be ironed with care, but be warned that the steam from it is poisonous. Place the cloth onto the covered board. Arrange the things you want to print. Prints can be made from almost any flat object. As a first trial, try out leaves, dried flowers, grass, ferns, feathers, lace, curtain scrim, onion bag, paper doily and cut-outs from various kinds of paper. Put the sheet of glass over the top. Window glass will do, or an old car windscreen. I tape up the edges for safety's sake. Glass with a solar film is not suitable. Expose the cloth in the sun. As exposure times are slow, I suggest 5 minutes in noon summer sun, but an hour or more in winter. In June I angle the board to the north at something like 35 degrees for maximum effect (Adelaide is latitude 35 degrees south). You will notice the green change to dark green, then blue, then to a bronze-grey, or a silvery blue-grey. Over-exposure could mean loss of de-

tail, and under-exposed cloth looks faded. An ultra violet lamp can be used, but exposure times will have to be worked out depending on the size of the print, strength of the light, distance between the light and the print, etc.

Developing the image is done in cool running water. Take care removing the cloth from under the glass, as it is possible a poisonous gas is trapped there. Wash the cloth for about 5 minutes to remove any greenish stain, and watch the colour change to blue. Then soak the cloth for 5 minutes in a colour intensifier. For this purpose, you can use a 2% solution of Solution B above; or you can dissolve 5 gm of potassium dichromate in 1 litre of water. I am told that a 3% solution of hydrogen peroxide will do the trick as well. Return the cloth to the wash for another 20 minutes. Longer washing times do not seem to harm the prints in any way. In workshops we have carried out the whole wash procedure outdoors, in the shade. The blueprint is now quite stable to light.

To print photographs onto cloth it is necessary to have made a large negative on graphic film. I have made use of both Kodalith film from Kodak, and Lithex from Agfa. A dark room is necessary, and I hire one when needed. Considerable savings in film and time can be made by making high quality photocopies from old pictures, magazine cuttings, pictures from books or anything else you might want to use. The photocopy can then be transferred to film by making a contact print. But even more interesting, dark photocopy images themselves can be used for blueprints. It is also possible to make your own 'film' by drawing or painting images onto stiff clear plastic. Very black ink, or artist's acrylic black paint work best. Most felt-tip pens are not opaque to the sun, but charcoal and pencils 6B, EB, or EEB are.

It is possible to convert the deep Prussian blue so characteristic of blueprints to a milk-coffee colour by removing the blue, then toning the print with a toner. There are a number of ways to do this in the books listed, but try this one first. Soak the print in a solution of 40 gm bicarbonate of soda (from the supermarket) in 1 litre of water until the image has bleached to a pale straw colour. Rinse for 10 minutes. Paste up 28 gm of tannic acid powder in distilled water, and make up to 1500 ml with water. Soak the cloth in this until the image is restored. The colour can vary from charcoal, sepia, or brown to purplish brown. Wash in running water for 15 minutes. It is possible to stop this process at any point by washing. The toning process can be used on only sections of a print, with care, by isolating the area with a resist.

Of course, the blue will be influenced by colour underdyed in the cloth. Providing that all the normal fixing procedures are carried out, the original colour should appear as the 'white' in the print. Naphthols on silk, however, seem to change in unpredictable and nasty ways whether applied under, or over the blueprint. Naphthols underdyed on cotton work well, and so do Procions. The best dyes on silk seem to be the acid silk dyes that are steam-fixed, applied after blue-printing. I find that pure linen is hard to get, so I cannot say how it will behave. However, beautiful results were obtained on union cloth, which is a mixture of cotton and linen. The easiest way I've found to tint colour into blueprints is to use dilute Permasets, and heat set them in the usual way.

I have heard that blueprints are washable, and thus suitable for clothing. Beware — tests done by the Creative Group in Adelaide found that they washed out very easily. If you must wash them, we found the *only* thing to use is Softly laundry powder, *with vinegar added.* Much better to label things *dry-clean only,* as this seems to be quite safe. The prints are very stable in the light, and do not readily fade.

You may want to keep your print as a finished object, but the medium on textiles is very suitable to padding, quilting and stuffing. The surface of the cloth retains all its flexibility, softness and draping qualities. Most books deal with the medium on paper, so try prints on your own handmade paper. It is interesting to know that this process was first invented by Sir John Herschel, about 1840. It became tremendously fashionable towards the end of last century, and today there is a renewed interest, stimulated, one suspects, by the inflated cost of silver. I strongly suggest that you read some of the books listed below for more information about this process, and the dozen or so other related processes.

References

Suda House, *Photograph Processes,*
  Amphoto Books, N.Y. 1981
Ernst Lietze, *Modern Heliographic Processes,*
  A Van Nostrand Co N.Y. 1888, reprinted 1974, Visual Studies
  Workshop
Thelma Newman, *Innovative Printmaking,* Crown Publications
Sandra Sider, 'Blues in the Light: Cyanotype on Fabric', *Fibrearts
  Magazine,* September/October, 1986
Joanne Mattera, ed., *The Quiltmaker's Art,* Lark Books, USA,
  1982

The 'Silk Dyes'

Marie-France Frater

This technique, which can be applied to silk, wool, cotton and cellulose fibre, is unique in fabric design. It is closely similar to working in water colours on paper or canvas, except that the dyes pass through the fabric. The combination of an easy-to-apply dye and resist, the former in a range of vibrant colours, brings unparalleled ease to producing patterns, designs and drawings.

This article is about two main types of dyes, supplied by 'Marie-France' of Adelaide, South Australia: one which requires fixing by steaming (Princecolor) in either a pressure cooker or a specially designed fabric steamer, and one which does not require fixing after painting (Princefix), but instead is diluted with a fixative prior to application. If good quality dyes and a fixative are used, both techniques leave the dyes colour fast, with no discharge and no residue. Both the Princecolor and Princefix dyes are very concentrated and must be diluted with water (Princecolor) or a fixative (Princefix) before being used. There is a large diversity of colours in the Princecolor (46 colours) and Princefix (29 colours) ranges and these may be further mixed to produce hundreds of tones.

For painting, the fabric is stretched on a frame, and if the fabric has sizing in it from manufacture, it needs to be washed and rinsed before painting. The dyes are applied with a brush, cotton bud or cotton wool. Because the dyes diffuse evenly, painting is very easy, and it is not even necessary to paint to the edges. Special effects can be obtained by such methods as sprinkling dry salt onto the fabric immediately after painting; the salt absorbs the colour dye and produces beautiful and unpredictable migration effects. Some of the other techniques to obtain special effects include using ethyl alcohol, Javanese wax (as in batik), or a mouth vaporiser. Very nice effects can be obtained by grading shades as in water colours to mix on the fabric in the absence of a resist. If totally dissatisfied with a design, in the case of steam-fixed dyes, the fabric can be washed and the dye removed so as to recover the fabric.

When the dyes are applied to the fabric they migrate with ease. If this effect is not desired, an inhibitor can be used as a 'fence' to prevent the colour from spreading. The technique uses a rubber based compound known as 'gutta' (pronounced goota) to outline the drawing or pattern. To apply the gutta, a plastic dispenser is held like a pen while being gently squeezed so that a constant flow of gutta outlines the design or drawing. The gutta acts as a barrier so as to give sharp defined edges to the areas coloured. After painting, the gutta can be removed by dry cleaning or by washing the fabric in white spirits. Various coloured guttas are available for use if it is desired to enhance the pattern or drawing by retaining the gutta outline. An alternative to using gutta as an inhibitor, is to use an antifusant. The latter is a fluid that can be either mixed with the dye or can be brushed onto the fabric before painting. It has the effect of thickening the dyes so that painting becomes more typical of painting on canvas, i.e. the colours do not fuse, and one colour can be applied over another without mixing the two.

The fixing process is very simple. Steam fixing involves wrapping the fabric in paper and steaming in a pressure cooker or a fabric steamer. The fixing time varies according to the type of fabric and the steaming utensil used, e.g. silk in a steamer requires thirty minutes; for wool the fixing time is longer. The Princefix dyes are not steam fixed but are diluted with a fixative at the time of use, one volume of colour to one volume of fixative being the minimum dilution.

Note: people wishing more information on 'silk dyes' can obtain a slide kit (rental or purchase) from AFTA P.O. Box 77, University of Queensland, St Lucia Q4067. The slides were prepared by Thel Merry of Montville, Qld.

Dyes in Nature

Introduction

There are probably hundreds of recipes for using plants to get colour on fibre. Rather than print some of these, it was thought preferable to indicate something about method, but also to show the fascinating history of dyestuffs (not to mention the dyers themselves) — and to suggest directions and approaches.

Thus Edith Neilsen of New Zealand gives very practical advice on setting up a 'dyeing day' for a group — so many experiments can be done at once. She also discusses the fresh versus the dried plant as a colour source. The eucalypt has been chosen for special attention because so many species are found in Australia and so many wonderful colours can be obtained. Jean Carman, one of the foremost researchers in this area explains the dye procedure, plus the less usual ways to apply the dyes (Kangaroo Press has published an entire book by Jean Carman, *Dyemaking With Eucalypts*). Ian and Mikki Glasson

are also expert in these dyes, and have very good advice on conducting your own researches.

Alick Smith extends the questioning mind to the humble 'soursob' and gets some surprising results. And Janet De Boer reviews the methods of mordanting — preparing the fibre to bond with the dyestuff, one of the most important aspects of using dyes from plants.

The 'mineral' dyes are another field of exploration, described by James N. Liles from the USA, who also tells of Edward Bancroft, a remarkable dyer from the 18th century who gave us the 'one pot' approach to mordanting. Neta Lewis of Adelaide expands this knowledge of dyes developed before 1857, which still has great use today. And Joyce Burnard provides a look at the traditional dyes of India, giving dyers yet another link with the history of colour and decoration, indeed with human history.

Drying for Dyeing

Edith Neilsen

Plant dyeing was the only form of dyeing until the mid-1850s, and naturally enough nearly all materials would have been gathered in season and dried. At times my garage must look like an early dyer's shed. When the cottage industry gave way to the

commercial looms and dyeing was done commercially with vast amounts of cochineal, indigo, and logwood chips being imported and exported every year, the home dyer was no longer so important. But colour is the most important factor in textile design, and for those who like to use plant dyes, drying of favourite plants is necessary.

You can approach it with cool detachment in a businesslike manner, or you can let your collection accumulate and use it as the spirit moves you. I am a mixture of both types.

For the former you need to be reasonably experienced and know the range of colours you use the most, and which plant produces that range, and then at the correct time you can go out and do your harvesting. As each plant type is brought in you will weigh it and label it noting the plant's name, the date, when and where gathered, and of course its weight. Then you will hang that plant type in a dry airy place, or store it on netting racks to allow the air to circulate. Holidays are interesting gathering times as you have the opportunity of accumulating plants not found in your own area, and summer is the best gathering time. Most of your material, when thoroughly dried can be broken up and placed in paper bags or cartons. I favour cartons as they stack neatly. Never use plastic as it tends to sweat and a soggy mildewed mess is only fit for compost, and all that time and effort wasted. I have used dried flax flowers when mouldy, and they were just as good as when fresh, but most books say *no* to mouldy plants.

Barks are best when gathered in the spring as the sap is rising, though they will yield dye at any time. Never mutilate a living tree, not even for a sample. If a supply is not available, why have a sample? This is the collection to build up on holiday as you often see fallen trees in parks, on roadsides where roadworks are in progress, or if you are lucky, at a sawmill (though they are likely to be on holiday too). Dry your bark and pack in cartons, complete with labels. Most barks will produce brownish colours. Most leaves will produce yellows, but quite a lot give greens. Once you have found your favourites, decide whether or not it is necessary to collect and dry them, as some are with us all year. My favourites are prunus and budlia for greens, but as the prunus is best gathered in the spring, then it must be harvested. Budlia, I gather in summer while in full flower, thus getting green from the leaves and a good yellow from the flowers. Experience will soon tell you how to weigh these. Six heads of flowers is approximately 2 oz or 50 gm.

Prunus leaves are fragile when dry, so can be crumbled and stored in quite a small container. Walnut husks can be dried as they leave the nut, for a good brown — but they must be kept really dry. Reds are hard to get in plant dyes but a good pink and a range of wine shades are obtainable from the root of the climbing dock, and you will do the world a favour if you root it out. It can be dried out in summer, but I keep mine in the hot water cupboard. Lichens are one of the nicest dyes to use as their colours are satisfactory and retain a slightly destinctive scent. But once again be careful of where you gather them, as other folk also like to enjoy things in natural surroundings. If gathered in the wet, dry thoroughly before storing. Onion skins are probably tucked away in every dyer's cupboard, so little needs to be said about them.

Silver dollar gum leaves are also likely to be found hanging around in the dyer's garage. They produce such a wide range of glowing colours that they are universally popular. Seaweed for most will be gathered on holidays and if you can stand the smell, it is a good dye. I found that to boil the dye liquor out in the open, remove the seaweed, and use only the liquor inside was acceptable.

Last mentioned is my favourite, New Zealand flax. It can produce such a wide range of colours and shades that it must rate number one as a dye plant. Depending on where you live it flowers from November to February, and it is best harvested when the flowers and pods are on the stalk together. That way you get them both, but you can take a stalk of flowers and leave another till all the seed pods are formed. The stalk can be used as well. The roots take a long time to dry, but with patient watching it can be done. It is easier though to plant a root in your garden and let it grow. The colours range through pinks to bricky reds, and pale to deep dirty purple.

Of all your dried plant material the only ones to require pre-soaking are the lichens and barks. It is sufficient just to pour boiling water on the rest and start releasing the dye. There are a lot of other things that can be dried, weeds from the roadside, as well as flowers from your garden — but I shall leave you to experiment for yourself. And I sincerely hope you do!

Organising a Dye Day

Edith Neilsen

Dye days are fun. Most guilds or groups have had such an event at some time or another, and all involved have voted them as the most fun day they have ever had (hopefully!). Sure, they are fun — dyeing is fun, and dyers are fun people. Dyeing should be enjoyed. But remember, dyeing is serious. Colour is a very important part of any craft, perhaps the most important part. Design on paper and the technique used can be perfect, but it is colour that you depend on to bring your finished piece alive. If you have to dye to get a specific colour, do your dyeing carefully, for if it fades it will alter the balance of that design completely.

So — if you are planning a guild dye day, you will either have a fun day with a serious intent; or you will plan a serious day and have fun. Taking the fun day first, here are some ideas:

Appoint someone in charge, or agree beforehand on a theme. Assuming it's an outdoor day over open fires, where everyone arrives with large pans and masses of plant matter (and lots of wool!), you really need to suggest firmly that one member supervises one fire. Don't have just one person to supervise the lot. The supervisor needs to say how much weight of a plant was used in his/her pot; and also regulate the amount of yarn to go into the pot. If people bring a prepared solution of dye colouring, ask for their recipe in preparing the stock solution. How often on these dyeing days you see too much wool go into one pot because it supposedly yields an unusual colour. What happens is that no one gets a good colour, or indeed knows at the end of the day just what they should have got.

Most people come with their own mordants and will stand over the pot with spoon in jar saying 'How much?' This is when you use the supervisor to show you how. Place an ounce of each mordant on a dish or lid (out of the wind). Divide this carefully into 8 portions. Most mordants need to be applied in the proportion of ½ ounce to a pound of wool. Thus each section is two ounces. (This is a start for knowing how much yarn can go into a pot with this much mordant.) Again, *suggest firmly* that everyone sees just how much (or how little) it is.

It's no use saying 'spoonsful' when spoons are all different sizes.

Another job to allocate is to have someone prepare several long lengths of yarn to put into pots for samples. Most members like to take samples and this is easier than snipping bits off hanks on a line. The sampling length stays at the fire where it was dyed.

Another person can organise the books. Go to the library before the dyeing day and gather as many dye books as you can, or have your members bring them. Keep them well away from the actual working area, and provide a towel for those with wet hands. Books are very important and a selection lets members see just what is available at the library, or on the market.

If you participate in a dyeing day, take plenty of wool and plant matter. The wool is not wasted if you don't use it, and surplus plants can be swapped afterwards. People get very keen after a day out, and welcome the chance to try different things. And, please clean up as you go — don't leave it all for your hostess.

Now for the serious day. Actually, I find them more fun than a 'fun day.'

You definitely need someone *in charge* with one or two assistants. Once again, you can work outdoors, or in a hall using cookers. Gas is best, as gas stoves are easy to regulate. Have members bring 1- or 2-oz hanks, and have the guild supply the mordants, with one participant in charge of them. To save time, prepared liquor can be used, but have some plants for comparison. For your theme for the day, answer some of the questions most commonly asked. These are:

1. Is there any difference between using prepared liquor and boiling it all up together?
2. Do you have to mordant first?
3. Does it matter what sort of pot you use?
4. Will unscoured wool dye?
5. Can you dye other fibres and things like feathers?

Those are but a few that have come my way, and make a good basis for a serious day. You can also have a time trial with a substantive dye plant such as gum leaves or lichens, or use one lot of plant liquor to explore its possibilities with each of the mordants — or try a combination of mordants — or after-rinses (with ammonia, for example, or cream of tartar).

In all these experiments, use the same size skeins (hanks), and record the amount of plant used. Carefully measure mordants and try to keep your temperature and time for coming to the boil and simmering the same.

To answer number one above, try to make sure the same amount of plant is used, whether you prepare the liquor first and strain it, or put everything in one pot.

The answer to number two is, you can get interesting results either way, so experiment.

The answer to number three is that different pots give different results, depending on whether you use stainless steel or enamel (non-reactive), aluminium, copper or tin (all reactive). Some pans have a lining, depending on the acidity of the product used in them. A galvanised bucket can be used but they usually have a ring underneath which takes a long time to heat. Iron pots are classic for 'saddening' a dye colour.

For number four, try unscoured wool, in all its dirt and grease. All that natural mordanting of

sweat and urine may give some interesting results once again — if you can stand the smell. This is definitely something to try outside. If you wash just a hank in cold water, it's all right for indoors too.

For number five, this can make a great day in itself — especially if you want certain weaving and embroidery effect yarns. Put all your experiments in one pot and see what comes out. If you use commercially spun yarn, be sure you pre-wash to get rid of manufacturer's additives. 'Other Things' is up to you. Some people try feathers, some try bones — both can be dyed with some plant dyes.

After a dyeing day, whether it was the 'serious' or the 'fun day,' you should always be able to use what you have dyed. So that is why it is so important to be serious. Use hanks of at least 1 oz and vary them from good, controlled spinning to bulky or 'primitive'; blended greys and whites; commercial yarns of different textures and synthetic blends; mohairs; silks; cottons. To me, a lot of coloured yarns suggest a project, whether it be a Fair Isle pattern, or off-loom weaving. But please don't go along to a dye day and leave it at that. Be creative with your results and take them along to the next meeting of your guild or group, to motivate someone else to try dyeing.

The Eucalypt Dyes

Jean Carman

My research with the eucalypt dyes began in Melbourne in 1968, when I, as a very new member of the Handweavers and Spinners Guild of Victoria, attended a seminar on spinning, weaving and dyeing, organised by the Guild. It was my first introduction to natural dyeing and I was fascinated by the experience and enjoyed listening to members talking about their dyeing experiments. But it was comments made about different dye colours obtained

from gum leaves — from unknown species of eucalypts — that interested me most. Perhaps it was because my daughter, Kathleen, a botany student at the University of Melbourne, had become interested in the eucalypts after reading Dr Trevor Clifford's article on the classification of the eucalypts in the Mt Dandenong area, which included Croydon where we were living.

On arriving home from the seminar, I decided to

test, for dye colour, the leaves from the eleven species of eucalypts growing around our home. Some were cultivated in our garden and others grew naturally in the bush around us. It was fortunate that the first two I tested gave such contrasting colours, red from the silver-leaf stringybark, *E. cephalocarpa*, and yellow from the messmate, *E. obliqua*. Leaves from the other species gave colour variations of yellow, orange and olive green. The bark gave brown shades.

At the beginning I only used alum as a mordant. The wool used was a Border Leicester cross and was spindle spun. Then, I obtained a copy of 'Home Dyeing with Natural Dyes', U.S. Department of Agriculture, from Mr J. Anderson, Chemistry Department, Royal Melbourne Institute of Technology, and decided to use other mordants. The tin mordant gave yellow hues, the copper green to brown, iron, grey brown and the colour from chrome was very similar to that obtained from copper. The leaves of the silver-leaf stringybark, without using a mordant, gave an unattractive greyish colour. So I decided, as it was colour variations I wanted, I would only use alum as a mordant.

My husband having brought home a copy of L.F. Costerman's little book, *Trees of Victoria*, I decided to test for dye colour leaves of all trees listed in the book. I thought it would be of interest to country spinners and weavers to know what dye colours could be obtained from trees growing in their locality. Mr A. Threader of the Forests Commission kindly offered to arrange a collection of leaves for me.

To make it easier for the collection of leaves and the postage of them, I decided on a set recipe — 1 oz leaves, 1 pint water, 1 yard spindle spun wool, as I was not then proficient with the spinning wheel. I treated each new species as an individual. If I noticed that the alum mordanted wool was showing signs of deepening in colour after simmering for 10 minutes in the dye bath, I left it in longer till the final colour was fully established, orange or red.

Most of these dyeing experiments were done during the hot summer of 1967-1968 and the leaves were not dried out, even those that came by post to me were comparatively fresh.

But an interesting thing happened at the end of that summer when the rains came. Jeanne Plummer had been weaving a cushion for an exhibition, using some of my eucalypt dyed wool. She rang one day asking for more of the red wool. It was raining, but I picked some leaves from *E. cephalocarpa*

and boiled them up. To my great surprise, the resultant colour on the wool was not red but a pink-orange. For interest sake, I tested leaves from the messmate and the colour was a drab instead of a clear yellow. Kathleen took samples of the dyed wool into the Botany Department and Dr Ashton suggested that I dry the leaves before extracting the dye. This I did and the original colour returned.

A similar thing happened in August, at the end of a long, wet winter. Leaves from the last two species of eucalypts to be tested arrived. They had come from the Alps district of Victoria, where there was still snow. The leaves were very thick and seemed full of moisture. Because we were then preparing for the move to Queensland, I did not dry out the leaves before processing them. The resultant colours were very pale, drab yellows. One lot of leaves had come from a species of snow gum, which, in the summer, had given a bright clear yellow colour.

Before leaving Victoria, I submitted a copy of the work I had done to Dr Ashton who sent a copy to Professor and Mrs D. Carr, Botany Department, Research School of Biological Studies, Australian National University, Canberra. Mr Threader advised me to contact Mr K. Cockley, Department of Wood Technology, Forestry Department, Brisbane. Dr Clifford was then at the Botany Department, University of Queensland. These people have, subsequently, been of great assistance to me.

On arriving in Brisbane, I was happy to find a number of species of eucalypts growing in the suburb where we were to live, but great was my disappointment when I found, that, with the exception of one species, the tallowwood, *E. microcorys*, they all gave a drab yellow colour. I decided to give up dyeing; but it was not to be.

In 1970, I was asked to weave a cushion from hand-spun wool dyed with dyes from Queensland eucalypts, for an exhibition in Brisbane at the time of the Captain Cook Bi-centennial celebrations. I was rather appalled at the suggestion as the dye colours I had obtained from the Brisbane eucalypts were not very attractive. So I then decided to use the other basic mordants, tin, copper, iron as well as alum. In some cases I mixed the mordants. The result was a very impressive range of colours, yellow, orange, red, varying shades of green and brown and grey. *E. microcorys*, which had given me the rust-red dye colour with alum as a mordant, also gave me a black using a copper mordant and adding a little ferrous sulphate to the dye bath.

From then on, I used the four basic mordants for

all my experiments. Even though I obtain the widest colour variations from alum as a mordant, copper and iron give a fascinating range of mixed, muted colours, rich and varied. I find it impossible to give a name to them. Tin as a mordant can give brilliant yellow colours. I have not found that consistant colours can be obtained from using no mordant. In some cases a red dye can be produced similar to that obtained from using alum as a mordant, but in other cases only a yellow dye colour or a pale orange is obtained instead of a red dye from using alum.

It was about this time I contacted the forestry departments in other States who willingly supplied me with samples of leaves from numerous species of eucalypts native to those States. Kathleen, who was then working in Papua New Guinea, sent me leaves from the five species of eucalypts native to that area. Later, she tested for dye colours the leaves of several species of eucalypts which had been introduced to Mt Hagen.

In 1974, I received a grant from the Australian Council for the Arts to continue my work with the eucalypt dyes and write a book. The Forestry Department was most co-operative in arranging a collection of leaves from all Forestry districts of Queensland. Other States contributed too, so that when the book was written, nearly 200 different species of eucalypts had been tested for dye colours.

The dye colours Kathleen obtained from some species of eucalypts that had been introduced to Papua New Guinea were very interesting. The trees that gave red hues when grown naturally in Australia, in Mt Hagen gave yellow-orange hues. A few tests that I was able to do in Brisbane from cultivated trees, gave similar results, but it was not always so. Species of eucalypts native to two or more States on the whole, gave the same dye colours, but some species, e.g. *E. camaldulensis,* gave a colour range from yellow to red. Botanists have told me that the colour variation may have been the result of variations in the species.

I am now wondering if the change in dye colours within a species is due to the tree flowering. In Brisbane, I have found that the leaves of the tallow-wood, *E. microcorys,* are very good for demonstration purposes as, using a range of mordants, a wide range of colours is available. When I tested leaves from one tree, monthly for a year, I did notice that the dye colour was paler when the tree was flowering — mordant used, alum. The flowers and buds of some flowering eucalyptus give a reddish colour.

When I started testing the eucalypts for dye colour, I thought the different groups of eucalypts, gum, box, stringybark, peppermint, bloodwood, may give distinctive colours. On the whole there is a colour pattern, but certain species within the group give different colours. The eucalypts that give the red dyes seem to come from all groups with the exception of the bloodwoods.

Dye solutions from wood chips, with mordanted wool added, give soft colours. But if ferrous sulphate is added to wood chips soaking in cold water, the solution immediately turns blue or blue-grey, depending on the species of eucalyptus. Wool from this dye bath comes out grey or grey-blue.

Dye colours from the roots of *E. cineria* give yellow, brown and black shades. From that species, the same dye colours can be obtained if each mordanted wool is put in different dye baths; if they are put in the one dye bath, one after the other; or if they are all put in one dye bath together.

By using different mordants, using exhaust dyeing and mixing mordants, the colour range of the eucalypts is immense. What overseas visitors notice is the fact that they are so like the colours of Australia, inland from the lush coastal fringe, the colours of earth, rock, vegetation and sometimes sky.

During the latter part of the last century, a chemist, Henry Smith, was very enthusiastic about the yellow dye he extracted from a few species of New South Wales eucalypts. He believed that the dye would be of great economical value to Australia. But the synthetic dyes were developed and his dream was not realised.

During the past year, I have been using the eucalypt dyes in various ways. Previously, I had been using wool for all my experiments. I have now used other fibres for dyeing with varying results. Cotton has not been very satisfactory — perhaps I am not using the right mordant or method. Sisal and corn husks and other basketry fibres dye well, also feathers. My greatest success has been with silk — it dyes beautifully and does not need a mordant and is fast to washing and good to light. The eucalypt dyes can be used for tie-dye and batik. The powder left after evaporation can be mixed with a Permaset base and used for block-printing and screen printing. Commercial wool takes the dye better than hand-spun wool.

Dye solutions can be used for painting water colours and an artist suggested that the powder could be mixed with oil for oil painting.

Certainly we shall all have to do our utmost to

preserve the remaining eucalypts and embark on a vast replanting scheme. I do not look upon myself as a pioneer; people like J.H. Maiden and Henry Smith last century and isolated dyers throughout Australia have contributed much of value to this research. Perhaps I have blazed a

colour trail around Australia and in other countries where the eucalypts are growing so extensively. There is still so much to be done, so many questions that remain unanswered, that I hope more people will do a deeper research into the eucalypt dyes.

The Extension of the Eucalypt Dyes

Jean Carman

Since 1980, I have been experimenting with the eucalypt dyes by using them for dyeing fibres other than wool, and for various techniques other than weaving, knitting and crochet.

Dyeing Cotton

The mordant was 30 gm alum, with 7 gm washing soda in 4.5 litres water on 120 gm cotton material.

Dissolve alum and washing soda in a little boiling water and add to the remainder of the water. Add the clean wet cotton material and slowly bring to the boil stirring occasionally. Boil the material for an hour and leave in the solution overnight. In the morning, remove the material and squeeze out the excess liquid — it is advisable to dye the material immediately. New material must be thoroughly washed before placing it in the mordant solution.

Prepare the dyebath in the usual way and strain thoroughly. Place the damp material in the dyebath and simmer for 30 minutes, stirring frequently. Rinse well and hang in the shade to dry. Always use a large pot for dyeing to avoid streaking of the material.

Painting Cotton Material

Dampen clean cotton material and paint it with paint brushes, using dye solution like watercolour paints.

When using leaves of eucalypts, prepare dye solutions as for dyeing wool. For painting, only small quantities are required. Various grey tones may be obtained from wood chips or shavings.

40 gm wood shavings plus 1 litre water plus 1 tsp. ferrous sulphate is the recipe.

Soak shavings in cold water, with ferrous sulphate added, for 24 hours or longer. Strain, and use dye solution for painting. Blue-grey can be obtained from the wood of *E. pilularis* and *deanii*. To obtain a grey-grown tone or one with a suggestion of green, add ½ tsp. copper sulphate to the above recipe.

Dyeing Silk Material and Thread

Wash silk in a warm water solution of soap powder, suitable for washing wool. Rinse and add to the dyebath. Raise the temperature of the dyebath to 85 degrees C; to preserve the lustre quality of the silk don't go higher. Leave in the dyebath for 20 minutes, stirring frequently. Rinse in warm water and hang in the shade to dry. Iron when still damp.

Silk does not require a mordant with eucalypt dyes, but mordants may be added to the dyebath to give a greater range of colours. Because of the lustre of the silk the result of dyeing with the eucalypt dyes is very beautiful — earth colours with something extra added. The colour fastness to light and careful washing is good.

As with cotton, grey tones may be obtained from wood chips with ferrous sulphate added to the water. Copper sulphate may be used to give a different tone. Silk is then dyed in the strained dye solution.

Black may be obtained by dyeing the silk first in a dye solution from leaves of *E. tereticornis,* then over-dyeing the silk in a dye from the leaves of *E. crebra,* with ferrous sulphate added. A similar result might be obtained with wood chips from another species of ironbark.

I have dyed 2½ metres of silk in 18 litres of dye solution and have redyed it to get a deeper colour.

Painting on Silk

Very interesting effects were obtained when I painted the eucalypt dyes on unwashed silk from China.

Tie and Dye

Cotton and silk material may be used for tie-dyeing with eucalypt dyes.

Cotton dyed with the eucalypt dyes gives paler hues than those obtained from dyeing wool, using alum as the mordant. Overdyeing can be done with dyes from various species of eucalypt, or bark or wood chips, giving different colours. The depth of colour too will depend on the proportion of material to dye stuff. Different colours may be obtained by adding ferrous sulphate to the dye solution, or copper sulphate, or both.

Batik

Method used: wash new cotton material thoroughly to remove any dressing. For batik, better results are obtained if cotton material is pre-mordanted.
1. Paint cotton material with dye, dry, then wax. Repeat, using different dye colours, till required design is obtained.
2. Immerse cotton material in a dyebath (cold), dry, then wax. Repeat using different colours.

When the design is completed, dry the material, then iron it between sheets of newspaper to remove most of the wax. Next iron it under a cloth dampened with a solution of acetic acid and cold water. White vinegar may be used, 1 tsp. vinegar to 1 litre of cold water. This is intended to fix the dye. Following that, boil the material in a detergent solution to remove the remainder of the wax.

Other Approaches

Basketry — plant fibres for basketry take the eucalypt dyes well.
   Corn husks — boil in dye solution for 10 minutes.
   Sisal — wash in soapy water, rinse and boil in dye solution for 10 minutes.
   Feathers — wash in soapy water, rinse and then simmer in dyebath for 10 minutes. Dry, then shake the feathers to loosen fibres.
   Painting on paper — the eucalypt dyes may be used like water colours for painting on paper.
   Embroidery — painted or dyed silk or cotton material may be embroidered by hand or by using a sewing macine.
   Dyed wool can be used for hooked rugs and wall-hangings.

Block-printing and Screen-printing with Eucalypt Dyes

Printing Pastes

1. Reduce dye solution to a thick paste by boiling or standing solution in the sun. Then add it to the Permaset Printing Base. This may then be used for the normal techniques of screen-printing and block-printing on material or paper — drawing paper gives good results.

Methods I have used for different effects   Press printing paste unevenly through the screen with the squeegee, then add markings to the print with hakea needles or paint brushes. Leaves and sprays of fine-leaved plants or small flowers may be placed on paper or material, and then the screen placed on top and printed.

Iron the material 24 hours later, to fix the colour in it.

2. **Eucalypt dye solutions thickened with Manutex**   1 cup of dye solution to 2 teaspoons of Manutex. Heat dye solution to hot and add the Manutex very slowly, stirring all the time. Cool before using. More Manutex may be added if a thicker paste is required.

I have used this paste for block-printing on paper. The paste is applied to the wooden block by paint brushes. More than one colour may be used. The paper is pressed down on the block and then gently lifted off. The resultant pattern will depend on which corner of the paper is lifted, or which side. It is advisable to cover the paper with another piece of paper to prevent any dye coming on the underside of the print, especially if the print is to be used for a card.

Using Sawdust from the Eucalypts for Block-printing

Mix sawdust with Permaset Printing Base and place small areas on the wooden block with a paint brush. Wash the spaces between with either a dye solution or the Manutex thickened dye. Press paper on the block very firmly and follow the same technique as with the Manutex-thickened dyes. Small pieces of silk may also be printed in this way.

Dyes

Dyers in each State will need to experiment with the eucalypts available. In Queensland, for the strongest red paste, I have used the black bark from the mugga, *E. sideroxylon,* or any other ironbark that has a dark grey bark. Ironbarks grow along the eastern coast of Australia.

The bark is broken up into small pieces and soaked in cold water for a few days. Then it is brought slowly to the boil and simmered for 2 hours. Strain, then reduce it or thicken it with Manutex.

The coloured sap from various species of eucalypts may be suitable for making this printing paste.

Sawdust from different species of eucalypts will give tonal variations. A little ferrous sulphate added to the sawdust before the printing base will give a grey-black colour, and copper sulphate will give a green tone.

Different tones of black for the printing pastes may be obtained by soaking small wood-chips in cold water and adding ferrous sulphate. Soak for 7 days, pour off the liquid and either thicken it with Manutex, or reduce it and add it to the Permaset Printing Base.

It is very important that all natural dyes be tested for colour fastness before being used for art and craft work.

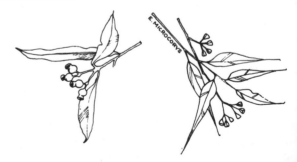

Cloth dip-dyed, then silk dyes used for a 'bled' effect plus gutta outlining. Thel Merry.

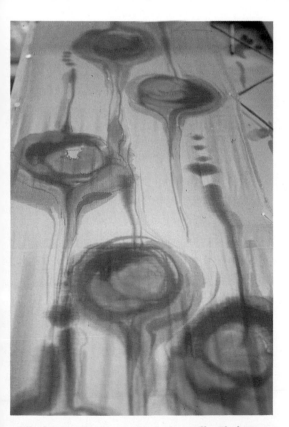

Silk dye brushed onto dry Indian silk. Thel Merry.

Coat, dip-dyed fine silk with designs painted with silk dyes, gutta resist.

Wool dyed with cochineals, various mordants and indigo overdyeing. James Liles.

Shades of indigo on cotton and wool. Background is 'Turkey Red'. James Liles.

Shades of Prussian Blue. 12″ × 15″. James Liles.

Mineral dyes, James Liles.

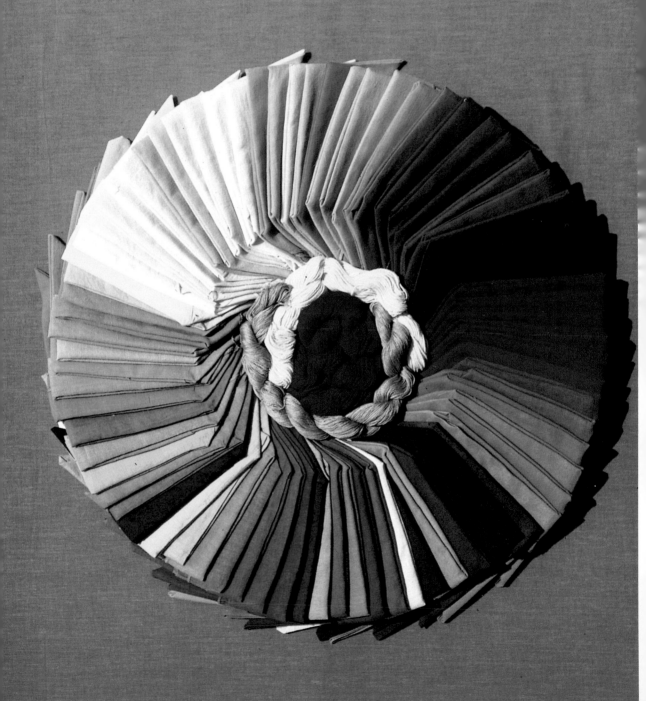

Cotton handkerchiefs, 21" diameter, 80 pieces. *Centre:* 'Turkey Red', Indigo and Chrome Yellow. James Liles.

A Eucalypt Dyer's Handbook

Mikki and Ian Glasson

Adjective and Substantive Dyestuffs

Natural dyeing is actually a chemical process. During this process the dye becomes a part of the fibre being dyed. In other words it forms a 'lake' of colour in the structure of the fibres. Certain chemicals — metallic salts for which wool has an affinity, are used in this process, and are called mordants. The function of a mordant is to form a union between the fibre and the dye. Therefore, when wool fibres have absorbed metallic salts in the form of a mordant, they will also absorb the dye and the colour will remain reasonably fast in those fibres.

Natural plant dyes are classified as two types — adjective or mordant dyes, and substantive or nonmordant dyes. The adjective dyes have to be used with a mordant to insure permanent colour. The substantive dyes do not require the addition of a mordant to permanently colour wool, there is usually some chemical substance in the dye plant which acts in a similar way to a mordant.

Eucalyptus leaves contain a substantive dye and this is one of the things which make them so simple to use.

Chemical Composition of Leaves

Our investigations into just what component in the leaf acts as dye and mordant led us to Mr E. Lassak, Chemist-in-Charge in 1973 at the Museum of Applied Arts and Sciences in Sydney. From his analysis of leaves from *E. nicholii,* Mr Lassak stated that the 'leaves contain a number of aromatic acids such as gallic acid (1), gentisic acid (2), caffeic acid (3),

and chlorogenic acid (4). They also contain appreciable amounts of ellagic acid (5), and of the flavonoid quercetin (6).' He goes on to say that in his opinion the quercetin is responsible for the wool-dyeing properties of the leaves.

From what we know of the use of oak galls as a source of tannic acid mordant by early European dyers, it would seem logical to assume the substantiveness comes from the gallic and ellagic acids. After five or six years of researching this subject we still cannot tell by the appearance of a leaf whether it will be a good one for reds and oranges or just another khaki or string colour. That is nature's secret and the mystery of it keeps us searching.

There are many naturally occuring conditions which can affect the colour potential of eucalyptus leaves. Similar varieties of trees may produce quite different colours in different areas of Australia, and the same tree can give better colours in some seasons than in others. For instance, in summer the colour could be red and in winter it might change to a dull yellow or fawn. The same thing happens in wet and dry seasons, high and low altitudes, hot and cold climates, and with varying types of soil. These changes can only be discovered by experimenting. By trying small samples from all the trees in your particular area in all seasons you should get a reasonably good idea of their potential. Almost all plants contain some dye, but it is not always readily available, or in a suitable form for the home dyer to make use of it. There is another aspect to be considered here, and that is fermentation. Many discoveries are made by accident and we like to think this is how we may have discovered that fermenting can produce colour from eucalyptus leaves. On a trip through the arid areas and two deserts in central and west Australia (in a wet season), we collected a few leaves from many trees and stored them in plastic bags in the luggage. Weeks later they were opened and found to be mouldy. When these leaves were tested with wool and no mordants we were delighted to find over one third gave oranges, pinks and reds. This was a surprising result because trees growing in arid areas do not usually produce the variety of colours which can be obtained from higher altitude country. More research and experimenting is needed in this category of dyeing with eucalypts.

Cream of Tartar

Quantities: 6%   1 oz cream of tartar to 1 lb wool
30 gm cream of tartar to 500 gm wool
2 gm cream of tartar to 28 gm wool

Cream of tartar is not harmful and it does not matter if these quantities are increased.

Additives

These can be added to a gum leaf dye-bath to alter a colour in a similar manner to the way in which a chemical mordant alters a colour. These additives are easy to use and readily available for people who do not have mordants on hand.

Copper Mitts   This is the mitt made from one long narrow strand of copper woven into a ball and sold as a saucepan cleaner. Copper mitts added to a dye-bath will give bronze tonings to a red dye, and green to a yellow or greenish dye. The mitts can be used over and over again and work better when they are not shiny. They take the place of a copper sulphate mordant. One or two mitts to an ounce of wool is usually sufficient, but the number used varies according to the strength of colour required.

Steel Wool   Sold in grocery shops as Steelo, these pads, without soap impregnation, do a good job of darkening the colour, thus taking the place of iron (ferrous sulphate). It is possible to organise shades of pale grey through to black according to the quantity of mitts used. Beautiful colours can come from using them with leaves giving red. They are not re-usable. The ratio is approximately 1 in 15 or 7%; increase the amount for darker shades. It is mainly a matter of experimenting, as some eucalypt dyes are more readily influenced by steel wool than others. Always tear the mitts apart rather than cutting them, and remember that Steelo will stain an enamel pot, so keep one pot just for iron.

Citric Acid or the juice of a lemon will often help to brighten colours and make them clearer.

Bark, Wood Chips, Twigs, Sawdust

Best colours from bark usually come from the thin pieces which peel off the branches (not the main trunk) of some eucalypts. Soak these pieces overnight and use the mixture as a dyebath next day. If you are not using a mordant it is a good idea to add a few leaves from the same tree when you put the wool into the bath. Bark from iron barks and stringy barks needs long soaking. Decocting will hurry up the process. To decoct means to release the dye and to do this the bark is put into a pot with water and brought slowly to the boil. Allow it to boil for half an hour, then stand aside at least overnight or till required. Another way to get the colour from iron bark is to use extended soaking. In this case the bark is soaked in water in a loosely lidded jar for up to 3 months, and the mixture used as the dyebath with more water added.

Wood chips need soaking or decocting and long boiling.

Sawdust can at times yield enormous amounts of colour. One example of this is swamp mahogany, *E. robusta*, from the Kempsey area in New South Wales. At one dye school, a bath, after five or six exhaust dyeings was still giving colour.

If a tree such as yellow box, *E. melliodora*, gives a good red from its leaves, it is almost certain that the twigs, irrespective of how old and weathered they are, will also produce good reds.

Ratios

One of the rules of natural dyeing is that quantities of all ingredients are relative to the weight of wool to be dyed. With eucalyptus leaves the ratio of leaf to wool is most important because it governs the intensity of the final colour. The ratios to be used will vary considerably according to the strength of colour expected by the dyer. The strongest colour from one dyeing procedure requires at least ten times as much leaf by weight as wool to be dyed, i.e. 10 oz of leaf to 1 oz of wool, or a ratio of 10:1. Ratios higher than 12 or 15:1 do not appear to add any more strength to the colour, and the quantity of leaf becomes cumbersome. More colour can be gained by re-dyeing or over-dyeing the wool a second or third time using fresh leaves and water at the same ratio as was used in the original bath.

Equal quantities of leaf and wool, ratio 1:1 gives a pale shade; 2:1 a little darker; 5:1 about midway and 10:1 is the optimum ratio for one dyeing.

Boiling Times

The length of time the wool is in the dye bath with the leaves is very important to the colour fastness of the finished product. It needs 1½ hours of simmering or gentle boiling to complete the dyeing operation. During the first half hour the mordanting properties are boiled out of the leaves and transferred to the wool; during the first hour the dye comes from the leaves and the last half hour sets it in the wool. Tougher leaves from trees growing in the hotter drier areas of the continent need soaking and boiling to get the dye. When leaves have given up the dye they usually change colour, and boiling longer than 1¾ hours will then tend to produce kino, which spoils the colour in the wool by darkening and dulling it. Kino is the dark red, sometimes almost black 'gum' which is found in veins and pockets in the timber, making it practically valueless for commercial purposes. Kino leaves a strong aroma in the wool which is most noticeable when the wool is wet, even years after dyeing.

If the wool is taken from the dyebath after, say, half an hour, because it is a delicate colour and that is the colour you want, it will fade because it has not boiled for long enough. The way to get pale colours is by using a lower ratio and not by less boiling time.

The wool can be left in the dye bath overnight or till the bath is cold. It may take up a little more colour, but if it is the colour you like when the boiling is finished it is a good idea to remove it from the bath as soon as it is cool enough to handle, otherwise you might end up with a different colour.

Vegetable Dyeing

Alick Smith

There is an indigestible plethora of dye books, under various titles, with the same old recipes and the same old 'do's' and 'don'ts', which I believe are prescriptive and stifling. In this article I hope to interest readers to do something that is not the commonplace standard approach.

'Every plant is a dye-pot' is quite true, but it requires interest and energy to find the best, and it is very likely that a source of beautiful colour could be obtained from the most despised of plants. I am sure most vegetable dyers have walked over dye-rich plants without even troubling to test them. Your own home garden is an excellent place for you to make a start. Common weeds, fruit tree prunings, green vegetation (sweet peas), duranta hedge clippings — are but a few.

Most vegetable dyeing requires mordants (chemicals), plus a few pieces of apparatus. If you wish to try vegetable dyeing consult any of the standard texts. When beginning, follow the instructions, but do not continue the routines suggested for the remainder of your life without the slightest deviation. Change the order of mordanting, and enjoy the results that will surely follow. Do not be disappointed if all your trials are not successful. If you obtain one good colour in every ten experiments, you will be doing quite well. Don't forget to record in detail all your successful dyeing experiments. I hope that some of my experiences and observations will illustrate the challenges and pleasures there are in vegetable dyeing.

The Soursob Story:

The effects of making the dye-bath acid or alkaline

For non-South Australians I should explain that soursobs *(Oxalis pes caprae)* were originally brought from England, possibly 100 years ago, to be grown as a home garden flower. They are now to be found State-wide, and in the more fertile areas around Adelaide, during late winter and early spring, they literally inundate the pasture paddocks with their brilliant flowers. They regenerate both from seeds and from bulbs.

Having stripped off the flowers, taking care not to have a bee or two in the handfuls, I went home with a bucket full. Anticipating some skeins of that brilliant yellow, I put the bucket in the shed where I did my dyeing. But alas, something rather important intervened and the soursob waited in the bucket for some days. When I finally inspected them I found them in a sorry state. They had changed into a rotting, brown sloppy mess with a few yellow blotches here and there, but oh — *the smell!*

However, like all true dyers, I 'gave it a go', and placed the bucket plus water of course, on my old kerosene burner. When boiling point was reached the obnoxious odour disappeared and I proceeded as usual:

a. After boiling for perhaps 1 hour, the contents were strained through some fly-wire into another bucket.

b. These were strained again through a funnel with a fine brass-wire sieve. I prepared to dye the wool, alum-mordanted. The bath was brought to the boil, then simmered.

Final colour — *brilliant deep orange!* I expected brilliant yellow, as I had some weeks before admired very much some skeins of wool dyed with soursobs. The deep orange was a pleasant surprise, but what had happened to the yellow dye?

Naturally I tried again with fresh flowers, and this time I obtained that brilliant yellow. In the meantime I had been discussing my dyeing with a knowledgeable old friend, who informed me that the 'foul odour' indicated organic decomposition, and further that this would have made the dye-bath alkaline.

At this stage some mention must be made of 'litmus paper.' Litmus paper is made from a lichen. *Roccella tinctoria* (dye stuff is the translation). It is a chemical indicator showing whether a solution is acid or alkaline. Red litmus turns blue if in contact with an alkali, while blue litmus turns red if in contact with an acid. Nowadays a 'universal litmus' is available which detects both acidity and alkalinity.

From the local pharmacy I bought a small quantity of glacial acetic acid (very strong!), which I diluted to about 5% (vinegar is about 2%). Washing soda is a mild alkali which is obtainable from any grocer.

Wool can tolerate quite strong acid dyebaths, but with alkalis care must be taken not to add too much. An excess will destroy the strength of the wool fibres (it strips off the platelets).

To ensure an excellent yellow from soursobs, add acid to the dyebath. Addition of washing soda, small dose-by-dose, followed by stirring to dissolve the crystals, causes a very interesting change, as the dyebath becomes deeper and deeper orange. Trial and error plus the use of your litmus paper will inform you how far you can go without damage to the wool fibre. Having obtained orange, the conscientious dyer will automatically try for *red*. Red and blue are two of the more difficult colours to obtain from vegetable matter.

Orange = red + yellow. If the yellow can be removed from the orange dye then you would naturally expect to get *red*. With soursob dye, made strongly alkaline, the addition of a very small quantity of tin (stannous chloride) will cause an instant chemical change. A cloudy precipitate forms, and if undisturbed will sink to the bottom of the dyepot. As this precipitate is insoluble it will not affect the dye. Using this method I have obtained a bright orange *red*. *Note:* Stannous chloride is most useful in the search for reds, but it is *not the only way*.

I feel rather ashamed to admit that I have not tried to produce the soursob red in larger quantities. Perhaps it is because I don't need it, as I grow my own *Rubia tinctorum* (madder) which I harvest every year. Madder is the best vegetable red, without any doubt.

Mother Nature is consistent as well as bountiful,

and I feel sure there must be many more plants which respond to acids and alkalis in a manner similar to the troublesome soursobs. Why not 'give it a go'? You may be pleasantly surprised. Soursobs can be picked with their long stems, tied into bundles and hung up to dry. The dried flowers give the same result as the fresh ones. Soursobs are still used in South Australia although they are not as popular as they were, because they do fade if exposed to strong sunlight.

Testing for fastness is quite simple:

1. Wind a quantity of your freshly dyed and dried wool around a rectangular piece of thick cardboard, approximately 15 cm × 6 cm, beginning at one end and finishing at the other end.

2. Cover one half of the wool with another piece of cardboard, approximately 7.5 cm × 6 cm. Secure on 3 sides with sticky tape of some sort.

3. Expose the uncovered wool to full sunshine. Check every 2 days.

Extraction of Chlorophyll Fill a jar (1 or 2 litres) with green leaves. Jacaranda or oak leaves have both given good results, but try others that may be available. Pour in enough methylated spirits to cover the leaves. Screw on the lid and leave for 24 hours. Pour methylated spirits (now light green) into another jar of *fresh* green leaves and go on repeating this procedure until the liquid is very dark. Mix 50/50 with water, and use this as a dyebath.

Warning: Do not try the above method if you use a flame (gas or kerosene) to boil your dyes. Methylated spirits boil at a lower temperature than water, and if too much heat is applied, gas bubbles could splash some of the dyebath out of the dyepot, thus causing a fire.

Fermentation Fermentation takes place in moist places (see 'The Soursob Story'). This can simply be in water, or in water with chemicals added. The chemicals are lime (ashes), lye — these are alkaline. Or they can be acetic or oxalic acids.

Oxalic acid is often used when trying for those elusive 'blues'. Green = yellow + blue. Removal of yellow from green will give *blue*. (Oxalic acid may precipitate out the yellow influence.)

The Mineral Dyes

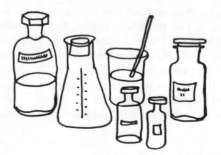

James N. Liles

This article was reprinted with permission of Shuttle, Spindle and Dyepot magazine, USA

The traditional dyestuffs were not all of vegetable and animal origin. Indeed, mineral dyes (iron containing mud, iron water, copper ores) were used from the beginning of dyeing history.

Mineral dyes reached the peak of their use at the beginning of the 19th century, but were used into the early part of the 20th century.

The term *mineral dye* may be a misnomer. In addition to mineral pigments, this group contains coloured inorganic chemical precipitates and oxides, deposited on and in yarn and piece goods. All of the mineral dyes, then, are termed *inorganic;* the animal- and vegetable-derived dyes, which contain carbon molecules, are called *organic.*

The majority of the best mineral dyes were not developed early because the chemicals necessary for their production were not available. For example, Prussian blue was not discovered until 1749, and potassium dichromate (chrome), used for rich chrome yellow, until about 1800.

With the exception of Prussian blue and manganese brown, the mineral dyes were used almost exclusively on cellulose, i.e., cotton, linen, wood, and paper. Wool and cellulose fibres can both be dyed with the mineral dyes which precipitate, depositing color equally well on either. However, this process makes wool somewhat harsh to the touch. The organic dyes which did not produce this effect were more frequently used on wool. The effect of harshness occurs to a much lesser degree when cotton is mineral-dyed. The mineral dyeing process on cotton is also much shorter than that required for organic (plant and animal) dyes. Mineral dyes were a practical way to get colour on cotton.

Characteristically, the mineral dyes are quite fast to light, exposure, and washing compared to the other traditional dyes, and are purer in colour. This latter aspect probably appealed to our forebears, just as many of the soft non-pure colour vegetable dyes appeal to some of us now. In addition, the mineral dyes are easy to apply and reproduce.

This article will concentrate on iron buff, the Prussian blues, and manganese brown.

Iron Buff

Also called nankeen, nankin, or rust, has probably seen longer continuous use than any other dye, with the possible exception of the tannins. It was used as far back as c. 6000 BC by the Swiss Lake Dwellers, and by the Egyptians as early as 2500 BC. It was also used by the Japanese as late as 1912, and as late as 1940 in an isolated village in Germany, according to *The Art of Dyeing in the History of Mankind.*

In 1912, iron buff was the one ancient dye still quite important compared to the then existing synthetic dyes, says C.E. Pellew in 'Dyeing for Craftsmen, I'. The reason for this was its extreme fastness to washing, exposure, and light. Iron buff is rust (hydrated ferric oxide). Have you ever tried to get a rust stain out of cotton or wool? It takes reasonably strong acid to discharge rust.

According to Pellew, the sails of many of the fishing boats on the Mediterranean around the turn of the twentieth century were dyed dull shades with buff. It was used by colonial Americans on

their homespuns and in rugs and covertures by the French inhabitants on the St Lawrence River into the early part of the twentieth century.

Methods of iron buff production can include iron water, and iron containing muds, but easier techniques are available.

The Egyptians and colonial Americans used similar methods. First, the yarn, or piece goods, was steeped in iron acetate solution, produced by dissolving small pieces of scrap iron in vinegar. Then the material was wrung out, steeped in an alkaline solution, and exposed to the air. The Egyptians probably used lime water for the alkaline solution, while the colonial Americans used wood ash lye or a very alkaline lye soap solution. The easiest and most economical method for the home dyer now is to use the nineteenth century method of copperas (hydrated iron sulphate or ferrous sulphate) for the iron source and washing soda solution for the alkali.

The shade depends upon the amount of rust deposited, and will vary from a light orange to a reddish brown. Once well washed with soap, buff is definitely wash- and light-fast, but it is not advisable to produce the heaviest shades because they may not be entirely rubfast.

Method

The first step in *all* cotton or linen dyeing is to scour the material extremely well, since all but the most highly processed and mercerised yarn is full of pectic substances, wax, and oil. It is likely that most cotton dyeing failures, whether the dye be modern or traditional, result from improperly scoured yarn *or* yarn that is not thoroughly wet. If in doubt, drop the well-tied skeins of yarn into a bucket of water.

If the yarn wets immediately and sinks, you can assume that it is well-cleaned. If the yarn floats, it should be scoured thoroughly with washing soda. To do this, dissolve one level tablespoonful of washing soda for each ounce of yarn in hot water in a porcelain-lined pail or stainless steel vessel. (The general rule is at least one quart of water per ounce of yarn.)

Also, tie the cotton skeins very carefully, but not with wool yarn. Cotton yarn can tangle in a way that wool never dreamed of, and the strongly alkaline washing soda may disintegrate woollen ties.

Next, heat the pot to a simmer or slow boil and keep it at that temperature for at least two hours. If the wash water is very dark, a second scouring is advised. In the old days, cotton was often scoured at the boil for 6-8 hours! After rinsing the scoured yarn, leave it wet or bleach it with clorox and rinse again. *Note:* It is inadvisable to do iron buff on cotton lint because it will be hard to card and spin.

Dyeing procedure: Work the material 30 minutes in a bath prepared by completely dissolving two level tablespoonsful of copperas ger gallon of warm water. Squeeze and work the material for about 15 minutes in a bath containing three level teaspoonsful of washing soda per gallon of hot water (120-180°F). The iron will precipitate as a light greenish-gray coating (ferrous hydrate). Squeeze, and expose the material to the air. In a few minutes the greenish-gray colour will change to orange or reddish-brown (ferric hydrate). Finally, wash the material in a warm-to-hot soap or detergent bath. If the colour is too deep, dilute the copperas for the next run or discharge the colour (Note 3 below). If not deep enough, repeat the entire process as many times as necessary or make the copperas bath stronger.

Note 1: Ferric salts may also be used (ferric chloride, nitrate, or sulphate). In this case, the air oxidation step is omitted.

Note 2: Wear rubber or disposable gloves. Iron-buffed hands, and especially fingernails, remain so for at least a week or two. Dilute acid or straight lemon juice will probably get it off, with work.

Note 3: It is possible to discharge iron buff completely, but great care must be exercised because the process requires strong acid (about a 'one normal' solution; pH less than one).

To do this, carefully pour one part of concentrated hydrochloric acid (muriatic acid) into eleven parts of water in a glass vessel and mix. *Never pour water into acid. Preparation of the acid solution should be done outside or in a fume hood.* Concentrated hydrochloric acid is '12 normal'.

Next, work the wet material with rods (wood or glass) for a few minutes in the solution. Then pick up the material with rods and rinse two or three times, at least. A rinse with alkaline washing soda solution or diluted ammonia will help remove all traces of acid, which is mandatory. If strong mineral acids are permitted to dry on cellulosic materials, the fibres will be destroyed or, at the least, greatly weakened.

Prussian Blue

Prussian blue was very extensively used on cotton, wool and silk during all of the nineteenth century. It was especially employed for the dyeing of army uniforms, according to J.M. Matthews in *Application of Dyestuffs to Textile, Paper, Leather and Other Materials.* By the beginning of the twentieth century, it was outdistanced by the early aniline blues. It is doubtful that the early aniline (coal tar) colours were all that good, but they were brilliant, cheap and easier to apply than the traditional dyes. Also, Prussian blue is decomposed by hot alkaline solutions, and the turn of the century laundry soaps were just that. By contrast, many of our modern detergents are nearly neutral.

Prussian blue is very fast to light and exposure, and fairly fast to ordinary washing. In very heavy shades it may not be entirely rubfast. It is also fast to dilute acids, but is decomposed by strong acids. As mentioned previously, it is decomposed by strong alkalis, leaving iron buff. This latter reaction was used for discharge work in printing at least as late as 1918, says Matthews. Prussian blue is still used as a pigment, and as a test for the presence of iron (for the dyer in samples of alum).

Prussian blue was used as a self colour on cotton, wool, and silk, and as a 'bottom colour' in the dyeing of feathers and silk for full shades of black. In addition, Prussian blue overdyed with chrome yellow produced the green dye of American 'greenback dollars' from about 1850 to 1900.

Prussian blue can be produced in many shades, almost from a reddish purple, through the blues from light to dark, to almost blue-black. If prepared with nitric acid, a teal or greenish blue may be obtained. Many of these shades assumed different names, such as Berlin blue, Napoleon's blue, Raymond's blue, sky blue, royal blue, and Chinese blue.

Prussian blue was first discovered by Nacquer (France) in 1749, and apparently rediscovered accidentally by two young German chemists in 1788. The chemists sought refuge at a country inn during a rainstorm. Behind the inn was a blacksmith's shop which they visited after the rain had stopped. They found a deep blue puddle in a depression on the paving stones. They soon discovered that the blue colour developed whenever a trickle of water from a pile of rusty horseshoes in one corner of the yard came in contact with water draining from a pile of ashes from the forge. The ashes contained not only burned charcoal, but also scraps and shavings from the hooves of horses. They later determined that the 'Prussian blue' resulted from the combination of iron salts with a yellow salt, potassium ferrocyanide (yellow prussiate of potash), formed by the action of fire on the potassium carbonate in the wood ashes with the nitrogen of the hoof scrapings and the iron from the scales of the horseshoes, says Pellew.

Dyeing Cotton

To dye cotton with Prussian blue, take some wet iron buff-dyed yarn or cloth and work it in a cold, acidified solution of potassium ferrocyanide (yellow prussiate) for about 15 minutes. The colour develops almost instantaneously; if it does not, the prussiate solution is not acidic enough. The amount of prussiate needed depends upon the depth of colour desired, although the final depth of colour is even more dependent upon the amount of iron buff present. Different yarns will vary, too. A suggested amount is one teaspoonful of yellow prussiate (well dissolved) and four teaspoonsful of good vinegar or two millilitres of concentrated acid (any kind) per gallon of water. Work the material for about 15 minutes. Remember that if the blue does not develop very soon, the solution needs a little more acid. Following the dyeing, work the material in a solution of one ounce of alum per pound of cotton in four to five gallons of cold water. Finally, wash and dry.

Dyeing Wool

Wool may be dyed Prussian blue with potassium ferrocyanide (yellow prussiate) or potassium ferricyanide (red prussiate). Place the material in a solution of about 20 percent of the weight of the yarn of yellow prussiate along with a small amount of alum and cream of tartar (about ½ teaspoon of each per gallon of water). Next, heat the bath slowly until it simmers and keep it at that temperature for 15 minutes.

The old dye manuals indicate that red prussiate is preferable for wool. Try placing the wool into a cold bath containing about 10 percent of the weight of the wool of red prussiate and 20 percent of the weight of the wool of concentrated sulphuric acid, for a bath volume of five gallons of water

per pound of wool. (One liquid ounce of concentrated sulphuric acid weighs about two ounces.) The temperature should be gradually raised to simmering during the course of an hour and kept at the simmer or boil for another half hour. The wool turns green first and then blue. If one or two percent of the weight of the wool of tin (stannous chloride) is added along with the other ingredients at the beginning or during the last half hour, the colour is brighter and somewhat more reddish-purple.

Acids other than sulfuric may be used which will affect the shade slightly. This is part of the reason for the different names, e.g. royal blue, Napoleon's blue. Nitric acid makes the shade greener.

Manganese Brown

Manganese brown (bistre) was used extensively on cotton, but it also works well on wool, skins and fur.

As it is very fast to light and to washing, be careful not to dye your hands. It can be discharged by strong reducing agents such as sodium hydrosulphite and thiourea dioxide ('spectralite').

Pellew considered the dye to be especially useful to craftsmen not only for dyeing full shades of brown but also in light tan shades, as a cover, or to soften and blend harsh combinations of other colours.

Pellew considered the dye to be especially useful not only for dyeing full shades of brown but also in light tan shades, as a cover, or to soften and blend harsh combinations of other colours.
front as possible, including the famous Scots Greys, who rode on white or light grey horses. Someone in the British War Dept. thought that white horses would be too good a target for the Boer marksmen, so a dye chemist was consulted.

The chemist advised that several kegs of potassium permanganate be sent down to the troopships. Each trooper was instructed to sponge his horse with a weak solution of the chemical every morning. Apparently it worked, because the skin and hair of the horses was a nice soft shade of brown long before the troopships reached South Africa.

Manganese brown or bistre is the easiest of all the dyes to produce, in my experience, if done by the potassium permanganate method as developed by Pellew.

To dye cotton or wool with bistre, prepare a permanganate dyebath by completely dissolving up to one teaspoon of permanganate crystals in a quart of hot water. Mix with one gallon water.

In order to prevent oxidisation (tendering) of the fibre (the possible problem with this method), a second bath should be prepared. This bath should contain two teaspoonsful of glucose (dextrose) or three to four teaspoonsful of Karo syrup or molasses per gallon of water.

Work the scoured, wet yarn for about five minutes, squeeze out, and plunge the material directly into the syrup bath for about one minute. The colour develops instantly, and the oxidising action of the permanganate is stopped. If the colour is not deep enough, the process may be repeated as many times as necessary. Finish by washing with soap or detergent and rinse. *Note:* much heavier shades of brown result by premordanting with tannic acid, about 1 oz per pound of cotton.

Since the mineral dyes seem to have been largely neglected by traditional dyers for the past 80-100 years, some of the chemicals may not be readily available. Red prussiate is carried by photographic suppliers and by Cerulean Blue. A pharmacist can get all of the chemicals listed, and all are available from biological and chemical supply companies.

Bibliography

Brunello, F., *The Art of Dyeing in the History of Mankind*. Vicenza: Neria Pozza Editore, 1973. (Cleveland: English translation made available by the Phoenix Dye Works, 467pp.)

Horsfall, R.S., and L.G. Lawrie, *The Dyeing of Textile Fibres*, London: Chapman and Hall Ltd., 2nd ed., 1946, 438 pp

Hummel, J.J., *The Dyeing of Textile Fabrics*, London; Cassel and Co. Ltd., 1885, 534 pp

Matthews, J.M., *Application of Dyestuffs to Textile, Paper, Leather and Other Materials*. New York: John Wiley and Sons, Inc., 1920, 768 pp

Napier, J.N., *A Manual of Dyeing and Dyeing Receipts*. London: Charles Griffin and Co., 1875, 420 pp

Pellew, C.E., 'Dyeing for Craftsmen, I. The Dyestuffs of the Ancients.' *Handicraft* 5(5):63-71, 1912

Pellew, C.E., 'Dyeing for Craftsmen, II. The Dyestuffs of our Ancestors.' *Handicraft* 5(6):87-96, 1912

Dyes Used in the 19th Century Before 1857

Neta Lewis

Dyes that were derived from natural sources and required a mordant

The dyers of the early 19th century had the accumulated knowledge of centuries of experiments as man had searched for colour in textiles. Where colour sources were expensive or rare they were the prerogative of royalty or the church. *Exodus* tells of purple, scarlet and blue, the more expensive and difficult colours to obtain. The dyers were skilled craftsmen who guarded their secrets and were proud of their standards. Where written texts from that period exist they need to be examined carefully as the terminology has changed although the ingredients have not. The chemical action taking place as the dyeing proceeds was not understood as such, but was closely observed. The four main fibres of cotton, linen, silk and wool were dyed as fibres and as woven cloth. In so far as chemistry was developed, the master dyer would closely observe effects of his work and try to find chemical explanations. We have to accept that there were two classes of dyers.

First: the itinerant dyers, who could not standardise their methods because of their habits, which were against them arriving at any considerable degree of perfection. *Second:* the public dyer (or master dyer) as in England, where the colouring was generally performed by public dyers who employed 'foremen as managers who were usually taken from the common workmen'.
'When the owner of a dyeing establishment perceives in any of his men a more than ordinary capacity, and at the same time, approves of his general conduct, he will propose, if he wants a foreman, to instruct him in the business, when this is mutually agreed upon, the man is bound for a term of years, say fifty, or sixty, on conditions subject to a heavy penalty, to serve his employer faithfully during the stipulated period, and never to make known to any other person the secrets communicated to him, or which he may attain during his practice. As a compensation for losing his liberty, he generally has double wages secured to him, and this is mostly advanced as his services become valuble.'

In America each woollen mill employed a boss dyer who 'seldom remained in the same situation more than one or two years' thereby affecting the quality of the dyed goods produced, as it was thought time was needed to secure dyeing-wares and to prepare them in uniform ways and to become familiar with the water conditions available.

William Partridge, the second son of a family of dyers from Bowbridge, England, immigrated to America in 1808 and worked at his art of dyeing; he subsequently published a book in 1823, *A Practical Treatise on Dyeing.* This was a comprehensive book covering the woollen industry as well as dye recipes and comments, and comparisons between the established practices in England, and the new industries in America. Partridge was a practical dyer in contrast to Bancroft and Cooper who had each published works on dyeing. He sums up their publications as 'none deserving of notice that is sufficiently practical'. Bancroft and Cooper were not practical dyers but theoretical writers on chemistry, whom Partridge suggests could not be expected to know the small details of the art. It is 'necessary that every part of the workmanship should be given....The time of boiling the dye wares, of running the cloth in the furnace, and of boiling it therein; the preparation of different solutions preparatory to dyeing'. He points out that the above authors 'prescribe a given quantity of mordant in proportion to the weight of the goods dyed, without

any reference to the colour, or to the state of the goods'. Partridge states that the quantity of mordant used must be in proportion to the hue of the colour intended to be obtained' — so no general rule.

This is interesting because natural dyeing enthusiasts today prescribe a fixed amount per pound of mordants to be used. This could be the difference between a master craftsman and an amateur. Most craftsmen who are natural dyers today, however skilled, would seldom fit the master craftsman classification of that period.

William Partridge, while working with superior dyes of better quality, acknowledged that there existed dyers of 'common colours that are employed in low price goods.'

The Effect of Containers

The dye vessels were made from 'brass, copper or block-tin or wood. When done in brass or copper they must be kept very clean and the liquor must not be permitted to remain after a day's colouring was finished'. Wooden vats were also common and had the advantage that wood has no effect on dyes. 'Obviously they could not be heated by a fire underneath, which meant they could only be used if steam heat was available or dyeing done cold'. They were also more difficult to clean.

'The material from which dyeing vessels should be made had long been a problem. Most metals have an effect on dyes which is why metallic salts are used as mordants, some good, some bad. As cochineal needs a tin mordant to get the best shade, a tin vessel can do nothing but good'.

'For the dyeing of scarlet and other bright and delicate colours they had baskets made to fit the furnace to prevent the goods from coming in contact with the metal and being soiled. The baskets were made of willow and finished about 2" above the level of the top with clean white canvas attached to reach over the curb of the furnace so that the cloth may never come in contact with the metal'.

Mordants in Use

Alum was by far the most used mordant.

Cream of tartar (acid potassium tartrate) was widely used in Partridge's recipes. It was sold as hard colourless crystals or crystalline powder.

Argol was crude cream of tartar and was basically red or white depending on whether it had been deposited during fermentation of red or white wine. It was widely used in the 19th century as an addition to the mordanting bath, especially with alum and stannous chloride and the colours were certainly fuller and brighter.

Vitriol was the old name for sulphuric acid. Oil of vitriol, a concentrated form of sulphuric acid, was widely used in wool dyeing after 1850 (for synthetic dyes).

Copper sulphate Blue crystals for mordanting and after treatment.

Verdigris, a green deposit naturally forming on copper or brass — or it could be obtained by the action of dilute acetic acid on thin copper plates. It was therefore copper sulphate and was used as a copper mordant.

Copperas was ferrous sulphate and the most common iron mordant. Also known as green vitriol because of its pale green colour. Before the coming of chrome, copperas or ferrous sulphate black was very important.

Tin liquor. In medieval centuries, scarlet was the most expensive colour, so much so that in England cloths dyed with it were especially taxed. 'Tin is always obtained from Cornwall in stamped blocks and none other can be depended upon as being genuine... The blocks weigh about 300 lbs each.' They were broken into small porous pieces by melting and pouring into water from a height of 10 ft above the tub. The tin pieces were drained and carefully dried as they must not be wet when put in the acid. 'Aqua fortis' (nitric acid) was put into stone pots. 'Into each pot is put four pints of the single aqua fortis, two pints of water and a handful of white blown salt, and each requires about 8 oz of granulated tin.' The tin was slowly added and stirred constantly over 8 hours. A rod of basket willow or glass was used to stir the acid. This would be used the next day as it would not keep.

Partridge does not mention chrome as a mordant — it was shortly to be used, and to become the most important of all mordants.

Dye Sources

Kermes   The dye kermes came from an insect found on the oak trees in the Eastern Mediterranean and was often called Venetian Red because Venice controlled the export of the dye.

Shell lac   Shell Lac was a cheaper but somewhat similar dye to kermes and cochineal. It came from an insect, the *Coccus lacca* or *ficus*. It was known also as lac dye. Stick lac was a cheaper cruder type which contained the bugs upon which the insects lived, as well as the insects themselves. The dye was used in combination with cochineal. The same tree that was a home to the insects which produced the dye also produced the well-known shellac which was of course used for making varnish. Grained was the name given to the product after the twigs had been removed.

Cochineal   The dyer again had to ascertain that the goods brought to him were of a quality suitable for producing good colours. 'That which is called Sylvester, having a white down covering the outside, is never used by the best scarlet dyers, the large black-grained cochineal being always employed by them. Cochineal, being a costly article, is subject to great adulterations; there is often found in it a gummy looking substance, having no colour, sometimes stones are found in it as large as the fly. Every sample, before purchasing, should be scrupulously examined, and all suspicious substances separated from the real fly and broken, which will disclose the imposition and enable the consumer to judge of the adulterated percentage'.

Brazilwood came from a tree known as the 'caesalpine', used in calico printing as an extract under the name of sappanwood.

Madder, from the ground root of the herbaceous perennial *Rubia tinctorium.* The best qualities were said to come from plants grown in calcareous soil. The plants must be left in the soil for 14 to 28 months because old roots were richer in colouring matter. As a cotton dye it produced the famous Turkey Red shade. The colouring matter in madder was *alisarin* plus a closely allied chemical, *purpurin.* Three years after Partridge published his book, that is in 1826, two chemists, Robriquet and Cole, isolated alizarin and in 1868, first two German chemists, Grabe and Lieberman, then the great English chemist W.H. Perkins, who a little earlier had discovered the first real synthetic dye, synthesised alizarian, and the manufacture of it in synthetic form began — the first of the major successes of

the man-made dyestuff industry vis-a-vis the natural.

Fustic   Usually called old fustic *(Chlorophora tinctoria)* to distinguish it from a quite different dye called young fustic *(Cotinus coggyria)*, this dye was obtained from the trunk of a tree found in America and was, after logwood, the most important new dye found in America. Fustic was widely used on wool and before the coming of synthetic dyes was the base of khaki and similar shades.

Weld   *Reseda luteoia* was possibly the oldest of all dyes and the universal yellow before the discovery of America. Mixed with indigo it was in medieval times the yellow basis of green.

Quercitron bark, or black oak bark is preferred on silk.

Logwood   *Haematoxzlin campechianum* was the most important dye discovered in America. At first it was used on an alum mordant to produce a blue much cheaper and much less satisfactory in fastness properties than indigo. Its use was rightly attacked. Later, however, first on a copper mordant and later, better still, on a chrome mordant, it gave an excellent black. Logwood remained in wide common use long after all other natural dyes had been replaced.

Indigo   The most famous of all dyes came from the leaves of the plant genus *Indigofera,* which was originally cultivated in India and later in most parts of the world. It was known to the dyers of antiquity but was very rare in the Western world until 1498, when Vasco da Gama discovered the sea route to the East. During the following years woad was the common blue dye and woad, botanically speaking *Isatis tinctoria,* and quite different from indigo, contained the same colouring principle.

Dyers greenwood   *Genista tinctoria* was frequently combined with woad to obtain green.

Sumac shoots of *Rhus* were dried and chopped.

Cutch, *Cicacia catechu* was used on cotton for brown.

Walnut Husks.

These dyes provided the yellow, red and blue from which other colours were mixed.

William Partridge was aware of the problem of putting a name on compound colours. 'Blue, red and yellow can be easily described so as not to be misunderstood, but in the compound colours, this is not so easy and I have felt the impediment very sensibly throughout that branch of the work'. 'Take cinnamon brown — there would be 20,000-22,000 different shades. In nearly all of them yellow would dominate and it is impossible to describe more than three of them in any work published on the art of the light, the dark and the middling cinnamon.' The only other way would be to attach patterns to the recipe which would be laborious and expensive. Partridge had contemplated such a catalogue and found it would have to be sold for over $100 (American) each copy, and would have taken five years to complete. To solve this difficulty he was arranging 2000 patterns in a large book, in regular order, with the design of matching any that may be sent by dyers or manufacturers'. To those who purchased dyestuffs there would be no charge, but to all others 50 cents for each pattern that is matched, suggesting an advisory service.

The Effect of Water on Dyeing

Partridge, whose ancestors were dyers in England, found when he immigrated to America that the effect water had on colours was considerable, while the general opinion had always been that soft water was necessary. Partridge concluded that his family in England held the notion of soft water, but their practice was in direct opposition, as they had used spring water (hard) to achieve their success. Almost 'any water is calculated for dyeing, provided the supply be regular, and always in the same state, and that water, however soft, that is subject to alterations from season and rain, or any other cause, is not fit for the purpose.' The regular supply was important if the dyer had to scour the wool or goods prior to dyeing and most necessary for the rinsing after dyeing, particularly for dark colours.

While mill stream water may have been soft it would not have been consistent either in hardness or softness or cleanliness as the streams were fed from distant areas with changing weather patterns.

The biggest problem in cleanliness was the dye-houses themselves, because they were often clustered near together and all drew water from the nearby river and then emptied their effluent, which usually contained residual dye, back into the river. One man's fresh was therefore another man's waste. If the dyers upstream had been dyeing black the one downstream had difficulty in dyeing a pastel colour.

The use of Urine in the Scouring of Wool

Partridge was critical of the American factories' understanding of scouring greasy wool. In general, they did not make the liquor strong enough to decompose the whole of the yolk and grease; when this happens, the wool will turn yellow in drying, and if handled when dry, it will feel greasy. These practices tended to make American cloth compare unfavourably with foreign fabrics.

Urine was the main material to be used because of its availability and low cost. Wool scourers were very familiar with its use and observed that the volatile alkaline which combined with the yolk did not injure the wool unless too much heat was applied. Fresh urine would not scour well and that from persons on a plain diet was stronger than that from 'luxurious livers'. The cider and gin drinkers were considered poor quality and beer drinkers best. The urine had to be kept in closed vessels to allow the ammonia to develop. A factory could have six closed vessels, each holding 2000 gallons which were worked from the oldest and filled as they emptied. A clear understanding of the chemistry of scouring was understood, as Partridge refers to 'Vauquelin's Analysis of Wool and Urine'. 'They will there see, that nine-tenths of the salts of fresh voided urine are acid, whilst in a stale state, they are altogether alkaline, eight-ninths being ammoniacal. The material to be detached from wool is principally an animal fat, which forms a soponaceous compound with the ammonia of the urine, which will readily wash out in water. The ammonia, if any remains about the wool in an uncombined state, is so volatile as to escape while the wool is drying, leaving it free from oil or salts. When the practice corresponds so exactly with the chemical analysis, it proves that the operation pursued by the manufacturer has obtained its utmost degree of perfection.'

The public dyer had to be his own supplier and preparer of plants for dyeing and so he needed to gain a knowledge of agriculture. In preparing woad leaves for the blue colour, the preparation was long and needed careful watching along the way. Where he could grow and prepare his own dye source he was on familiar ground, even when the crops failed — but where he had to rely on buying the dried roots of madder, for example, he could often be trapped into using inferior plants and so ruin the colour, incurring considerable losses.

Bibliography

Partridge, William, *A Practical Treatise on Dyeing of Woollen, Cotton and Skein Silk*. Originally published in New York in 1823 by H. Walker and Co. for the author and printed by J.W. Bell, 70 Bowery. Reprint, Pasold Research Fund Ltd., Edington Wiltshire, 1973

Robinson, Stuart, *A History of Dyed Textiles*, The M.I.T. Press, Cambridge, Massachusetts, 1969

Bancroft's Mordant
A Useful One-Pot Natural Dye Technique

James N. and Dale Liles

By the 1700s, empirical dye technology was in an advanced state in many parts of the world. The burst of scientific knowledge which occured in many fields in the late 1700s was also occuring in the area of dye technology. The chemistry was being explored and understood.

Most who were writing about dye technology at this time were European. There was one exception. Dr Edward Bancroft, who was born in Massachusetts in 1744. Dr Bancroft moved to England in 1768 or 1769.

He was a remarkable self-educated researcher and entrepreneur, with a love of money, apparently stronger than his devotion to his native country or to England. His activities as a counter-spy during the Revolution are reported by Edelstein *(Am. Dyestuff Reporter,* 1954) as are his researches into the dyeing capabilities of the bark of the American black oak *(Quercus velutina).*

Bancroft did two major things for the dye industry. Prior to or in 1771, he discovered the dye potential of black oak bark as a money saving replacement for the yellow dye weld, and in 1794, he wrote a book, *Experimental Researches Concerning the Philosophy of Permanent Colours* (he expanded his work with a second volume in 1813). The dye extract of black oak, quercitron, was more economical than weld and was thus much used, becoming an important trade item between America and Europe for 100 years. His writings, however, were unfortunately ahead of the times, and were not appreciated until later.

In 1973-4, Fred and Willi Gerber published an article in two parts in *Shuttle, Spindle and Dyepot,* titled 'Quercitron, The Forgotten Dyestuff, Producer of Clear, Bright Colors'. At that time the Gerbers were investigating the use of American black oak bark, and had just gained access to the two volume work by Bancroft.

In his work, Bancroft concluded that the best and clearest black oak yellows were obtained by a one-pot method which he had developed. This conclu-

sion was confirmed by the Gerbers, i.e., they made comparisons using conventional mordanting methods. Any readers wishing to use black oak bark (quercitron or flavin) are advised to read these two articles by the Gerbers.

These works by the Gerbers fed our continuing interest in one-pot dyeing methods — a technique used by commercial dyers with certain dyestuffs throughout the traditional period, especially for cochineal reds and scarlets with tin mordants.

To understand the principles involved in one-pot dyeing methods, it is helpful to review some mordant basics. Most natural dyestuffs require a mordant to produce relatively washfast and lightfast colours. The mordant is a chemical (most are metal oxides) which bonds both with a chemical grouping in the dye molecule and with a chemical grouping in the fibre molecule. The mordant serves as a chemical bridge between the fibre and the dyestuff.

In the majority of cases, the fibre is treated with the mordant prior to dyeing, but there is an alternative. In one type of one-pot method, the dyestuff is dissolved (if a natural dyestuff extract) or the dyestuff is cooked up, then the mordant or mordants are dissolved directly in the strained dyebath. The yarn or fleece is added, and the bath is heated to the required temperature over a given period of time.

The main reason for not always using one-pot methods in natural dyeing is this. Chemical combinations of part of the dyestuff and the mordant occurs, producing an insoluble material which does not combine with the fleece or yarn. Thus, a certain amount of the dyestuff and mordant is lost. This is more true of certain dyestuffs and mordants than others. In addition, alum as a mordant usually produces a better finished dye if it is applied to the fibre as a premordant some days prior to dyeing, i.e., a certain amount of 'ageing' is beneficial.

With quercitron, Bancroft found the one-pot method to be superior with respect to production of clear, clean yellows (yellows relatively free of gold, greenish, or brown tinges). He also determined that these yellows produced very nice green when overdyed with indigo or indigo sulphate.

As the Gerbers reported, the amounts of mordant judged to be best by Bancroft were reasonably different from those usually prescribed then and now. The 'Bancroft mordant' was a combination of tin, alum and tartar; the unusual thing was the extremely small amounts of alum and tartar. With quercitron, Bancroft even suggested eliminating the tartar for a yellow which lacked a then much admired slight greenish tinge!

The Bancroft mordant we use is an adaptation of that outlined in Bancroft's writings. He used 'tin spirits' (a solution of feathered tin dissolved in hydrochloric and nitric acids) which was one of the tin mordants of his time. The Gerbers substituted an equivalent amount of stannous chloride, the usual wool tin mordant of modern natural dyers.

To use the Bancroft mordant for one pound of wool, prepare the dyestuff material in the usual way to produce a 4 to 6 gallon dyebath. Dissolve 9 gm of alum (aluminium potassium sulphate) in the dyebath. Then dissolve 6 gm of cream of tartar (potassium bitartrate) in the dyebath. Finally, dissolve 9 gm of tin (stannous chloride) in a quart of hot water and add this to the dyebath. (The tin solution will not be clear.) Stir for a few minutes, add the wet, scoured yarn or fleece, and slowly heat to a simmer (do not exceed 190°F, in order to avoid felting). Thirty to forty five minutes at the simmer should be enough. In fact, some nice yellows can become dingy brown or greenish if left in the dyepot too long. Remove the wool and when it is cool, give it a careful wash with a mild detergent, and rinse well.

Note 1: Always add the alum and tartar to the dyebath before adding the tin. Alum and tartar are both acidic, and this facilitates solution of the tin.

Note 2: If you lack a balance, one level teaspoon of powdered tartar and granular alum weigh about 4 gm each. One level teaspoon of granular tin weighs about 7 gm.

Note 3: Seal the tin container with tape following each use, and store it in a cool, dry place to prevent water absorption.

No problems with harshness or brittleness of wool have ever resulted for us in using this mordant. Tin, in excess of about 14 gm per pound of wool can cause damage, but 9 gm never has this effect. Alum can make wool sticky, but not with less than approximately 3½ ounces (100 gm) per pound of wool. In addition, this is a very economical mordant even though tin is used, because of the extremely small quantities required.

There are some disadvantages with almost all one-pot methods, in that some dyestuff and mordant will be lost as unfixed dye-mordant complex. Also, as Crews determined (*Shuttle, Spindle and Dyepot,* 1981), chrome and copper are the two most lightfast mordants with most natural dyestuffs, especially yellows, while tin and alum are usually the least. We have not encountered fading problems in normal use, but we have not subjected our materials to strong sunlight for extended periods.

The primary advantages of the Bancroft mordant are time saved, economy of chemicals, brightness and clarity of colour, and with fleece, decreased tendency towards felting because the material is heated only once.

Initially, we used Bancroft's mordant to exhaust the colour in dyebaths previously used with premordanted yarn. Light bright colours often result but, if not, the Bancroft mordanted yarn or fleece is then a premordanted partially dyed product, and can be overdyed in another exhaust bath without additional mordant, or used with a weak indigo overdye.

Because of the beautiful yellows obtained with the 'Bancroft mordant' with black oak bark, we tried it with other commonly used yellows, following standard procedures for cooking up dye material to make a full strength dyebath (Davidson, *The Dyepot;* Adrosko, *Natural Dyes in the U.S.*) A lighter, brighter yellow usually resulted with this method. It was obvious from the residue left in the dyebath that some mordant had combined with some dye material and precipitated out, not attaching to the wool. What portion of the dye this was, we do not know, but the lighter, brighter yellow portion is what attached to the wool.

Following Bancroft's suggestion, the same one-pot mordanting procedure was used, but tartar was omitted. In about one half of the natural yellows tested, (seven in all) the colour was improved even more. Thus, this option provides another alternative. Several Bancroft mordanted yellows were overdyed with indigo with excellent greens being produced.

Note: It is usually better to dye with the indigo first and then the yellow to produce greens. The acidity of the mordant neutralises any remaining alkali from the indigo vat and the heated yellow dyebath removes any free indigo blue which would crock (rub off) later.

Another use of the Bancroft mordant is in the production of reds, scarlets, and oranges. Early traditional dyers often used one-pot methods in the production of cochineal reds and scarlets. This was usually a tin spirit one-pot bath, including one or more dyestuffs. One-pot or no, many of the traditional dyes were used in combination, and often with more than one mordant. Combinations giving good results with Bancroft mordant include: cochineal alone; cochineal plus madder; cochineal plus old fustic; madder alone; brazilwood alone; brazilwood plus old fustic; madder, brazilwood, and old fustic.

When working for a colour range from one dye source, use of the Bancroft mordant will give another related shade in addition to those produced with the use of the standard mordants and modifiers such as suggested in the Gerber Investigative Method (*Shuttle, Spindle and Dyepot*, Winter, 1974; spring and fall, 1975). Frequently the shade will be between that obtained with tin-tartar-oxalic acid, and alum-tartar.

The Bancroft mordant is particularly useful in dyeing fleece for spinning because the decreased handling of the fleece in a one-pot reduces felting tendencies. Also, if other mordants are used to dye fleece, a little Bancroft mordanted fleece of the same dye stuff carded into the other dye lot has a 'highlighting' effect in the yarn because of its clarity and brightness of colour.

This one-pot method originated by Dr Edward Bancroft in the 18th century for use with his patented dye discovery, black-oak bark (quercitron) should be a tool for experiments by today's traditional dyers, particularly with the red and yellow dyestuffs.

References

Adrosko. R., *Natural Dyes in the United States*, Washington D.C.: Smithsonian Inst. Press., 1968. 160pp

Bancroft, E., *Experimental Researches concerning the Philosophy of Permanent Colors*, Philadelphia: Thomas Dobson Publ. 1814. Vol. 1, 401 pp. VOl. II, 394 pp

Bemis, E., *The Dyer's Companion*, New York: Dover Publ., Inc., 1973. Unabridged re-publication of the second (1815) ed., by E. Duyckinck, New York, intro. by Rita Adrosko. 307 pp

Crews, P., 'Part 1. Considerations in the Selection and Application of Natural Dyes: Mordant Selection', *Shuttle, Spindle and Dyepot*,' 12:2 (Spring. 1981): 15 and 62

Davidson, M.F., *The Dye-Pot*, Gatlinburg. Ten. 37738. 2nd ed. 1976, 53 pp

Edelstein, S.M., *The Dual Life of Edward Bancroft*, Am. Dyestuff Reporter. 43:22, 712-735, 1954

Gerber, F. and W., 'Quercitron. The Forgotten Dyestuff. Producer of Clear, Bright, Colors', *Shuttle, Spindle and Dyepot*, 5:1 and 2 (Winter, 1973 and Spring. 1974)

Gerber, F., 'Investigative Method — A Tool for Study', *Shuttle, Spindle and Dyepot*. 6:20, 21, 24. (Winter, 1974. Spring and Fall. 1975)

Liles, J. and Dale. 'Bancroft's Mordant — A Useful One-Pot Natural Dye Technique', *Shuttle, Spindle and Dyepot*. (Summer. 1984)

Boiling up plants to get dye liquor.

Straining dyebath (plant materials).

Adding mordant to dyebath (madder).

Adding mordant to dyebath.

Dyeing yarns outside. Logwood dye.

Dyed, tagged skeins, vegetable dyes.

Indian 'patempore' from the collection of the Power House Museum, NSW. Handpainted cotton calico, made on the Coromandel Coast of India for the European market between 1740 and 1780. Bears the stamp of the British East India Company on the reverse. 'Courtesy of the Trustees of the Museum of Applied Arts and Sciences.'

Traditional Indian Dyes — The World's First Fast Dyes!

Joyce Burnard

As importers of Indian handwoven furnishing cottons, two questions we are often asked by customers are: 'Do they fade?' and 'are they vegetable dyes?' The short answer to both is 'No'. Modern Indian handwoven dyed furnishing cottons coming from the best quality Indian hand-weaving establishments and sold on the international commercial market are as fast to sun and light fading, and to washing, as any 100% cottons can be. Best synthetic vat dye-stuffs are used, and the All-India Handloom Board issues a handbook with detailed instructions for their application. Indian universities are also training scientists with an up-to-date knowledge of dyes and methods. They work in laboratories attached to the big textile mills, and pass on knowledge throughout the industry, including the handweaving sector, which now accounts for quite a large proportion of the export trade. India also has its own well-established dye-stuff industry.

Vegetable, or 'plant' dyes, according to an article in *The Indian Textile Journal* (Bombay, 1982), have not been used in India for at least 30 years for textiles manufactured in the commercial area. For one thing, to use them properly would be quite impracticable and few dyers would know how to handle them anyway. However, it is likely that there are some dyers who can use plant dyes with skill and hereditary knowledge and there are certainly many naturalistic-minded modern Indians who are trying to preserve and re-introduce old methods to save them being lost forever.

The irony of the situation is that the centuries-old Indian methods of plant dyeing with mordants probably produced the world's original fast dyes. Indian dyeing methods go back into antiquity. Proof of this lies in some fragments of woven cotton still retaining traces of madder dye, miraculously found during archeological diggings in the 1920s on the site of Mohenjo-Daro, a twin city of the Harappa culture in the Indus Valley, in what is now modern Pakistan. They are dated to circa 3000 BC. The fragments were analysed and found to be cotton similar to cotton grown today in India and because of the traces of madder it was thought that a mordant must have been used.

In the 5th century BC, a Greek physician, Ktesias mentioned the popularity of brightly coloured Indian textiles among the Persians; and St Jerome's 4th century AD translation of the Bible likens the lasting value of wisdom to the permanence of the dye colours of India.

From about 2000 BC, Indian dyed cottons and silks were exported to the Middle East, to Egypt, Persia and Rome. The Romans especially liked Dacca muslin, which they called 'woven wind' because of its miraculous fineness. Arab traders carried these treasures to the West, by sea, catching the trade winds which landed them on the Malabar coast in south-west India, and carried them back up towards the Red Sea six months later — or by land, travelling on the old caravan route through Afghanistan. In this way large textile centres grew up around the southern coastal towns of Cochin, and Calicut (whence calico gets its name). And they still exist, these centres, in the northwest province of Gujarat. In the 13th century there was such a demand from the West for block-printed fabrics (block-printing was introduced from China about the 7th century AD) that entire populations of villagers were employed in meeting it. Even to this day Patipur, a village (or town) north of Ahmedabad, is famous for block-printed fabrics. Gujarat is also famous for tie-dye weaving (ikat), called patola in that region.

Perhaps the most famous of all historic Indian textiles were the hand-painted kalamkari (open-work) palampores or wall-hangings, which were made for temples and palaces. When the European East Indian companies first went to India in the 16th and 17th centuries they marvelled at these fantastic painted cloths. Their luscious designs, consisting of fruit, flowers, birds, animals and trees were brilliantly coloured. They began to buy them for export. In England, embroiderers sought them to copy. The Tree of Life design was especially popular. In due course, the companies gave the Indian artists patterns to copy, designs that they knew they could sell on their markets (much the same thing often happens today). All-over floral designs were popular in England both for clothing and furnishings. In fact these textiles took the 17th-century European consumer market by storm. It was such a novelty to have cottons with colours that were fast, that did not fade or wash out. The East Indian companies, French, Dutch and English began to make a fortune out of them, and the demand in India had not only the hereditary weavers and dyers working overtime, but whole village populations, every man, woman and child, lending a hand.

In due course the extremely skilled and time-consuming method of painting the cloth by hand gave way to the cheaper labour and time-saving block-printing method, and the quality suffered greatly. When the English East Indian Company set up headquarters in Madras, a large fabric printing centre grew up at Masulipatam on the Coromandel Coast, and became an historic kalamkari printing centre. East India Company merchants commissioned weavers and dyers all around the district to fill their orders. The general term for the colourful floral cottons was 'chints' — chint being the Hindi word for 'spotted' or 'variegated'. The word would be used over and over again on the lips of the merchants, in the letters, invoices and ship manifests — thus the word 'chintz' came into the language. Today it applies to a plain glazed cotton, as well as to a patterned one.

The Indian cottons were widely used in England both for clothing and furnishings. Samuel Pepys made an entry in his diary for 5th September, 1663: 'Bought my wife a chint, that is a painted East Indian callico (sic) for to line her new study'.

Samples of these types of 17th century cottons are kept in the Victoria and Albert Museum, Indian Section, with the colours (reds and blues anyway) as vivid as ever; as I was to note on a recent visit. Yellows have tended to fade out.

In France also there was a huge demand for 'indiennes'. By the end of the 17th century in England and France Indian patterned cottons had so taken over the market to the detriment of the established local wool and silk industries that both Governments acted, introducing laws which completely banned the import of Indian cotton chintz, and even the wearing of it. It had become fashionable for dresses, especially in France. Now, anyone seen wearing cotton chintz could be arrested and severely punished. A blackmarket did develop but the Indian trade was broken. The tragic and long-term result of these, from the Indian point of view, iniquitous laws was that the industry there came to a sudden halt; whole areas had been geared to supply the West, the weavers and dyers were thrown out of work, ultimately starved to death, and with them went forever the centuries-old skills and dyeing secrets. The bans were not lifted in England and France until the early to mid 18th century.

Meanwhile, cotton printing in both countries had been developing in spite of everything, but European dyers had not yet discovered how the Indians got their colours fast. The French were the first to obtain these secrets which until then had been closely guarded. First, a French naval officer, M. de Beaulieu, sent his account from Pondicherry in 1734. He had witnessed the dyeing process, and sent samples of cloth with his notes. But it is a later, more detailed description sent by the Jesuit Father Coeurdoux, in 1742, which has become the most often quoted. He wrote down the methods used by dyers who were Catholic converts.

His notes were detailed and helpful, but it is probable that some steps were missing or misunderstood, some special ingredient omitted. The hereditary dyers, with their ancient knowledge and skill would, like experienced and inspired cooks, have no doubt added an extra pinch here, another ingredient there, achieving quality and density of colour not seen before, or since.

So, what were these dyeing secrets?

First, there was the preliminary bleaching. The woven cloth was soaked in lemon juice, then laid out on grass and left in the sun for a suitable period.

Then came the step-by-step method of preparing and painting the cloth. The following is a brief summary of the method of painting an early 'chint'.

1. The half-bleached cloth was prepared with an aqueous solution of fat and astringent (buffalo's milk mixed with the powdered root of myrobalan plant, also known as cadou) followed by 'beetling' (laying the cloth on one piece of smooth wood and beating it with another piece) which gave the smooth surface needed for painting.

2. 'Pouncing' of the pattern or design came next. It was first drawn on paper, either by free-hand from memory, or from a muster (pattern), the outline perforated, then powdered charcoal dusted through the perforations.

3. The charcoal-traced outlines were drawn over with a pen (kalam) made of two reeds pressed together and dipped in mordants (for black, acetate of iron; for red, a solution of alum tinted with sapan-wood).

4. The cloth was now dipped in a vat filled with red dye (derived from chay, a plant of the madder family) the effect being to blacken still further the lines already black and to develop the red outlines.

5. The whole cloth was now covered with beeswax except those parts wanted to appear blue and green. A bamboo brush fitted with metal points was used at this stage, the fluid wax being released from a ball of hair and twisted hemp wound round the stem.

6. The cloth was now dipped in a vat of indigo.

7. The wax was then removed in boiling water.

8. Now followed the waxing of lines required to appear as white within the areas of red, followed by the painting of mordants (consisting of a solution of alum, tinted with sapan-wood). The composition of the mordant varied according to tones required in the next stage; a weak solution of alum gave pink, a stronger one deep red; the addition of iron gave violet.

9. The cloth was dipped for the second time in a vat filled with red dye (chay).

10. Then there was the application by brush of a concoction of yellow dye of plant origin.

Lastly, the 'chints' were given a sheen to bring up the colours. The processes were starching, beetling and chanking (burnishing). Rice starch was used, the fabric being thoroughly impregnated. Traces of starch have been found in old chintzes. The chanking was done with a chank shell until the fabric had a satin like sheen. This was the forerunner of modern glazing. The method is still basically the same except that the 'polishing' is done by mechanical heat friction (calendering).

The earlier Beaulieu manuscript mentioned the soaking of the dyed cloth at various stages in a solution of kid dung, presumably to fix the dyes, then exposing the cloth to the sun. At Jouy, in France, at the printworks of the famous 18th century textile printer C.P. Oberkamphe who, from records, obviously followed the Indian madder-mordant methods, cow-dung solution was used to fix the dyes.

The French managed to keep the Indian dye methods secret for 30 years which gave them a lead in the industry they have never quite lost.

One invaluable aid to European dyers was indigo, a native plant of India, and a natural fast dye if handled properly. It was called 'English blue' because the English had the main access to it through the English East India Company, which made a fortune exporting it from India. Natural indigo was

used until the discovery and production of synthetic indigo at the end of the 19th century through the researches of the German chemist Adolf von Baeyer. Professor von Baeyer won the Nobel Prize in 1905 for his work. It is said that if synthetic indigo had not been discovered, half of India today would have to consist of indigo plantations to meet the vast demand. Indigo was also grown in America and used there widely in the 19th century.

Madder red was synthesised in 1869 as alizarin, also by German chemists, so that the growing of madder in France and Holland, where it had become a huge industry, was abandoned within a few years.

It is only in recent years that it has begun to be realised what an important heritage India has given us in textiles and dyes. A tribute to the genius of the Indian master dyers was a marvellous exhibition called 'Master Dyers of the World' presented by the Textile Museum of Washington, D.C. in 1982. Examples of painted cloths (palampores) from leading museums, including several in India, were shown, as well as tie-dyed cloths such as ikats (patolu, bandhu) and printed cottons (chints).

Bibliography

John Irwin and Katherine B. Brett, *Origins of Chintz*, HMSO, London, 1970

John Irwin and P.R. Schwartz, *Studies in Indo-European Textile History*, Calico Museum of Textiles, Ahmedabad, India, 1966

Joyce Storey, *Dyes and Fabrics*, Thames and Hudson, 1978

Stuart Robinson, *A History of Printed Textiles*, Studio Vista, 1969

Romila Thapar, *A History of India, Pt. 1*, Pelican 1966, reprint 1979

Kamaladevi Chattopadhyay, *Handicrafts of India*, William Morrow, New York, 1975

Gulati, A.N. and Turner, Arthur James, *A Note on the Early History of Cotton*, Indian Central Cotton Committee, Bulletin No. 17, Bombay, 1928

John Edwards, *Crewel Embroidery in England*, William Morrow, New York, 1975

Indigo

Introduction

The story of indigo finishes this book; indigo dye has been chosen because it links the various parts of the book. The history of natural indigo is vast — in the plant's cultivation and preparation, its part in economic and social developments, and the marvellous textiles and designs that arise directly from it. Moreover, it is now synthetic indigo which is chiefly used by the modern dyer, so it is truly a dye of the past and the present.

Traditional means of application include *shibori*, described by Inga Hunter who incorporates the method, and the wonderful indigo shades, in many aspects of her work, including that found in the colour section opposite page 64 in this book. She was influenced by Yoshiko Wada of the USA/Japan, who also influenced Janet De Boer, author of the article on this remarkable artist and teacher.

Finally, anyone who seriously studies indigo will always turn to Fred Gerber's researches into the dyestuff. From the USA, Gerber originally studied taxonomic botany, and sees dyeing as a marriage between the sciences and the arts, a cross-fertilisation of interests, a 'propagation of a form of alchemy'. With those words he may very well be summing up not only the magic of indigo, but the basis of this book.

Indigo — Science and Art

F.H. Gerber

One basic clue to the prehistoric distribution of the use of colour may be deduced from the evidence of the ochre burials. The placement of bodies on a layer of red ochre is documented as early as the Mousterian Period c.30 000 BC; among the Ainu of Japan, in southern Russia, in Italy and, significantly, among the early peoples in the Great Lakes region of North America.

Earth colours, white, limestone, black, charcoal and manganese earths; a wide variety of iron colours ranging from pale yellow to brightest red were early used for paintings and textile colouring. Linen has been coloured, permanently with impregnations of ochres in the twentieth century in Italy, the seat of much high and modern technical development of modern dyeing. And the use of the same colourants persists as a matter of deep seated tradition among most primitive peoples. These colourants are used by the Aboriginals of Australia, the Indos of Mato Grasso (Brazil) and as decorative applications on spears and weapons by the American Eskimos.

These are the same colourants used in the cave paintings of Altamira, Spain, and Lescaux, France.

Combinations of tannic acid and soluble iron to produce grey and black iron tannates, the earliest of the true dyes, appear in all cultures.

To consider in detail all the dyes which have been found to have been used by early man is to court confusion. However, there are dyes or dye groups which stand out as singularly significant in several dye categories.

These categories of dyes are separable on the basis of the mode of fixation as permanent colourants on textile fibres.

The most direct of the natural dyes are typified by the permanent stains of walnut and henna, related chemical compounds, juglone and lawsone (names derived by the chemists from the generic names of the plants themselves, *Juglans* and *Lawsonia*). These are called substantive dyes. They provide permanent colour sources with no intermediary additives: mordants.

In its simplest form, as plant extracts, indigo is also a substantive dye. The dye precursor content in even the richest plant source is so low that the discovery of this ancient dye remains a mystery. That the dye precursor was early discovered in such disparate plant groups as a mustard *(Isatis)*, the legume of West Africa *(Lonchocarpus)*, the dogbane of the Coromandel (Oleander or *Nerium*), a milkweed of Sumatra *(Marsdenia)*, and in several paleo-and-neo-tropical species of *Indigofera*, seems all but incredible.

The nature of the colour precursor of indigo sets the stage of even greater mystery in terms of the early resolution of the technology of the most complicated of all dyes. On exposure to atmospheric oxygen the glucoside rapidly combines with the oxygen to form the familiar blue colour; a colour singularly resistant to change. Until the era of the modern bleaching agents anything which would change and remove the colour would simultaneously destroy the fibres on which it was applied.

As a chemically resistant compound in an insoluble form it cannot be applied to fibres. Without a means of converting it to a soluble compound, it must be applied immediately upon extraction from the plant source or forever lost.

This disposition to convert so quickly to an insoluble compound and the resolution of the technology to convert the insoluble colour to a form which was able to be applied to textiles led, in prehistoric periods, to a division of labor and specialisation perhaps unparalleled in the history of man. Even in 'primitive' cultures the process of preparing indigo was separate from its application.

The application of indigo requires that the coloured molecule be chemically reduced and changed to what we term the white or leuco-indigo form. This form is soluble in an alkali.

Dyeing with the reduced (white) form which has been dissolved in an alkali is called vat dyeing. Indigo used from an alkaline vat *and* the development of the colour on exposure to oxygen is vat dyeing.

The remarkable fact is that the preparation of indigo from its several sources was accomplished by but two processes both of which are means for concentration of the insoluble compound. *Isatis,* the woad of Europe, *Marsdenia,* the milkweed of the eastern Archipelago, the *Lonchocarpus* of West Africa and the *Indigofera* of tropical America, were all subjected to a composting process. The plants were made into a compost; the glucoside oxydised to insoluble indigo, the bulk reduced without loss of pigment. The product was made into balls, dried and stored or shipped to the user. The same process survives today in Kyoto, Japan, with the buckwheat, *Polygonum.*

A second process of extraction and concentration was developed. This process involved the removal of the dye by steeping, removal of and discard of the producing plants, reservation and oxidation of the glucoside in the decoction with subsequent precipitation of the dye. After sedimentation the precipitate is collected, dried and stored or shipped. This purer indigo with an assay of perhaps 48% purity obtained from *Indigofera* and *Nerium* was also found to be the second process used by the natives of the New World. The assay for 'indigo balls' is seldom above 4% and often much lower, even absent in the northern parts of Europe using *Isatis.*

The presence of both methods among the pre-Columbian Americans argues against spontaneous development of either mode. Cultural diffusion is the more likely logical deduction.

The means used for applying indigo in ancient times are not understood as neatly, perhaps, as the methods of production, but it is essentially true that every cultural group which used indigo had mastered, however pragmatically, the reduction of the coloured compound to the leuco-form, its solution in alkali, followed by application and reoxydation *in situ*.

The action of bacteria and their ability to utilise the oxygen from water molecules, leaving free and nascent hydrogen has been used since earliest times. The free hydrogen, too active chemically to 'live alone', combines with the indigo molecules forming an hydroxyl group at two places called the termini of the chromophore. The internal molecular bondings shift produced the leuco-form. When dissolved in some alkali the leuco-form is applied to fibres, after which the fibres are re-exposed to atmospheric oxygen. The hydrogen rapidly combines with oxygen and forms water molecules. These either run off with the residue of the alkaline vat or evaporate. The leuco-form reverts to the blue phase.

The alkalis used over the millenia have not been many. The potassium hydroxide of ashes is undoubtedly the oldest. Quick lime was adopted in modern times, especially in cellulosic dyeings, i.e cotton and linen. Sodium hydroxide is the most modern and most efficient alkali.

The reducing agents have been several: bacteria, iron sulphate, arsenical compounds, and in modern times finely dispersed zinc metal or sodium hydrosulphite.

Many additives have been used which, although they did not contribute to the colour, nevertheless enhanced the process by fostering bacterial action. Among these additives have been sugar, molasses, fibrous materials, woad balls in 'true' indigo vats and madder.

Indigo, of all the ancient dyes, was the last to be chemically synthesised by modern chemistry. Synthetic indigo was prepared first in 1880 and became commercially practical eleven years later in 1891. Alizarin had been synthesised in 1869. The first synthetic dye of William Perkin had been produced in 1856.

A recent study of the 'cottonades' of the Louisiana Acadian exiles from Eastern Canada revealed that, unique in the annals of dyeing, these impoverished people, far removed from the market place, dyed indigo blues with fresh extracts of indigo plants.

Shibori: An Introduction

Inga Hunter

Shibori — a Japanese word coming from a verb meaning 'to wring, squeeze or press' — is Japanese tie-dye, akin to the better known *plangi* and *tritik* of the Malay archipelago, but more far-reaching in scope than either of these. There is no English equivalent for the word *shibori*, which applies to both the process of resist-dyeing fabrics by various means of manipulation with threads, and to the resist-dyed fabrics themselves. By far the best definition of the process comes from the only important textbook on the subject written in English, *Shibori: the Inventive Art of Shaped Resist Dyeing* by Yoshiko Wada, Mary Kellogg Rice and Jane Barton (Kodansha).,

Shibori is defined by the authors as 'cloth that is given three-dimensional shape and then dyed ... after the cloth is returned to its two-dimensional form, the design that emerges is the result of the three-dimensional shape of the cloth, the type of resist, and the amount of pressure exerted by the thread or clamp that secured the shape during the cloth's exposure to the dye. The cloth sensitively records both the shape and the pressure; it is the "memory" of the shape that remains imprinted in the cloth. This is the essence of *shibori*.'

The resist process gives a soft-edged image, quite different from that associated with stencils or wax. The process can be finely controlled, but there remains always some element of the unexpected, because of the number of variables inherent in the folded and bound cloth and its interaction with the dye. Six distinct ways to impose a three-dimensional form onto cloth are included in the term *shibori*: binding; stitching or gathering; capping; pleating and binding; folding and clamping; and wrapping around a pole, then compressing and binding. In her book, Yoshiko Wada says:

> Designs created in this way clearly reflect the touch of each worker. No two persons fold or bind or stitch in exactly the same way — the work of one may be very precise and even, that of another, looser and more free. Likewise, the amount of force exerted on the binding thread, or in drawing up the stitching thread, or in compressing the cloth into folds on the pole, varies from person to person. The effect of each person's hand, and indeed temperament, on the shaping of the cloth becomes imprinted by the dye in the finished piece. This characteristic makes for highly individual results, even within a traditional framework.

History

The origins of shibori go back to prehistory, when the Japanese already bound sections of cloth to resist the dye, although the first written records did not appear until the twelfth century. But it was during the fifteenth and sixteenth centuries that shibori reached its peak, with the famed *tsujigahana* textiles of the Muromachi and Momoyama periods. Shibori fabrics were bound, stitched, gathered and dyed numbers of times, with many colours used close together on a single piece. The use of natural dyes and mordants necessitated considerable binding and dyeing skills, and the shibori motifs were in turn augmented by painting, gold leaf, and embroidery to produce those fabrics of extraordinary beauty which have given the Momoyama period the reputation for being the high point of Japanese textile history.

Today we think of shibori on its own, dyed with the many blues of indigo, the dye traditionally associated with Japanese peasant clothing. One modern Japanese artist in particular, Itchiku Kubota works with the old methods of multi-coloured, painted and embroidered shibori, and has developed his own personal *tsujigahana* style. His work, a series of amazingly beautiful kimonos, shows us just what can be achieved by an essentially simple process. For this is the beauty of shibori: it is simple enough for raw beginners to have good results; and complex enough for a Kubota to use it as the basis for a lifetime's work. I think this is precisely why shibori has become so popular in the West.

The contemporary Western shibori movement is centred in the USA, and began in the mid-1970s, with workshops given by Yoshiko Wada, who was interested in shibori as a traditional folk craft. An interest in dyes and surface design had already been awakened in 1972 by an exhibition at the Museum of Contemporary Crafts, called 'Fabric Vibrations'. The exhibition showed works in tie-dyed fabric by artists such as Marion Clayden, Chunghi Choo, and Jennifer Lew and Richard Proctor (authors of a recent book on surface design techniques). That exhibition came to Australia too. I saw it myself, and I think the effect it had on me was to make me believe that artists could work in fabric; you didn't have to be a painter or a weaver — you could use fabric and dyes. Indian plangi had already invaded everyday life via the hippie movements through the East; but serious artists ended up developing the skills of shibori, so that you now have artists like Marion Clayden and Ana Lisa Hedstrom exhibiting sophisticated and exquisite clothing, the result of more than a decade of practice.

In Australia the shibori movement began as in the USA, with Yoshiko Wada, at the First Australian Fibre Conference in 1981. At this stage interest was awakened, but the means to put this interest into practice was not possible until the book, *Shibori: the Inventive Art of Shaped Resist Dyeing* became available. Wada, Kellogg-Rice and Barton are Australia's teachers in absentia. The practice of shibori is growing daily, but as yet there is no one who has mastered the dialogue between control and spontaneity which is necessary for shibori to be used as a major medium of artistic expression.

Techniques

What exactly *is* shibori? How is it carried out?

Shibori is a resist process like batik except that where batik requires a wax resist, shibori uses a combination of bound thread and fabric folds to produce designs. There are roughly six areas of technique:

1. Binding   Designs are made by drawing up the cloth and binding each shape with thread. The designs vary according to the type of cloth; the type, tension and amount of thread; the spacing of units; and so on. In cultures where small circles (made by binding tiny units of fabrics) are the major design element, some sort of tool is usually employed to facilitate the tying process. Indian plangi artists use a type of pointed metal finger stall, which pushes the cloth into a point, making it easier to bind. The Japanese use a series of tying stands for the same purpose, each one specialising in a particular binding technique. Some traditional designs rely on an overall coverage of small resisted white squares with a coloured dot in the centre — *kanoko* or *hitta*. On a kimono, the design might appear wherever the cloth is left untied, and the kanoko spots become the background texture. All the many types of tiny bound motifs are made with a continuous thread, and a series of *kamosage* knots which will come undone when the cloth is pulled taut. This sort of binding requires practice, and few Western artists use it as a major patterning device.

2. Stitching   This is flexible, and easily controlled. It produces designs varying from rhythmic patterns to representational images. The effects vary according to the type of stitch; whether or not the cloth is folded; the type of thread; arrangement and contiguity of the stitches; efficiency in pulling up gathers; and so on. The principal stitch is the running stitch, which is used in a way not unlike a quilting stitch, except that the stitched cloth is pulled up into tight gathers, secured, and then dyed. The pattern comes from a combination of the stitch and the folds of the fabric created by the pulling up. Stitching is used to outline shapes, for overall textures, patterns, borders, spots, squares, curved shapes, and to help mask out big areas of fabric from the dye. It is an enormously versatile technique, but needs some skill with a needle, and practice in pulling the gathers tight enough to give

a good sharp image. It was the development of stitched motifs that made possible the multicoloured designs of the *tsujigahana* textiles (stitching is the basis of Kubota's work).

3. Capping and stitching   Covering the design motifs or background with a material which will resist the dye — combined with stitch resist, was an integral part of the *tsujigahana* process. A modern variant can be seen in Itchika Kubota's kimonos. Modern capping involves stitching and binding with plastic lined with lightweight paper; the insertion of rigid or flexible cores; and selective dyeing. It is used both to resist small and large areas in order to keep them white, or to reserve them for detailed work later on. It greatly extends the design possibilities of stitch resist.

4. Pleating and binding   In shibori, pleating and binding are much more sophisticated than in the Western tie-dye tradition. Used in Japan for more than 300 years, pleated and bound designs are based on the weave of the cloth. Fabric is pleated along the warp, and bound (using a stand) either by itself, or wrapped around a flexible or rigid core. The basic pattern resulting from pleated cloth is stripes. By use of binding; or of covering parts of the pleated cloth with paper; or by pleating and dyeing several times; or by the use of a core — an enormous number of variations on the striped theme can be achieved. Practice and accuracy with folding are needed before one can either visualise the sort of patterns possible to achieve, or realise the patterns one has visualised. The results are worth the effort.

5. Folding and clamping   Results come quickly with this method, and can be spectacular; much fabric can be ruined quickly as well. Even if only one method of folding is used, the patterns will vary greatly, depending on the size and shape, position and tension of the clamp; and the degree of penetration of dye into the fabric. Controlled results require the cloth to be damp, both when folded and when dyed. Accuracy in folding is important, and it is vital to have some knowledge of the dyes. Time in the dyebath is crucial too.

This is one of the most subtle and interesting shibori techniques — its speed of execution balances the much slower stitching and binding procedures.

6. Pole-wrapping, or arashi shibori   This is by far the most popular shibori technique in the

West, one that you could spend a lifetime developing, and one which by its very nature is suited to the patterning of long lengths of fabric. 'Arashi, "storm", is the name the Japanese have given patterns resist-dyed by an ingenious process of wrapping cloth around a pole, compressing it into folds, and dyeing it. Indeed, many of the diagonal patterns suggest rain driven by a strong wind. The particular quality and subtlety of the patterns are fully revealed only in a length of cloth. Small samples are insufficient. These patterns are by no means haphazardly achieved, but not even the most skilful worker has complete control over the process, making slight irregularities of pattern inevitable. To be sure, if complete control were possible, the results could hardly be called arashi, for it is precisely the irregularities, like those in the changing patterns of wind-driven rain, that give these fabrics their special beauty.' (Yoshiko Wada)

Arashi shibori in Japan, dates from the late nineteenth century, when Kanezo Suzuki, in the village of Arimatsu, invented the process in order to dye lengths of cotton in indigo dye. The cloth was wound around the cloth-wrapped pole, and two workers then compressed the cloth into tight folds. The process was continued until the pole was filled, and the whole thing was immersed into an indigo dye vat.

Artists in the USA have adapted this process to their own conditions by substituting plastic drainage pipe for the pole. A heavy duty plumbing pipe will even withstand hot dye baths, enabling a wide range of dyestuffs to be used. Cloth is either wrapped around the pipe and held in place with tape, or a loose sleeve is stitched and fitted onto the pipe. Strong thread is then wrapped evenly around the cloth, which is compressed into tight folds after each few inches of binding (any more and the cloth would be impossible to compress). A short length of pipe will take many metres of fabric, and fit neatly into a small dyepot. Once dyed, the pattern that results is of rhythmic stripes: dark, where the folded edge meets the dye; white, where the binding thread resists the dye; and half-tone where the cloth folds partially resist the dye. The pattern will vary according to the type and width of cloth; the diameter of the pole; the type, tension and spacing of the thread; the direction of wrapping; the tension of the compression and whether it is twisted or pushed up straight — and whether the process is done once or many times. Cloth may also be pleated or bound or stitched before pole-wrapping; the variations are endless. Even raw beginners can have good results; in the hands of an experienced arashi artist, the patterning is exquisite.

Australians, like the Americans, are attracted to arashi, and it is easy to see that this is the most popular shibori technique in this country. We are already developing our own variations, as batik artists work with naphthol dyes to produce rich and exciting results.

Dyes

This article is no place to discuss dyes, and indigo needs a whole study of its own. However, it is enough to say that you can use any dye for shibori, depending of course, on your fabric type and your fastness requirements. It is wise to start with one dyestuff and stick to it, since each dyestuff has different penetration qualities, and dye penetration is crucial with shibori. I would suggest too that you stick to one colour at first, until you know what you are doing. There is plenty of time to make colour decisions once the patterning is under control.

Bibliography

There are four books which are relevant to shibori itself; all are expensive publications.

Shibori: The Inventive Art of Shaped Resist Dyeing by Yoshiko Wada, Mary Kellogg-Rice, and Jane Barton; Kodansha. (History and technique, work and biographies of modern American artists. This is an excellent textbook, one which you could use to learn the skill. Well worth paying for if you are seriously interested in the subject.)

Tsujigahana: The Flower of Japanese Textile Art, by Toshiko Ito. Kodansha. (Purely historical)

Opulence: The Kimonos and Robes of Itchiku Kubota, ed. Tomayuki Yamanobe. Kodansha. (Gorgeous, with some photos of technique)

Kosode: Sixteenth to Nineteenth Century Textiles From the Nomura Collection, by A.M. Stinchecum. Japan Society and Kodansha. (Historical, with notes on traditional techniques and dyestuffs)

Some books on indigo

Japanese Stencil Dyeing: Paste Resist Techniques, by E. Nakano and B. Stephan. Weatherhill

The Dyers' Art, by Jack Lenor Larsen. Van Nostrand Reinhold

Hand Block Printing and Resist Dyeing by Susan Bosence. David & Charles

A Dyer's Manual, by Jill Goodwin. Pelham Books

Indigo from Seed to Dye, by Dorothy Miller. Indigo Press, Aptos, California

Nature's Colors, by Ida Grae. Macmillan

Natural Dyes and Home Dyeing by Rita Adrosko. Dover

Japanese Ikat Weaving by Jun and Noriko Tomito. Routledge and Kegan Paul

Indigo and the Antiquity of Dyeing, by Fred Gerber. Published by the author

Magazine articles on shibori and indigo

'Indigo — The All Time Fabourite Blue', *Handwoven,* May, 1981

'Indigo, The Devil's Dye', by S. Blumrich, *Surface Design Journal,* Spring, 1983

'The Chemistry and Use of Indigo: The Mystery Removed', by Fred Gerber, *Surface Design Journal,* Winter, 1983 & Spring 1984

'Dyeline — Shibori', by Inga Hunter, *Fibre Forum* magazine, Vol 3, no. 1, 1984 & Vol. 3, no. 2, 1984

Yoshiko Wada and the Art of Synthetic Indigo Dyeing

Janet De Boer

In January, 1981, I was pleased to be a lecturer/participant at the First Australian Fibre Conference, held in Melbourne. One of the overseas guests at the Conference was Yoshiko Wada, and it was in her workshop that I had my first experience with indigo dyeing. The techniques we learned were weft *kasuri* (resist binding lengths of weft yarn and dyeing); and *shibori* (which is cloth resist). These are some notes on the workshop, which was a very productive one.

It takes a full day for the synthetic indigo dyebath to prepare itself, and this time of waiting can be used to measure and tie skeins of yarn. We were going to be working with two large plastic garbage bins (50 litre) to hold the dyebaths, one prepared for a fairly dark colour, and the other for a lighter colour. Yoshiko's recipe calls for the use of calcium hydroxide (calx) and zinc dust to reduce the dyebath, or remove the oxygen from it. Several things affect the life of the dyebath (including the amount of tender loving care you give it!) so it's difficult to say how much fibre a given amount of dyestuff will in fact dye. However, for the quantities we used, one tub of dyebath might do about 10 pounds of medium weight cotton fibres.

I first watched Yoshiko mix the 'basic bath'. This is a mixture of calx and zinc which forms the

volume of the dyebath, and eventually receives the synthetic indigo stock solution. The quantities used were 50 gm calx and 15 gm zinc, and the liquor ratio (or amount of water to use) was 1 litre of water for every gram of calx. Consequently we ended up with 50 litres of water (or about 13 gallons) in our plastic garbage bin. The procedure for mixing the basic bath is to paste up the calx and zinc with a little water and add it to the 50 litres of *cold* water in the plastic bin. Stirring for a few minutes will dissolve the mixture completely. This is then covered and allowed to settle for 4-5 hours before anything else can happen to it. The zinc reduces or de-oxygenates the bath and the calx (alkali) renders the dye substance soluble, when it is added.

While the basic bath is settling, you can mix your stock solution of dyestuff, because it also needs to sit 4-5 hours. For this a heat source is needed, as the solution is brought to 140°F. For the stock solution we use 50 gm synthetic indigo, 100 gm calx, and 30 gm zinc dust. The liquor ratio is 1 litre of water for every 60 gm of dyestuff, so it will be 3 litres (because you total the quantity of indigo, calx and zinc, which comes to 180 gm using the above recipe). Use a stainless steel or enamel dyepot.

Again, you make a paste with the calx and zinc, using cold water. Set this aside, and in another container (glass preferred) mix the indigo with enough methylated spirits to make a soft paste. I was again peering over Yoshiko's shoulder at this stage, and saw she was pasting the indigo with water, as she didn't have methylated spirits on hand. She said this was a difficult procedure and only to be done if you have experience with the dyestuff. From watching her I'd agree!

The indigo paste is then dissolved in the heating water when it is between 90 and 100°F. Stir till all lumps disappear. Now you can add the calx/zinc paste and also dissolve it. Stir this for 5-10 minutes but try not to aerate it. As Yoshiko showed us, there are ways of stirring which move the dyebath but don't let nearly so much air into it. If one thinks about cooking experiences, it's obvious there are ways of stirring in which the point is to add a lot of air, but that is not the point here!

After this time, the solution should have reached 140°F, so you remove it from the heat, cover it and let it settle 4-5 hours. Please note these instructions are *not* for Centigrade temperatures.

After both the basic bath and stock solution have done their 4-5 hours resting, you mix 1/5 of the stock solution in with the large basic bath in the garbage bin, if you want to start with light colours. With this kind of dyeing, you keep on re-dipping to darken your colours, but if you want to start light, you must not add too much stock solution initially. As we didn't have a lot of time, Yoshiko added ½ the stock solution to the basic bath, which meant even our first dip went fairly dark.

Stir the basic and stock solutions without aerating, until they are very well blended, and let the dyebath settle another 5 hours. From then on you will add stock solution to the basic dyebath whenever it starts to look exhausted. We students decided there is a direct relationship between our exhaustion and the dyebath's! Do remember to keep your stock solution undisturbed while it's waiting to be used again.

The way to use your synthetic dyebath efficiently of course, is to have lots of items ready to dye when you open the dyebath. This is because you cannot leave it open continuously, but only for an hour or two, when you must close it again and let it rest 4-5 hours. And of course you need not use so large a bath for only one person, but can cut all the quantities down proportionately. If well cared for, the bath will last several months however, so you can think in terms of how much dyeing you would like to do over an extended period of time. The dyebath is especially suited to most of Austra-

lia's climate, as it must not be allowed to freeze! And of course, once it's mixed up, it's always there for you, over a period of months.

We students had many items ready to dye the moment the dyebath opened, but it still cannot be used immediately. During its sitting period, it should have formed what is called a 'flower' on its surface, which is really scum, but 'flower' seems a much nicer name for it. This flower is strained from the surface and saved in a separate container, to be added back to the dyebath when it is closed at the end of the day's dyeing. By observing the condition of the flower you can tell certain things about your bath. It will have a metallic sheen to it when healthy, and a kind of reddish glare.

Yoshiko removed the flower by straining it through a piece of muslin stretched over a shaped coat hanger. It's a good idea to use rubber gloves throughout these various processes, and of course while dyeing. We found the synthetic indigo does not have an intense desire to stick to the skin, and will come out of clothing if you rinse straight away (well usually). A full smock would have been better for me; and I found I preferred to use surgeon's gloves because you can feel through them with much greater sensitivity than thicker rubber gloves. This becomes important when you are manipulating your material in the dyebath to make sure the dye penetrates evenly throughout.

You have probably worked out by now that Japanese indigo dyeing has a number of rituals associated with it, and a religious metaphor is apt, because you must perform the necessary rituals religiously or your bath won't last. There is a certain feeling of communion too as we all gathered around the baths and worked our materials in them, not to mention the silent prayers I muttered, hoping my resist ties wouldn't come undone.

The ceremony of dyebath preparation is nearly complete. If you opened a dyebath which seemed too weak, you could add stock solution, but then must stir the bath and allow it to settle overnight before using again.

To close the dyebath, pour back the 'flower' you skimmed off earlier, and sprinkle a tablespoon of calx into the bath, stirring vigorously from the bottom for a few minutes. Yoshiko taught us the knack of stirring in a circle to form a whirlpool, then reversing direction, which gathers the flower into the centre, where it should sit well if the bath is healthy. If the bath seems weak, a teaspoon of zinc is added as well as the calx.

Summary

Equipment
1. 50 litre plastic garbage bin with cover
2. Stainless steel or enamel dyepot
3. Long stirring pole for mixing large dyebath
4. Scales

Basic Bath
50 gm calx (calcium hydroxide)
15 gm zinc dust
Liquor ratio of 1 litre water to every gram of calx
(50 litres)
Paste calx and zinc with a little cold water and add
to water in garbage bin. Stir to dissolve. Cover and
let settle 4-5 hours.

Stock Solution
50 gm synthetic indigo
100 gm calx
30 gm zinc dust
Liquor ratio of 1 litre water to every 60 gm of dry
ingredients (3 litres)
Paste calx and zinc with cold water. Set aside.
Paste synthetic indigo with methylated spirits.
Then dissolve in heating water (90-100°F). Stir to
get rid of all lumps.
Add calx/zinc mixture and dissolve.
Stir gently 5-10 minutes till bath reaches 140°F.
Remove from heat. Allow to settle 4-5 hours.

Dyebath
Mix quantity of stock solution into basic bath.
Use 1/5 stock solution for light bath; ½ for dark
bath.
Stir without aerating until well blended, and let dye-
bath settle 5 hours.

Suppliers

Artmat Pty Ltd, 21 Queens Ave, Hawthorn, 3122
Batik Oetero, 201 Avoca St, Randwick, 2031
Commission Dyers, 7 Pinn St, St Marys, SA 5042
Earth Palette, PO Box 315, Stawell, 3380
Kacoonda Enterprises, PO Box 6, Somers, 3927
Kirsten Loom and Yarn Co., 138 Pittwater Rd, Boronia Park, 2111
Kraft Kolour, Shop 7/74 Tobruk Ave, Heidelberg West, 3081
Marie-France French Dyes, 92 Currie St, Adelaide, 5000
The Shearin' Shed, 24 Mulgrave Rd, Mulgrave via Windsor, 2756
Spindle and Loom, Arcade 83, Longueville Rd, Lane Cove, 2066
Steadyrep, 715 Ann St, Ft Valley, 4006
Wondoflex, 1353 Malvern Rd, Malvern, 3144

Magazines

Australian Handweaver and Spinner, GPO Box 67, Sydney, 2001
Newsletter of the Batik and Surface Design Association of Australia Ltd, PO Box 85, Coogee, NSW 2034
Newsletter of The Craft Dyers' Guild, PO Box 28-168, Remuera, Auckland, New Zealand
Fiberarts 50 College St, Asheville, NC 28801, USA
Textile—Fibre Forum PO Box 77, University of Queensland, St Lucia, Q4067
Handwoven Interweave Press, 306 No. Washington, Loveland, CO 80537, USA
Journal for Weavers, Spinners and Dyers, The Secretary, Association of Guilds, BCM 963, London, WC1N 3XX, UK

Shuttle, Spindle and Dyepot, 65 LaSalle Rd, West Hartford, CT 06107, USA
Surface Design Journal, subscriptions to: Membership Dept., 4111 Lincoln Blvd, Suite 426, Marina del Rey, CA, 90292, USA
Threads, Box 355, Newtown, CT 06470, USA
The Weaver's Journal, Dos Tejedoras Press, P.O. Box 14-328, St Paul, MN 55114, USA
The Web, PO Box 187, Lyttelton, New Zealand.

Bibliography

Adrosko, Rita J., *Natural Dyes and Home Dyeing*, New York: Dover Pub.

Ainscow, Margaret, *Cotton Dyeing, a guide to using Fibre Reactive Dyes*, from M. Ainscow, School of Art, TSIT, PO Box 1214, Launceston 7250

Arnow, Jan, *Handbook of Alternative Photographic Processes*, New York: Van Nostrand Reinhold. 238pp

Baily, Catherine, *Natural Dyeing Notes*, 1906 Preble Road, Preble, NY, 13141, self-published

Bancroft, Edward, *Experimental Researches Concerning the Philosophy of Permanent Colours*, 2 volumes, London, 1813 (rare book)

Berthollet, C.L., *Elements of the Art of Dyeing*, Edinburgh, 1792 (rare book)

Birren, Faber, *The Textile Colorist*, New York: Litton, and Van Nostrand Reinhold. 1980

Bliss, Anne, *North American Dye Plants*, New York: Chas. Scribner and Sons.

Bliss, Anne, *Weeds — A Guide for Dyers and Herbalists*, Juniper House, Boulder CO. 1978

Bliss, Anne, *Rocky Mountain Dye Plants*, Juniper House, Box 2094, Boulder, CO, 80306, USA

A Handbook of Dyes From Natural Materials, New York: Chas. Scribner and Sons, 1981

Bolton, Henry Carrington. *A Select Bibliography of Chemistry*, Smithsonian Institution, Washington D.C. (books on dyeing and mordanting ltd)

Bolton, Eileen M., *Lichens for Vegetable Dyeing*, London: Studio Books

Briggs, Rose L., *Notes on Vegetable Dyeing*, Massachusetts: Rogers Print, 1941

Bronson, L. and R., *The Domestic Manufacturer's Assistant in Weaving and Dyeing*, L. and R. Bronson, 1817. Reprint 1950 by Charles Branford and Sons Co., Boston, Mass.

Brooklyn Botanical Gardens, publishers, *Dye Plants and Dyeing*, Brooklyn, New York, 11225

Bruandet, Pierre, *Painting on Silk*, EP Pub. Ltd, 1982, 64pp. Available from EP Publishing, Bradford Rd, East Ardsley, Wakefield, West Yorks, England WF3 2JN; or Ivy Craft Imports, 5410 Annapolis Rd, Bladensburg, MD 20710

Brunello, F , *The Art of Dyeing in the History of Mankind*, Vicenza: Neri Pozza Editore, 1973. English translation from The Phoenix Dye Works, Pub. Cleveland. 467pp

Bryan and Young, *Navajo Native Dyes*, US Dept. of Interior, Bureau of Indian Affairs; available from Publications Services, Haskell Institute, Lawrence, KS

Buehler, A. and Eberhard, F., *Clamp Resist Dyeing of Fabrics*, Calico Museum, 1977

Carman, Jean, *Dyemaking with Eucalypts*, Australia: Kangaroo Press

Casselman, Karen L., *Craft of the Dyer: Colour From Plants and Lichens of the Northeast*, Toronto: University of Toronto Press, 249pp

Colton, Mary, *Hopi Dyes*, Museum of Northern Arizona, Flagstaff, AZ, 1965

Conley, Emma, *Vegetable Dyeing*, Penland School of Crafts, Penland, NC, USA

Crookes, William, *A Practical Handbook of Dyeing and Calico Printing*, Longman Green and Co., London, 1874

Davenport, Elsie, *Your Yarn Dyeing*, London: Sylvan Press, 1955

Davidson, Mary Frances, *The Dye Pot*, Rt. 1, Gatlinburg, TN 37738, USA

Dick, W.B., *Dick's Encyclopedia of Practical Receipts and Processes, or How They Did it in the 1870's*. NY: Funk and Wagnalls, 1974, 607pp

Dick, Barbara Ann, *Welcome to the World of Natural Color*, Fleece and The Unicorn, Rt. 5, Box 368, Stillwater, OK 74074, USA, 1981. US$2.00. Simplified manual on natural dyes

Dryden, Deborah M., *Fabric Painting and Dyeing for the Theatre*, NY: Drama Book Pub., 821 Broadway, NY, 10003, USA, 1982. 176pp

Duncan, Molly, *Spin Your Own Wool and Weave It and Dye It* NZ: A.H. and A.W. Reed, 1972

Furry, Margaret S., and Viemont, Bess M., *Home Dyeing with Natural Dyes*, Bureau of Home Economics, No. 230, U.S.D.A., Washington D.C., 1935

Gerber, Fred, *Cochineal and The Insect Dyes*, Self published, 1978. 70pp *The Investigative Method of Natural Dyeing. Indigo and The Antiquity of Dyeing*. All self published

Gittinger, Mattiebelle, *Master Dyers to the World, Techniques and Trade in Early Indian Dyed Cotton Textiles*, 1982. The Textile Museum, 2320 S. Street N.W., Wash. D.C. 20008, USA. 207pp

Grae, Ida, *Nature's Colors, Dyes From Plants*, 1979. NY: Collier; paperback

Glasson, Ian and Mikki, *A Eucalypt Dyer's Handbook*, Self published. Stanfield, Carcoar, NSW

Handweavers and Spinners Guild of Victoria, *Dyemaking with Australian Flora*, 1974. Australia: Rigby

Hartung, Rolf, *Colour and Texture in Creative Textile Craft*, 1964, Batsford Books

Haynes, William, *The American Chemical Industry*, 6 volumes, 1945-54; New York. (History from colonial times)

Hummel, Prof. J.J., *Dyeing of Textile Fabrics*, 1906, London: Cassell and Co. Ltd

Jacobs, Betty E.M., *Growing Herbs and Plants for Dyeing*, 1977, Select Books, Tarzana, CA (USA). 126 pp

Jenkins, Catherine L., *Precautions for Craft Dyers*, NY: Art Hazards Project. 5 Beekman St, New York, 10038, USA

Johnston, Meda Parker and Kaufman, Glen, *Design on Fabrics*, 2nd edition, New York: Van Nostrand Reinhold

Kampert, Carol, and Henrikson, Sue, *The Dyer's Book (Cushing Dyes)*, Mountain Fiber Studio; US$50.00 (includes samples)

Kierstead, Sallie Pease, *Natural Dyes*, Boston: Bruce Humphries Inc.

Knutson, Linda, *Synthetic Dyes for Natural Fibres*, Interweave; 1986, (2nd edition)

Kramer, Jack, *Natural Dyes: Plants and Processes*, NY: Scribners, 1982

Krohn, Val Frieling, *Hawaiian Dye Plants and Dye Recipes*, 1978, 1980, University Press of Hawaii, 2840 Kolowalu St, Honolulu, HI 96822, USA

Larsen, Jack Lenor, with Alfred Buhler, Bronwen and Garrett Solyom, *The Dyer's Art, Ikat, Batik, Plangi*, New York: Van Nostrand Reinhold

Lee, R., ed. *Printing on Textiles by Direct and Transfer Techniques*, 1981, Noyes Data, Park Ridge, NJ 07656, USA. 418pp

Leechman, Douglas, *Vegetable Dyes from North American Plants*, Southern Ontario, Unit of Herb Society of America and Toronto, Canada. 1968

Lesch, Alma, *Vegetable Dyeing*, 1970. NY: Watson-Guptill

Leggett, William, *Ancient and Medieval Dyes*, 1955. NY: Chemical Pub.

Mairet, Ethel, *Vegetable Dyes*, 1916, London: Faber and Faber Ltd

Mathews, J.M., *Application of Dyestuffs*, 1920. NY: John Wiley and Sons

Miller, Dorothy, *Indigo From Seed to Dye*, Indigo Press, 5950 Fern Flat Road, Aptos, CA 95003, USA. 56pp

Miller Mary Ann, *A Rainbow in Your Hands*, 1981, Flexible Fibers, PO Box 34013, Omaha, Nebraska, 68134, USA, 25pp

Morrow, Mable, *Magic in the Dyepot*, Mrs Carl F. Murray, 713 Quaker Drive, Friendswood, Texas, 77546, USA

Murphy, Edith Van Allen, *Indian Uses of Native Plants*, Mendocino County Historical Society, 243 Bush St, Fort Bragg, CA 95437, USA

Nakana, Eisha, and Stephan, Barbara B., *Japanese Stencil Dyeing*, NY and Tokyo: Weatherhill. 143pp

Napier, James, *A Manual of Dyeing and Dyeing Recipes*, 1975, London: Chas. Griffin and Co.

Nash, Dominic, *Warp Painting, A Manual for Weavers*, 1981, Unicorn, Box 645, Rockville, MD 20851, USA. 33pp

Partridge, William, *A Practical Treatise on Dying (sic) of Woollen, Cotton and Skein Silk with the Manufacture of Broadcloth and Cassimere*, 1973 reprint by Pasold Research Fund Ltd, Edington, Wiltshire, US. 264pp

Pellew, Charles E., *Dyes and Dyeing*, 1918, NY: M. McBride and Co

Polakoff, Claire, *Into Indigo: African Textiles and Dyeing Techniques*, 1980, NY: Anchor Books, 269pp

Proctor, Richard and Lew, Jennifer, *Surface Design for Fabric*, 1984, University of Washington Press, Seattle, WA 98105, USA. 192pp

Proud, Nora, *Textile Dyeing and Printing Simplified*, 1974, NY: Arco Press

Reed, Joyce Lloyd, *Dyes From Plants*, Aust. and NZ: Reed, 1971

Rice, Miriam and Beebee, Dorothy, *Mushrooms for Colour*, 1980, Mad River Press Inc., Route 2, Box 151B, Eureka, CA. 95501, USA. 150pp

Robertson, Seonaid, *Dyes From Plants*, NY: Van Nostrand Reinhold

Schultz, Kathleen, *Create Your Own Natural Dyes*, 1982, NY: Sterling Pub. Co., paperback

Schwartz, Paul, *Printing on Cotton at Ahmedabad, India, in 1678*, Calico Museum, 1969

Scott, Guy, *Transfer Printing Onto Man-Made Fibres*, 1977, London: Batsford

Simmons, Max, *Dyes and Dyeing*, 1984, 2nd edition, Melbourne: Thomas Nelson

Singer, Charles, *The Earliest Chemical Industry*, 1948, London, (Dyeing in the Middle Ages)

Spee, Miep, *Traditional and Modern Batik*, Kangaroo Press, 3 Whitehall Rd., Kenthurst, 2156

Storey, Joyce, *The Thames and Hudson Manual of Dyes and Fabrics*, 1978, New York and London, 192pp

Thurston, Violetta, *The Use of Vegetable Dyes*, 1964, England: Dryad Press, 8th edition

Tidball, Harriet, *Color and Dyeing*, Shuttlecraft Guild Monograph no. 16, distributed by Craft and Hobby, CA

Tomita, J. and N., *Japanese Ikat Weaving: The Techniques of Kasuri*, 1982, Routledge and Kegan Paul, 128pp

Trendall, Kath, *Dyes From Western Australian Plants*, WA: Fremantle Arts Centre Press, 1981

Van Nostrand Reinhold, *Manual of Textile Printing*, 1974, NY: Van Nostrand Reinhold

Vinroot, Sally, and Crowder, Jennie, *The New Dyer*, 1981, Interweave Press, 306 No. Washington, Loveland, CO 80537, USA

Wada, Yoshiko, and Mary Kellogg Rice, and Jane Barton, *Shibori, The Inventive Art of Japanese Shaped Resist Dyeing*, 1983, Kodansha, Ltd 303pp

Walsh, Joan Lee, *Introduction to the Eucalypts: Substantive Dyes*, 1978, California: Straw Into Gold, 15pp. Includes swatches

Weigle, Palmy, *Ancient Dyes for Modern Weavers*, 1974, NY: Watson Guptill

Wickens, Hetty, *Natural Dyes for Spinners and Weavers*, 1983, London: Batsford

Worst, Edward, *Foot Power Loom Weaving*, 1918, Milwaukee, WI: Brud Pub. Co., (Chapter 12 is on dyes)

Index

Aboriginals, 100
absorption, 28
Acadians, 102
acetate rayon, 20
acetic acid, 7, 15, 22, 26, 32-3, 35, 48, 52-3, 57, 62, 68, 79, 85, 91
acid, 5, 15, 20, 22, 26, 32, 34, 39-40, 45, 61, 81, 84, 86-8, 91, 93, 95
bath, 53-4
conditions, 31
fumes, 43, 48, 53
neutralising of, 8, 42, 53
releasing salts, 22
acid dyes, 9, 18, 20, 22, 25, 31, 48, 50
acid levelling dyes, 15
acid milling dyes, 15, 22
acid potassium tartrate, 91
Acrylan, 20, 22
acrylic fibre, dyeing of, 20, 22
acrylic paints, 65
additives, 81, 82, 102
Adelaide, South Australia, 70, 71, 84
adjective dyestuffs, 81
Adrosko, R., 95

aerating, 107-8
Afghanistan, 97
after-treatment, 29, 43, 75
Agfa, 69
Ahmedabad, 97
Ainscow, Margaret, 53
Ainu, 100
airbrush, 36
Albegal B, 31-3
algae, red, 65
alisarin, 91
alizarin, 22, 91, 99, 102
alkali, 11-12, 21, 26, 29-30, 34, 38, 40, 42, 45, 51-2, 53, 61, 63, 84-7, 93, 101, 102
alkaline lye soap, 86
All-India Handloom Board, 97
Altamira, Spain, 101
alum, 66, 67, 76-9, 87-8, 91-2, 94-6, 99
America, 90, 92
American Association of Textile Chemists and Colorists, 31
American Dyestuff Reporter, 94
Americans, colonial, 86
amino acids, 30

ammonia, 11, 14, 16, 26, 32-5, 53, 61-3, 75, 87, 93
ammonium acetate, 22, 26-7, 33-5
ammonium hydroxide, 11
ammonium sulphate, 7, 22, 27, 33, 64
amphoteric, 32
Amway, 9
Anderson, M.J., 76
aniline, 18, 23, 87
Anthrosol, 53
antifusant, 71
'Aqua fortis', 91
Arab traders, 97
arashi shibori, 104-5
argol, 91
Arimatsu, 105
arsenical compounds, 102
aspen leaves, 16
astringent, 98
Australian National University, 76
Australian Wool Corporation, 50, 52
auxiliaries, 32-4, 62
azo dyes, 21, 25
azoics, 9, 20-21, 43-6, 49-51

back staining, 63
Baeyer, Adolf von, 99
Bains, Karma, 67
Bancroft, Edward, 90, 94-6
bandhu, 99
barks, 16, 73, 79, 82
Barton, Jane, 102-3
BASF chemical suppliers, 57
basic dyes, 20
basic properties, 32
Basilan DC, 57
basketry, 79
batik, 20-1, 29, 38-41, 43, 46, 49, 55-7, 60, 65, 71, 77, 79, 104-5
Batik and Surface Design Association, 41, 50
Batik Oetero, 36, 41, 50, 52, 64-5, 67
Bayer, 31
Beaulieu, M. de, 98
beeswax, 56, 99
beetling, 98-9
Benzyl chemical dyeing, 5, 19
Berlin blue, 87
bicarbonate of soda, 8, 12, 29, 52, 69

binders, 23
binding, shibori, 102-3
Bio-Gleem, 9
Biru, 55
bistre, 88-9
black oak bark, 92, 94-5
Blake, Don, 65
bleaching, 38-40, 63, 87, 98, 101
bleeding, 13, 32
blends, fibre, 4, 57, 68, 70
Bliss, Anne, 13
block-printing, 79-80, 97-9
bloodwood, 72
blueprinting, 68-70
Boer War, 88
boil fastness, dyes, 21, 41, 43
boiling out, 56
Bombay, 97
bonding, 31
bones, natural dyeing of, 75
Border Leicester, 48, 76
brand names, 19, 31
Brazil, 101
Brazilwood, 91, 96
brightness, dyes, 20-22, 25, 31, 60, 96

brilliance, dyes, 19, 29, 37, 87
Brisbane, 76
Bromberg, Kay, 12
buckwheat, 101
budlia, 73
buffer, 26
burn test, 36
burnishing, 99

cadium, 9
cadou, 98
caeselpine, 91
caffeic acid, 81
calcium hydroxide, 106-8
calendering, 99
Calgon, 11, 29
calico, 91, 97
Calicut, 97
calx, 106-8
Canada, 102
canting, 55
capping, 102-3
carbon dioxide, 50
carbon molecules, 85
Carr, Professor and Mrs D., 76
carragem, 67
carragheen, 65-7
carriers, 22
caustic soda, 8-9, 12, 24, 29, 30, 44, 50, 57
cave paintings, 101
Celanese, 22
cellulose, 12, 20-22, 29, 43, 49, 51, 55, 63-4, 71, 86-7, 102
cellulose acetate fibre, 22
Cerulean Blue, 89
chains, molecular, 30
chanking, 99
'chay', 99
chiaps, 55
Chine (Chene), 63
Chinese blue, 87
chints (chintz), 98-9
chlorination, 53, 57
chlorogenic acid, 81
Chlorophora tinctoria, 92
chlorophyll, 85
Choo, Chungi, 103
Chromacryl, 65
chrome, 9, 86, 91, 95
  after-chrome method, 22
  chromium dyes, 25
  chrome mordant, 25, 76, 92
  chromium salts, 23
  chrome yellow, 87
Cibacrolan, 31
Ciba-Geigy, 31-2, 61
Cibalan, 25
Cicacia catechu, 92
citric acid, 82
Clayden, Marion, 103
Clifford, Dr. Trevor, 75
climbing dock, 73
coal tar, 43, 87
cobalt, 25
Cocchus ficus, 91
Cocchus lacca, 91
cochiu, 97
cochineal, 16, 72, 90-91, 94, 96
Cockley, Mr K., 76
cold pad batch process, 58-64
cold water dyes, 29, 49-54
Cole, 91
Colophon Book Bindery, 65
colour, charts, 37
  circle, 19
  complementary, 19
  compound, 92
  index, 18, 25, 31
  mixing, 19, 37, 54
coir, dyeing of, 20
Condys crystals, 39-40
contact print, 69
Coomassie, 19
Cooper, 90
copper, 9, 40, 76, 85, 92, 95
  mitts, 82
  sulphate, 78-9, 80, 82, 91
copperas, 86-7, 91
corn husks, 77, 79
cornstarch, 66

Coromandel, 98, 101
Costerman, L.F., 76
Cotinus coggygria, 92
'cotonades', 102
cotton, 4, 14, 102, 105
  batching of, 63-4
  batiking on, 41, 55-7
  blended, 36, 57
  blueprinting, 68-70
  cotton/polyester, 68
  furnishing, 97
  headcloth, 68
  lawn, 68
  lint, 87
  marbling, 66-7
  mordanting of, 89
  natural dyes on, 75, 77-9, 86
  scouring of, 12
  synthetic dyes on, 20-21, 24, 29, 38, 41, 43, 53, 70, 71
covalent bonds, 30-31, 58
Crafts Council, 49
Crayola, 36
cream of tartar, 14, 16, 75, 81, 88, 91, 95, 96
Creative Group, Adelaide, 70
Crews, P., 95
crochet, 78
Croda chemicals, 57
Crossbred fleece, 11
cross dyeing, definition, 4
cutch, 92
cuticle, 30
cyanine, 19
cyanotype, 68-70

Dacca Muslin, 97
dacron, 22
Davidson, M.F., 95
decocting, 82, 101
defoaming agent, 33-4
Deka dyes, 36
Derivan, 65
detergent, 9-11, 13, 24, 26, 53, 63, 67, 87, 89
Dettol, 50
developing bath, 41
dextrose, 89
diazo salts, 39, 43-6, 54
dip dyeing, 29, 35, 41, 46, 49, 53, 59
direct dyeing, 49-54
direct dyes, 20-22, 24, 50, 64
discharge dyeing, 38-40
disperse dyes, 20, 22-3, 35-8, 50
dogbane, 101
DR33, 49, 51-2
dressing, 46, 61, 68
Drimafix, 64
Drimalan, 31
Drimarene K, 29, 49, 51, 61, 64
dripping, 45
drying box, 69
duranta, 83
dyepots, 6-7, 13, 16, 48, 90
dyes, commercial naming of, 18, 31
  concentration of, 32-3, 61
  hand application of, 49-54
  molecules, 30-31
  painting, 41-2, 50-52, 59, 63, 78-9
  pasting of, 24, 29, 34
  penetration of, 28, 61-2
  solutions, 7
  spraying, 41, 50-1, 53, 59
  stamping, 49-51, 53, 59
  storage, 6-7, 41, 43, 46
  waste disposal of, 9
Dylon, 31

Earth Palette, 58-9
East India Company, 97
E. camaldulensis, 77
E. cephalocarpa, 76
E. cineria, 77
E. crebra, 79
E. deanii, 78
Edelstein, 94
Edin, Karen, 38
Egyptians, 86, 97
ellagic acid 81
electrolytes, 34

embroiderers, 52, 98
embroidery, 49, 75, 79, 103
E. melliodora, 82
E. microcorys, 76-7
England, 84, 90-92, 94, 98
E. nicholii, 81
'entered' fibre, 23
E. obliqua, 76
E. pilularis, 78
E. robusta, 82
Eskimos, 101
E. sideroxylon, 80
E. tereticornis, 79
ethyl alcohol, 71
eucalypts, 74-83
eucalypt dyes, 75-83
evaporating tanks, 9
exhaust, dyes, 9, 16, 23-4, 34, 45-6, 51-2, 77
Exodus, 89

fabric paints, 65
fast dyes, 97-9
Father Coeurdoux, 98
feathers, natural dyeing of, 74-5, 77, 79, 87
fermentation, 16, 81, 85, 91
ferric ammonium citrate, 68
ferric chloride, 87
ferric hydrate, 87
ferric nitrate, 87
ferric salts, 87
ferrous sulphate, 76-80, 82, 86-7, 91
fibre reactive dyes, 7, 9, 20-21, 29-35, 36, 38, 41, 46, 50, 51-4, 58-64
finger stall, 104
First Australian Fibre Conference, 103, 106
fixation, dyes, 29, 51, 54, 59, 62
fixing agent, 24
Fixing Agent A, 58
flavin, 94
flavonoid quercitin, 81
flax, 12
Fletcher, Joan, 15
flowers, 16, 20
folding and clamping, shibori, 102-3
Forestry Department, 76
Forests Commission, 76
formaldehyde, 65
formic acid, 22, 35
formulas, 24, 37, 42
  auxiliaries, 32
  dye quantity, 23
  fibre reactive dyeing, 30
  indigosols, 42
  liquor ratio, 27, 31
  soga dyeing, 39
  strength of colour, 26
France, 98-9
fugitive dyes, 13
fur, dyeing of, 23, 88
fustic, 22, 92, 96

gallic acid, 81
gelatine, 66
Genesia tinctoria, 92
genesic acid, 81
Gerber, Fred and Willi, 94
Gerber Investigative Method, 96
Germany, 86
glacial acetic acid, 35, 84
glass measures, 6
glazing, 99
Glauber's salts, 7, 22, 24, 32, 34
glucose, 89
glucoside, 101
Grabe, 91
graphic film, 69
Green, David, 52
greenback dollars, 87
greenwood, dyers', 92
green vitriol, 91
Gujarat, 92
gum leaves, 74-5, 77, 82
gums, tragacanth, 66
gum, vegetable, 50
gutta, 71

Haematoxzlin campechianum, 92

handmade paper, 70
Harappa culture, 97
Harlequin paints, 65
hazards, health, 8-9, 13, 25, 26, 42, 44, 49, 68
heat setting, 70
Hedstrom Ana Lisa, 103
henna, 101
Herschel, Sir John, 70
hitta, 104
Hoechst, 31, 33, 51, 61
Holland, 99
Hostalan, 31, 33-4
Hostalan salt, 33-4
Hostapal, 34
hot water dye, 29
hue, 19, 90
Hunter, Inga, 56
hydrated ferric oxide, 86
hydrated iron sulphate, 86
hydrochloric acid, 9, 39, 42, 46, 53, 87, 95
hydrogen peroxide, 22, 69
hydrolysis, 29, 31, 52-3
Hydros, 39-40
hydroxyl group, 102
hygroscopic agent, 51, 62

ICI, 29, 31, 51, 61-2
ikat, 5, 49, 64, 97, 99
immersion method, 41
impregnation, 43, 49-51, 56, 99-100
India, 92, 97-9
Indian Textile Journal, 97
Indigo, 21, 72, 95, 103, 105
  'balls', 101
  basic solution, 106-8
  'flower', 107
  natural, 56, 92, 99, 101-2
  stock solution, 107-8
  sulphate, 95
  synthetic, 21, 99, 102, 106-8
Indigofera tinctoria, 21, 92, 101
Indigosol dyes, 41-2, 49-50, 53-4
Indonesia, 38, 43-4, 55, 57
Indos, 101
Indus Valley, 97
inhibitor, 71
inorganic, 71
intensifier, 69
ionic, 30
Irgalan, 25
Irganol, 25
iron, 9, 14, 28, 40, 76, 82, 85, 87-8, 91
  acetate, 86, 99
  buff, 86-9
  salts, 23, 88
  soluble, 101
  sulphate, 86, 102
  tannates, 101
ironbark, 79-80, 82
ironing, dye setting, 36-7, 52, 67, 79
Isatis tinctoria, 92, 101
Isolan, 25
Italy, 100

jacaranda, 85
Jakarta, 55
Japan, 100-101, 105
Japanese, 86, 103
Jogjakarta, 55
Jouy, France, 99
Juglans, 101
juglone, 101
jute, dyeing of, 20-21

kalam, 99
kalamkari, 97-8
kamosage knots, 104
kanoko, 104
Karo syrup, 89
kasuri, 5, 49, 60, 106
Kellogg-Rice, Mary, 102-3
kermes, 91
keratin, 30
kimonos, 103-4
kino, 83
Kitley, P., 54
knitting, 78
kodak, 69
kodalith film, 69

Kraft Kolour, 63
ktesias, 97
Kubota, Itchiku, 103-4

lac dye, 91
lake formation, 22, 81
Lanasol, 31, 32, 61
lanolin, 31, 35, 61
Lassak, Mr. E., 81
Lawsonia, 101
lawsone, 101
lease ties, 61
leather, dyeing of, 23
Lescaux, France, 101
level dyeing acid dyes, 22
levelling, 22, 24, 31, 33-4
levelling agent, 5
Lew, Jennifer, 103
lichens, 73-4, 89, 95
Lieberman, 91
lightfastness, dyes, 19-23, 25, 36, 41, 43, 58, 60-61, 79, 85-6, 94-5, 97
Linders, Olive and Harry, 12
linen, 14, 68, 70, 100, 102
  natural dyes on, 86, 89
  scouring of, 12
  synthetic dyes on, 21, 29, 38, 43
liquor ratio, 5, 23, 26, 28, 31, 57, 59, 106
Lissapol, 9-10, 50, 62
Lithex, 69
litmus paper, 84
logwood, 22, 56, 72, 92
Lonchocarpus, 101
loog, solution, 30, 44, 46, 51
Lorance, Merrilyn, 16

macrame, 51
madder, 22, 84, 91, 93, 96-7, 99, 102
Madras, 98
Maiden, J.H., 78
Malabar Coast, 97
Malay archipelago, 102
manganese brown, 86, 88-9
Manutex RS, 51-3, 62-4, 80
marbling combs, 67
  fabrics, 65-7
  inks, 67
  yarns, 63
Marsdenia, 101
Massachusetts, 94
master dyer, 89-90, 99
masulipatam, 98
Matexil PAL, 52
Mato Grasso, 101
Matthews, J.M., 87
mauveine, 20
McCann, M., 49
Mediterranean, 86, 91
melange, 63
Melbourne, 106
Merck Index, 8
merino, 10
Mesitol NBS, 63
messmate (eucalypt), 76
metachrome process, 22
metal complex dyes, 50
metal mordants, 9
metal oxides, 94
methylated spirits, 24, 50, 52, 62, 64, 85, 107
metric system, 5, 25
metallic salts, 13, 20, 22, 34, 81, 96
microwave oven, 15
Middle East, 97
migration of dye, 24, 27-8, 33, 61, 71
milkweed, 101
milling fastness, 19, 22
mineral dyes, 20, 33, 85-9
mineral khaki, 23
mineral pigments, 85
Modern Techniques in Batik, Art, 54
mohair, 16, 48, 75
Mohenjo-Daro, 97
molasses, 89, 102
monochrome process, 22
monoprint, 37
Monoyama, 103
mordant, 8, 12, 14, 16, 20, 74-9, 81, 83, 89-90, 94, 97, 99, 101, 103

mordant salts, 8
mordanting, natural dyes, 13-14, 94
one-pot mordanting, 14, 94-6
post-mordanting, 14
pre-mordanting, 13, 79, 89, 94-5
for marbling, 67
mottled dyeing, 5
Mousterian period, 100
mouth vaporiser, 71
Mt Dandenong, 75
mugga, 80
muriatic acid, 42, 87
Muromachi, 103
Museum of Applied Arts and Sciences, 81
Museum of Contemporary Crafts, 103
mustard, 101
MX15, 50, 54
myrobalan plant, 98

Nacquer, 87
nankeen (nankin), 86
Naphthol, 7, 30, 38, 43-6, 49-51, 54, 56-7, 70, 105
Napoleon's Blue, 87-8
natural dyers, 8, 13
natural dyestuffs, 9, 22, 25, 72-97, 101, 103
Neolan, 25
nerium, 101
neutralising, 46, 52-3, 57, 61, 95
nitric acid, 87-8, 91, 95
nitrogen, 88
Nobolaine DS, 57
nonionic detergents, 10-12, 34, 50
non-mordant dyes, 81
North America, 100
New South Wales, 77, 82
nuts, 16
nylon, 22, 35

oak galls, 81
oak leaves, 85
Oberkamphe, C.P., 99
ochre, 100
oleander, 101
onion skins, 16, 73
optical brighteners, 9-10
organic, 85
orlon, 20, 22
oxalic acid, 85, 96
oven-dyeing, 15
overdyeing, 54, 79, 95
over-printing, 38
ox gall, 65
oxidation, 18, 21-2, 87, 89, 101-2
oxidation dyes, 20, 22
oxidising agent, 53, 62
oxidising bath, 41

pad batch dyeing, 58-64
pad batch printing, 53, 60-64
padding, 70
Pakistan, 97
palampores, 97, 99
Palatine, 25
paper, transfer printing, 36-8
Papua New Guinea, 77
Partridge, William, 90-92
pastel shades, 23-4, 41, 44, 93
Patipur, 97
patola, 97, 99
pectin, 12, 86
Pelikan ink, 65
Pellew, C.E., 86, 88
pentel, 36
peppermint, 77
Pepys, Samuel, 98
Perendale, 48
Perkin, William Henry, 18, 20, 91, 102
Permaset, 9, 65, 70, 77, 79-80
Persians, 97
pH, 9, 12, 14, 16, 26, 33-5, 62-3, 87
photocopies, 69

photographic methods, 68-70
pigment, 21, 87, 101
dry, 65
dyes, 20, 23
printing paste, 9, 23
plangi, 102-4
plant dyeing, 72-3, 74-5, 81, 97
plastic, batching, 58-64
platelets, wool, 84
Pleasance, H.D., 50
pleating, shibori, 102-3
Plummer, Jeanne, 76
polyamide, 22
polychromatic screenprinting, 52
polyester, 22, 35-7, 41
Polygonum, 101
Polysol dyes, 36-7
Pondicherry, 98
potassium aluminium sulphate, 67, 95
potassium bitartrite, 95
potassium carbonate, 88
potassium dichromate, 8, 69, 86
potassium ferricyanide, 68, 88
potassium ferrocyanide, 88
potassium hydroxide, 102
potassium permanganate, 39, 88-9
'pouncing', 98
precipitation, 101
pre-Columbian Americans, 101
Premissima, 55
pressure cooker, 71
Prima, 55
primaries, colours, 25, 31, 48, 54
Princecolour, 71
Princefix, 71
printing, pastes, 79-80
thickeners, 49-50, 52-3, 84
Procilan, 31
Procion, 29, 49, 51, 53, 61, 70
Proctor, Richard, 103
protein fibres, 13-14, 43, 49
prunus, 73
Prussian blue, 68-70, 86-8
purpurin, 91

Queensland, 76, 80
quercitron, 92, 94, 96
Quercus velutina, 94
quick lime, 102
quilting, 49, 65, 70
quilting stitch, 104

raffia, dyeing of, 20
Raymond's blue, 87
rayon, 4, 14, 29, 53, 55, 66
rayon acetate, 16
recipes
ammonium acetate, homemade, 26
azoic dyes, 51
chlorination of wool, 57
direct application, Indigosol, 53
DR33 printing paste, 52
hand application, fibre reactive dyes, 51-2
Manutex thickener, 52
naphthols, 44-5
screenprinting paste, 52
soga dyes, 39
stock paste, cold pad batch, 62
urea pad batch printing, wool, 53
red prussiate, 88-9
Red Sea, 97
reducing agent, 102
reduction, 52, 106-8
re-dyeings, 19
Remazol, 51, 61
Remol GE, 33-4
Remol GES, 33-4
Reseda luteoia, 92
resin, 56
resin printing, 23
resist dyeing, 102

resist salt L, 52, 62
resist, silk dyes, 71
Rhus, 92
Robriquet, 91
Roccella tinctoria, 84
Rome (Romans), 97
Rossell, Monona, 49
Royal Melbourne Institute of Technology, 76
rovings, 16
rub fastness dyes, 21, 58, 60, 86-7, 95
Rubia tinctorum, 84, 91
running stitch, 104
Russia, 100
rust, 86

'saddening', colours, 28, 75
salt, 5-6, 11, 14, 16, 20-21, 24, 29-30, 51, 71, 91, 93
Sandopan DKA, 52
Sandoz, 31, 51, 61
sappanwood, 91, 99
saponifying, 11, 93
satin, 66
sawdust, 80, 82
scales, 6-7, 44
scarlet, dyeing of, 90-91, 94, 96
scouring, fibres and fabrics, 101
recipe for Merino, 10
recipe of Crossbred, 11
wool, 11, 31
cotton, linen, 12, 86
silk, 12
prescouring, 34-5
screenpriting, 49-50, 52, 55, 59, 65, 77, 79
Scrubb's ammonia, 26, 35
seaweed, 65, 73
secondary colours, 34, 54
sedimentation, 101
sensitizer, 68
shades, 23, 32
depth of shade, 23
pale, 24-5, 29, 33, 41, 44, 51, 65
medium, 44, 53
dark, 44, 53
shell lac, 91
shibori, 49, 102-6
silk, batching of, 58-9
batiking on, 55
bleaching of, 39-40
blueprinting, 68
marbling, 66
microwave dyeing, 15
mordanting of, 13-14
natural dyes on, 75, 77-80, 87, 89, 92, 97
scouring of, 12
synthetic dyes on, 18, 20-21, 28-9, 41, 43, 48-9, 70
the silk dyes, 71
silver dollar gums, 73
silver leaf stringybark, 76
sisal, dyeing of, 20, 77, 79
sizing, 10, 65, 66, 71
Smith, Henry, 77-8
Snepp, Alison, 65, 67
soap, 10-12, 29, 56, 78, 89
Society of Dyers and Colourists, 18, 31
soda ash, 11, 29-30, 42, 46, 52-3, 63-4
sodium alginate, 62
bichromate, 22
bisulphtie, 50, 53, 57
carbonate, 11-12
dithionite, 39
hydrosulphate, 20
hydrosulphite, 24, 39, 52, 88, 102
hydroxide, 8, 102
nitrite, 41-2, 53
sulphate, 7, 32
sulphide, 21
Soga, 38-40, 56
solar dyeing, 16
Solo (Surakarta), 55
solubilizing agents, 53
soluble dyestuffs, 22-3, 101
solvents, 9
snowgum, 76
soursobs, 84

South Australia, 84-5
space dyeing, 15
spectralite, 88
Spee, Miep, 54
spinning oil, 31, 35, 61, 63
spot dyeing, 4
sprinkle dyeing, 15
St. Jerome, 97
standing bath, 11
stannous chloride, 84, 88, 91, 95
starching, 99
steamer, 15
steaming, 29, 49-50, 52, 59, 70-71
steel wool, 82
Steelo, 82
stitching, shibori, 102-3
stock dyeing, 5
stock solution, 6, 15, 61, 62
strength, dyes, 19, 26, 37
stringybark, 77, 82
stripping salts, 20
substantive dyestuff, 32, 74, 81, 101
Sudachmir, Saad Ibny, 38
sulphonated castor oil, 44
sulphur dyes, 20-21
sulphuric acid, 22, 25, 42, 88, 91
sumac, 92
surface design, 49
Suzuki, Kanezo, 105
swamp mahogany, 82
sweet peas, 83
swelling agents, 22, 62
Swiss Lake Dwellers, 86
Sydney, 81
Sylvan Katherine, 15-16
synthetic blends, 75
dyes, 22, 24, 48, 55, 77, 86, 91-2
fabrics, 36-7, 46, 53
fibres, 55, 68

tallow, 56
tallowwood, 76, 77
tannic acid, 68-9, 81, 89, 101
tannins, 88
tapioca size, 66
tartaric acid, 28
tartartic acid, 28
Teepol, 9-10
'tendering', 89
termini of the chromophore, 102
Terric BL8, 10
tertiary colours, 54
terylene, 22
tetron, 22
Textile Artists' newsletter, 15
Textile Museum, Washington D.C., 99
Textile — Fibre Forum, 65
Threader, Mr A., 76
thiourea dioxide, 88
thickeners, 49-50, 51-4, 62, 71
tie dyeing, 5, 20, 59, 77, 79, 102
tin, 76, 84, 88, 90-91, 95-6
tin spirits, 95
tint colour, 70
tints, 19
tone, 19
toner, 69
top dyeing, 4
transfer crayons, 36-7
transfer printing, 35-9
Trees of Life design, 98
tri-chromatic sets, 25
trisodiumphosphate, 11
tritik, 102
tsujigahana, 103-4
Turkey Red Oil, 44, 50, 91
tying stands, 104

union cloth, 70
union dyeing, definition, 4
universal litmus paper, 84
University of Melbourne, 75
University of Queensland, 76
urea, 7, 14, 51, 53, 62, 64
urine, 93

varicoloured dyeing, 5

Vasco de Gama, 92
vat dyes, 20-21, 24, 41, 50, 97, 101
solubilised, 9, 21, 41, 49, 53-4, 56
vegetable dyes, 72-3, 97
Venetian Red, 91
verdigris, 91
verofix, 31
Victoria and Albert Museum, 98
videl black dye, 21
Videl, Raymond, 21
vigourex printing, 63
vinegar, 8, 14-16, 26, 30, 35, 45, 48, 52, 57, 70, 79, 84, 86, 88
vinyl sulphone, 33
viscose rayon, 20-21, 35, 41, 43, 63
vitriol, 91
viyella, 57
Voilissima, 55
volumetric solutions, 25, 2
Vonwiller, Eva, 41

WRBE (Wax Resist Batik Effects), 55-7
Wada, Yoshiko, 102-7
wallpaper paste, 37, 62, 66
walnut husks, 73, 92, 101
warping board, 61
warping mill, 61
warps, ground, 60
movement, 60
painting of, 59-64
printing, 64
preparation, 61
supplementary, 60
washfastness, dyes, 19-25, 29, 31-2, 36, 58, 60-61, 79, 86, 94, 97
washing soda, 6, 10-12, 29, 52, 63, 78, 84, 86-7
water, distilled, 65
hard, 28, 34
sized, 65
softeners, 10, 12, 28-9, 31, 92
'sprinkling', 67
wax capping, 56
cracking, 56
Javanese, 71
outline, 56
paraffin, 56
weave structures, 60
weaving, 49, 51, 59-64, 75, 78, 97
wefts, 60
weld, 92, 94
wetting agents, 10, 13, 27, 44, 51, 53, 61-4
wetting out, 10, 27-8, 46, 51
white spirit, 67, 71
woad, 92, 101-2
wood ash lye, 86
wood chips, 77-80, 82
wood, dyeing of, 20, 86
woods, 16
wood shavings, 78
wool, acids on, 84
bleaching of, 39
chlorination of, 53, 57
fleece, 48, 58-9, 96
lightfastness test, 85
mordanting of, 13-14, 95
natural dyes on, 74, 77, 79, 82, 86-9
pad batching, 53, 58-64
scouring of, 10, 31, 35, 93
solar dyeing, 16
staples, 63
synthetic dyes on, 18, 20-22, 24-5, 29-33, 43, 48-9, 53, 71

Xylene, 19

yarn, handspun, dyeing of, 58
construction of, 61
yellow box, 82
yellow prussiate, 88

zinc dust, 106-8
zinc metal, 102